Help Me! Guide to the iPh

By Charles Hughes

Table of Contents

What's New in iOS 11? 11

  1. Using the New Notification Center - Cover Sheet 11
  2. Using Music Controls on the Lock Screen 12
  3. Accessing Quick Settings through the Control Center 12
  4. Capturing a Screen Recording 12
  5. Enabling Do Not Disturb While Driving Mode 12
  6. Typing a Search in Siri 12
  7. Translating a Phrase Using Siri 13
  8. Application Store Redesign 13
  9. Editing Live Photos 13
  10. Marking Up and Sharing Screenshots 13
  11. Switching Between Applications 13
  12. Opening the Most Recent Note from the Lock Screen 14
  13. Entering an Alternative Character on the Keyboard 14
  14. Adding a Drawing in an Email 14
  15. Deleting Unused Applications Automatically 14
  16. Accessing Control Center Quick Actions Without 3D Touch 14
  17. Disabling In-App Ratings and Reviews 14
  18. Scanning a Document in the Notes Application 15
  19. Answering a Call Automatically 15
  20. Connecting to a Wi-Fi Network Automatically 15
  21. Managing Notification Settings 15
  22. Sharing a Wi-Fi Password Over the Air 15
  23. Making an Emergency SOS Call 16
  24. Moving Multiple Application Icons at Once 16

25. Shutting Down Your Phone without
   Using the Sleep/Wake Button 16
26. Viewing a List of All Attachments in Messages 16

Getting Started 17

1. Button Layout 17
2. Charging the Phone.. 20
3. Turning the Phone On and Off.. 21
4. Installing a SIM Card 21
5. Navigating the Screens 23
6. Organizing Icons... 24
7. Creating an Icon Folder... 24
8. Using Wi-Fi... 26
9. Accessing Quick Settings through the Control Center 31
10. Using the Cover Sheet... 33
11. Accessing Application Shortcuts Using 3D Touch.......................... 33
12. Searching the Phone or Web for Content 40
13. Managing and Using Widgets.. 40
14. Using Interactive Notifications 43

Making Voice and Video Calls 44

1. Dialing a Number 44
2. Calling a Contact 46
3. Calling a Favorite.. 49
4. Returning a Recent Phone Call 51
5. Receiving a Voice Call... 53
6. Replying to an Incoming Call with a Text Message 53
7. Setting a Reminder to Return an Incoming Call................................. 53
8. Using the Speakerphone During a Voice Call 54
9. Using the Keypad During a Voice Call 55
10. Using the Mute Function During a Voice Call 56
11. Putting a Caller on Hold (hidden button) 56
12. Starting a Conference Call (Adding a Call)... 56
13. Making a Call Over Wi-Fi... 58
14. Making an Emergency SOS Call 61
15. Blocking Phone Numbers 62

2

16. Starting a FaceTime Call 63
Managing Contacts 65
   1. Adding a New Contact... 65
   2. Finding a Contact 67
   3. Deleting a Contact 70
   4. Editing Contact Information 72
   5. Sharing a Contact's Information 72
   6. Changing the Contact Sort Order.. 76
Text Messaging 80
   1. Composing a New Text Message 80
   2. Copying, Cutting, and Pasting Text 85
   3. Using the Spell Check Feature 88
   4. Receiving a Text Message 88
   5. Reading a Stored Text Message 92
   6. Forwarding a Text Message... 92
   7. Calling the Sender from within a Text... 95
   8. Viewing Sender Information from within a Text......................... 96
   9. Deleting a Text Message 97
   10. Adding Texted Phone Numbers to the Phonebook 97
   11. Sending a Picture Message 100
   12. Leaving a Group Conversation 104
   13. Naming a Conversation.. 104
   14. Adding a Voice Message to a Conversation (iMessage Only) 104
   15. Sharing Your Location in a Conversation 106
   16. Viewing All Attachments in a Conversation 108
   17. Handwriting a Message.. 112
   18. Sending a Digital Touch 113
   19. Sending an Animoji 113
   20. Using Tapback in a Message 113
   21. Turning Read Receipts for a Single Conversation On or Off....... 113
   22. Using iMessage Applications 114
Using the Safari Web Browser... 116
   1. Navigating to a Website 116

2. Adding and Viewing Bookmarks 118
　3. Adding a Bookmark to the Home Screen 122
　4. Managing Open Browser Tabs 124
　5. Blocking Pop-Up Windows 126
　6. Changing the Search Engine 129
　7. Clearing the History and Browsing Data 129
　8. Viewing an Article in Reader Mode 129
　9. Turning Private Browsing On or Off 132
　10. Setting Up the AutoFill Feature 132
　11. Customizing the Smart Search Field 134
　12. Viewing Recently Closed Tabs 134
　13. Scanning a Credit Card Using the Phone's Camera 136

Managing Photos and Videos 137

　1. Taking a Picture 137
　2. Capturing a Video 139
　3. Using the Digital and Optical Zoom 139
　4. Using the Flash 139
　5. Focusing on a Part of the Screen 140
　6. Browsing Photos 140
　7. Editing a Photo 142
　8. Deleting a Photo 146
　9. Creating a Photo Album 146
　10. Editing a Photo Album 148
　11. Deleting a Photo Album 150
　12. Browsing Photos by Date and Location 150
　13. Searching for a Photo 152
　14. Recording a Time-Lapse Video 154
　15. Recovering Deleted Photos 154
　16. Managing People in Photos 155
　17. Managing Memories in Photos 159
　18. Capturing and Viewing a Live Photo 159

Using iTunes 161

　1. Registering with Apple 161
　2. Buying Music and Ringtones in iTunes 161

3. Buying or Renting Videos in iTunes	164
4. Searching for Media in iTunes	168
5. Sharing Your iTunes Account with Family	170
6. Adding Content to Your Wish List	174

Using the Music Application 176

1. Downloading Media	176
2. Playing Music	176
3. Using Additional Audio Controls	180
4. Creating a Playlist	180
5. Using the iTunes Radio	184

Using the Mail Application 186

1. Setting Up the Mail application	186
2. Reading Email	190
3. Switching Accounts in the Mail application	192
4. Writing an Email	194
5. Referring to Another Email when Composing a New Message	196
6. Formatting Text	196
7. Replying to and Forwarding Email Messages	199
8. Attaching a Picture or Video to an Email	201
9. Moving an Email in the Inbox to Another Folder	204
10. Flagging an Important Email	206
11. Archiving Emails	208
12. Changing the Default Signature	208
13. Changing Email Options	211
14. Unsubscribing from an Email List	211
15. Viewing Emails in Conversation View	212
16. Adding a Drawing in an Email	215

Managing Applications 218

1. Signing In to an iTunes Account	218
2. Signing In to a Different iTunes Account	221
3. Editing iTunes Account Information	223
4. Searching for an Application to Purchase	223
5. Buying an Application	229

Help Me! Guide to the iPhone X

6. Using Wi-Fi to Download an Application 232
7. Switching Between Applications 232
8. Closing an Application Running in the Background 234
9. Organizing Applications into Folders 234
10. Reading User Reviews 234
11. Changing Application Settings 235
12. Deleting an Application 235
13. Sending an Application as a Gift 236
14. Redeeming a Gifted Application 240
15. Turning Automatic Application Updates On or Off 240

Using Siri 241

1. Making a Call 241
2. Sending and Receiving Text Messages 242
3. Managing the Address Book 242
4. Setting Up and Managing Meetings 243
5. Checking the Time and Setting Alarms 243
6. Sending and Receiving Email 244
7. Getting Directions and Finding Businesses 244
8. Playing Music 244
9. Searching the Web and Asking Questions 245
10. Looking Up Words in the Dictionary 245
11. Application-Specific Phrases 246

Adjusting Wireless Settings 247

1. Turning Airplane Mode On or Off 247
2. Turning Location Services On or Off 249
3. Customizing Cellular Data Usage 252
4. Turning Data Roaming On or Off 254
5. Setting Up a Virtual Private Network (VPN) 254
6. Turning Bluetooth On or Off 258
7. Using Wi-Fi to Sync Your Phone with Your Computer 260

Adjusting Sound Settings 261

1. Turning Vibration On or Off 261
2. Turning Volume Button Functionality On or Off 265

3. Setting the Default Ringtone 265
4. Customizing Notification and Alert Sounds 267
5. Turning Lock Sounds On or Off 267
6. Turning Keyboard Clicks On or Off 267
7. Controlling Siri's Voice 268
8. Adjusting Siri Settings 271

Adjusting Language and Keyboard Settings 272
1. Customizing Spelling and Grammar Settings 272
2. Adding an International Keyboard 275
3. Adding a Keyboard Shortcut 278
4. Changing the Operating System Language 281
5. Changing the Keyboard Layout 284
6. Changing the Region Format 285

Adjusting General Settings 287
1. Changing Auto-Lock Settings 287
2. Adjusting the Brightness 290
3. Turning Night Shift On or Off 290
4. Assigning a Passcode Lock 292
5. Setting Up a Face ID Lock 296
6. Turning 24-Hour Mode On or Off 298
7. Resetting the Home Screen Layout 300
8. Resetting All Settings 302
9. Erasing and Restoring the Phone 302
10. Managing Notification Settings 303
11. Changing the Wallpaper 306
12. Restricting Access to Private Information 310
13. Turning Raise to Wake On or Off 312

Adjusting Accessibility Settings 314
1. Managing Vision Accessibility Features 314
2. Managing Hearing Accessibility Features 318
3. Turning Guided Access On or Off 318
4. Managing Physical & Motor Accessibility Features 320
5. Answering Phone Calls Automatically 321

Adjusting Phone Settings 324

    1. Turning Call Forwarding On or Off 324

    2. Turning Call Waiting On or Off 328

    3. Turning Caller ID On or Off 330

    4. Turning the International Assist On or Off 332

    5. Blocking Specific Numbers 332

    6. Editing Preset Text Message Responses 334

    7. Turning Wi-Fi Calling On or Off 336

Adjusting Text Message Settings 337

    1. Turning iMessage On or Off 337

    2. Turning Read Receipts On or Off in iMessage 340

    3. Turning 'Send as SMS' On or Off 340

    4. Turning MMS Messaging On or Off 341

    5. Turning the Subject Field On or Off 341

    6. Turning the Character Count On or Off 341

    7. Turning Group Messaging On or Off 342

    8. Setting the Amount of Time to Keep Messages 342

    9. Setting the Expiration Time for Audio Messages 344

    10. Turning Raise to Listen On or Off 346

    11. Blocking Unknown Senders 346

Tips and Tricks 348

    1. Maximizing Battery Life 349

    2. Taking and Editing a Screenshot 350

    3. Scrolling to the Top of a Screen 350

    4. Saving an Image While Browsing the Internet 350

    5. Inserting a Period 350

    6. Adding an Extension to a Contact's Number 350

    7. Navigating the Home Screens 351

    8. Typing Alternate Characters 351

    9. Quickly Deleting Recently Typed Text 351

    10. Resetting the Phone 351

    11. Calling a Phone Number on a Website 351

12. Taking Notes 352
13. Recovering Signal After Being in an Area with No Service 352
14. Changing the Number of Rings
    Before the Phone Goes to Voicemail... 352
15. Deleting a Song in the Music Application 353
16. Taking a Picture from the Lock Screen 353
17. Assigning a Custom Ringtone to a Contact.................................. 354
18. Opening the Photos Application without Closing the Camera 354
19. Inserting Emoticons 354
20. Hiding the Keyboard in the Messages Application...................... 355
21. Controlling Web Surfing Using Gestures 355
22. Navigating the Menus Using Gestures 355
23. Pausing or Cancelling an Application Download 355
24. Making a Quick Note for a Contact 356
25. Using a Search Engine that Does Not Track Your Searches 356
26. Preventing Applications from Refreshing in the Background..... 356
27. Leaving Your Home Screen Free of Icons 356
28. Call Waiting in FaceTime 357
29. Viewing Battery Usage 357
30. Attaching Any File Type to an Email... 357
31. Viewing Favorite Contacts Using 3D Touch.................................. 357
32. Moving the Text Cursor Like a Computer Mouse 357
33. Saving Data by Sending Smaller Pictures..................................... 358
34. Filtering Email to Customize Your Inbox....................................... 358
35. Using 3D Touch in the Control Center.. 358
36. Deleting Unused Applications Automatically 359
37. Disabling In-App Ratings and Reviews 359
38. Scanning a Document in the Notes Application 359
39. Sharing Your Wi-Fi Password Over the Air 360
40. Shutting Down Your Phone without
    Using the Sleep/Wake Button 360
41. Viewing and Deleting All Attachments in Messages 360
42. Capturing a Screen Recording 361
43. Enabling Do Not Disturb While Driving Mode 361

Troubleshooting 363

1. Phone does not turn on 363
2. Phone is not responding 364
3. Can't make a call 364
4. Can't surf the web 365
5. Screen or keyboard does not rotate 365
6. iTunes does not detect phone when connected to a computer 366
7. Phone does not ring or play music, can't hear while talking, can't listen to voicemails 366
8. Low microphone volume, caller can't hear you 366
9. Camera does not work 366
10. Phone shows the White Screen of Death 367
11. "DEVICE needs to cool down" message appears 367
12. Display does not adjust brightness automatically 367

Index 368

Other Books from the Author of the Help Me Series, Charles Hughes . 372

What's New in iOS 11?

Table of Contents

1. Using the New Notification Center - Cover Sheet
2. Using Music Controls on the Lock Screen
3. Accessing Quick Settings through the Control Center
4. Capturing a Screen Recording
5. Enabling Do Not Disturb While Driving Mode
6. Typing a Search in Siri
7. Translating a Phrase Using Siri
8. Application Store Redesign
9. Editing Live Photos
10. Marking Up and Sharing Screenshots
11. Switching Between Applications
12. Opening the Most Recent Note from the Lock Screen
13. Entering an Alternative Character on the Keyboard
14. Adding a Drawing in an Email
15. Deleting Unused Applications Automatically
16. Accessing Control Center Quick Actions Without 3D Touch
17. Disabling In-App Ratings and Reviews
18. Scanning a Document in the Notes Application
19. Answering a Call Automatically
20. Connecting to a Wi-Fi Network Automatically
21. Managing Notification Settings
22. Sharing a Wi-Fi Password Over the Air
23. Making an Emergency SOS Call
24. Moving Multiple Application Icons at Once
25. Shutting Down Your Phone without Using the Power Button
26. View a List of All Attachments in Messages

1. Using the New Notification Center - Cover Sheet

The Lock screen and Notification Center have been merged into one in iOS 11, and are now called the Cover Sheet. When you swipe down from the top of the screen, the lock screen now appears with all of your notifications. Swipe back up to return to what you were doing. Refer to "*Using the New Notification Center - Cover Sheet*" on page 10 to learn more.

2. Using Music Controls on the Lock Screen

The music controls no longer take up the entire lock screen while music is playing. Refer to *"Playing Music"* on page 175 to learn more about the Music application.

3. Accessing Quick Settings through the Control Center

The Control Center has a completely new look in iOS 11 and has been merged with the multitasking screen. You can bring up the Control Center by swiping up from the bottom with a single finger when viewing the Home screen or with four fingers when using an application. Refer to *"Accessing Quick Settings through the Control Center"* on page 11 to learn more about the Control Center updates.

4. Capturing a Screen Recording

You can record your screen while you perform various actions. The screen recording feature will also record the audio, such as music, in the applications that appear in the recording. Refer to *"Capturing a Screen Recording"* on page 328 to learn more.

5. Enabling Do Not Disturb While Driving Mode

You can enable the iPhone to automatically turn on Do Not Disturb mode while you are driving. While in Do Not Disturb mode, you will not receive any calls or notifications of any kind. Someone who really needs to reach you can always break through by texting the word "urgent." Refer to *"Enabling Do Not Disturb While Driving Mode"* on page 328 to learn how to use this mode.

6. Typing a Search in Siri

You can now type a search when using Siri instead of using your voice. You cannot enable both features at the same time. Refer to *"Managing Hearing Accessibility Features"* on page 285 to learn more.

7. Translating a Phrase Using Siri

You can now use Siri to translate phrases. Just say "translate", the phrase, and "to Spanish", "to Chinese", or whichever language you prefer. Refer to "*Using Siri*" on page 208 to learn more about acceptable Siri phrases.

8. Application Store Redesign

The Application store has been redesigned with a new Today tab and many other changes. Purchasing and downloading applications still works the same, just looks different. Refer to "*Managing Applications*" on page 185 to learn more about the application store.

9. Editing Live Photos

You can now edit a live photo just as you would edit a regular one. To edit a live photo, touch **Edit** while viewing the photo. You can crop it, apply effects, mute the sound, and mark it up. Refer to "*Editing a Photo*" on page 141 to learn how to edit photos.

10. Marking Up and Sharing Screenshots

You can now share, draw, and write on a screenshot immediately after capturing it. Refer to "*Taking and Editing a Screenshot*" on page 317 to learn more.

11. Switching Between Applications

The multitasking screen is now merged with the Control Center. To access this new screen and to switch between applications, touch the bottom of the screen with four fingers and slide up. Refer to "*Switching Between Applications*" on page 199 to learn more.

12. Opening the Most Recent Note from the Lock Screen

You can now open your most recent note from the Lock screen by touching the screen with the Apple Pencil.

13. Entering an Alternative Character on the Keyboard

Each letter key on the keyboard contains an alternative character (for example, the alternative for q is 1). To enter an alternative character quickly, touch the key and slide your finger down.

14. Adding a Drawing in an Email

In addition to attaching pictures and files, you can now insert a drawing into an email. This is especially easy to do on an iPad Pro using the Apple Pencil. Refer to "*Adding a Drawing in an Email*" on page 218 to learn how.

15. Deleting Unused Applications Automatically

When you do not use an application for a long time, your phone can now delete that application automatically. Refer to "*Deleting Unused Applications Automatically*" on page 359 to learn more.

16. Accessing Control Center Quick Actions Without 3D Touch

You can now access the same 3D touch quick actions by touching and holding an icon in Control Center (such as the Camera icon).

17. Disabling In-App Ratings and Reviews

You can now disable those pesky pop-ups that appear in applications asking you for a rating or review. Refer to "*Disabling In-App Ratings and Reviews*" on page 359 to learn how.

18. Scanning a Document in the Notes Application

The Notes application now enables you to scan a document using your camera. Refer to "*Scanning a Document in the Notes Application*" on page 359 to learn how.

19. Answering a Call Automatically

One useful accessibility feature added in iOS 11 is the ability to answer calls automatically after a set amount of time. Refer to "*Answering Phone Calls Automatically*" on page 321 to learn how.

20. Connecting to a Wi-Fi Network Automatically

Starting in iOS 11, your phone will no longer ask to join open Wi-Fi networks by default. Instead, Auto Join is disabled by default until you enable it in **Wi-Fi Settings**.

21. Managing Notification Settings

iOS 11 brings three new notification settings:
- You can make notifications remain on the screen until you interact with them by touching or swiping them away (Persistent setting).
- You can disable notification previews for each application. When a notification preview is disabled, the notification simply reads "Notification" and the name of the application.
- You can block applications from appearing in your Recent Notifications section on the Cover Sheet.

Refer to *"Managing Notification Settings"* on page 303 to learn how to customize your notifications.

22. Sharing a Wi-Fi Password Over the Air

Instead of having to write out a long and complicated Wi-Fi password, you can now send your Wi-Fi password directly to another phone. The phone that is trying to connect to your Wi-Fi network needs to have iOS 11 installed. Refer to "*Sharing Your Wi-Fi Password Over the Air*" on page 360 to learn how.

Help Me! Guide to the iPhone X

23. Making an Emergency SOS Call

Any iPhone running iOS 11 now has the ability to make an automated emergency phone call in case you are hurt or in trouble. To make an SOS call, press the Sleep/Wake button five times fast. Refer to "*Making an Emergency SOS Call*" on page 61 to learn how to enable this feature.

24. Moving Multiple Application Icons at Once

You can now move more than application icon at a time by touching and holding one icon and then touching the rest on at a time. Refer to "*Organizing Icons*" on page 24 to learn more.

25. Shutting Down Your Phone without Using the Sleep/Wake Button

In case your Sleep/Wake button stops working, you can now shut down your phone or iPad from a settings menu. Refer to "*Shutting Down Your Phone without Using the Sleep/Wake Button*" on page 360 to learn how.

26. Viewing a List of All Attachments in Messages

To free up space on your phone, you can now view a list of all attachments in all of your messages and delete them as needed. Refer to "*Viewing All Attachments in a Conversation*" on page 108 to learn more.

Getting Started

Table of Contents

1. Button Layout
2. Charging the Phone
3. Turning the Phone On and Off
4. Installing a SIM Card
5. Navigating the Screens
6. Organizing Icons
7. Creating an Icon Folder
8. Using Wi-Fi
9. Accessing Quick Settings through the Control Center
10. Using the Cover Sheet
11. Accessing Application Shortcuts Using 3D Touch
12. Searching the Phone or Web for Content
13. Managing and Using Widgets
14. Using Interactive Notifications

1. Button Layout

The iPhone X has three buttons and one switch. The rest of the functionality is controlled by the touchscreen. The iPhone X is the first iPhone without a Home button. Each button has several functions, depending on the context in which it is used.

The buttons perform the following functions:

Help Me! Guide to the iPhone X

Figure 1: Left Side View

Volume Controls
- Controls the volume of the ringer. Refer to "*Adjusting Sound Settings*" on page 261 to learn more about setting ringtones or the sound volume.
- Controls the volume of the earpiece or speakerphone during a conversation.
- Controls the media volume.

Vibration Switch
- Turns Vibration on or off
- Turns the Sound on or off

Getting Started

Figure 2: Bottom View

Lightning Connector - Connects the phone to a computer in order to transfer data. Connects the phone to a charger.

Help Me! Guide to the iPhone X

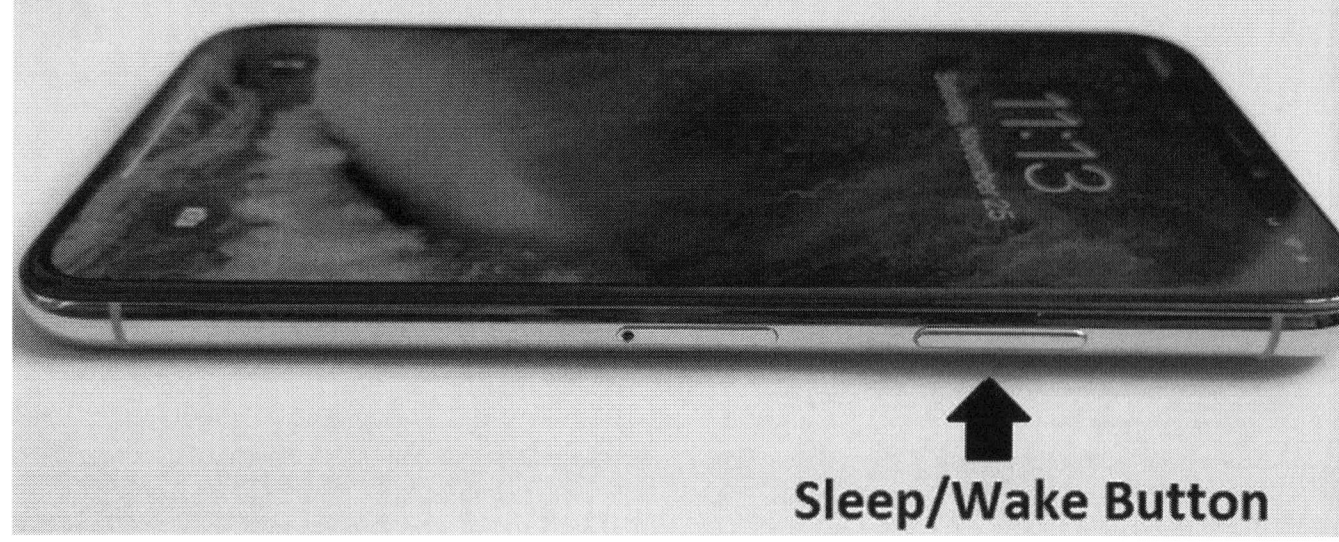

Figure 3: Right Side View

Sleep/Wake Button
- Turns the phone on and off when pressed together with either Volume Control button.
- Locks the phone and turns on the screen. This button is not necessary to turn on the screen when **Raise to Wake** is turned on.

2. Charging the Phone

To ensure that the phone works well, please follow these guidelines:

Note: You cannot use a cable that came with an iPhone 4S or earlier to charge an iPhone X.

When charging the battery, the meter in the upper right-hand corner of the screen (when unlocked) may show that it is fully charged; however, the charge is not complete until **100% Charged** appears on the lock screen.
Insert the Lightning cable into the Lightning Connector on the bottom of the phone. The lightning cable looks like this: . When the cable is inserted correctly, the indicator sound is played or the phone vibrates. Refer to "*Tips and Tricks*" on page 348 to learn about conserving battery life.

3. Turning the Phone On and Off

Use the Sleep/Wake button to turn the phone on or off. To turn the phone on, press and hold the **Sleep/Wake** button for two seconds. The phone turns on and the logo is displayed. After the phone has finished starting up, the Lock screen is displayed.

To unlock the phone, press the **Sleep/Wake** button while the screen is on, enter your password, or show your face.

Note: If the phone does not turn on after a few seconds, try charging the battery.

To turn the phone off, press and hold the **Sleep/Wake** button and either volume control button at the same time. The message "Slide to power off" appears. Touch the slider and move your finger to the right. The phone turns off. To keep the phone turned on, touch **Cancel**.

4. Installing a SIM Card

Insert the SIM card from an old phone to retain your personal information and phone number. The iPhone X is only compatible with nano SIM cards. The type of SIM card also depends on your carrier. For instance, you cannot insert a Verizon SIM card into an AT&T phone, and vice-versa.

To install a SIM card:
1. Insert the end of a paper clip or a SIM eject tool into the hole on the right side of the phone. The SIM card tray pops out, as shown in **Figure 4**.
2. Take out the old SIM card, if necessary, and insert the new SIM card with the short side facing away from the phone, as shown in **Figure 5**.
3. Re-insert the tray into the phone. The new SIM card is installed.

Help Me! Guide to the iPhone X

Figure 4: SIM Card Tray

Getting Started

Figure 5: SIM Card Inserted

5. Navigating the Screens

There are many ways to navigate the iPhone X screen. Use the following tips to quickly navigate the screens of the phone:
- Touch the bottom of the screen and slide your finger up to return to the Home screen at any time. Any application or tool that you were using will be in the same state when you return to it.
- When on a Home screen, slide your finger to the left or right to access additional pages. If nothing happens, the other pages are blank.
- Touch the center of the Home screen and slide your finger down to access the phone's search feature. You may search any data stored on your phone, including application data, as well as the web, iTunes, Application Store, movie show times, locations nearby, and much more. Refer to "*Searching the Phone or Web for Content*" on page 40 to learn more.

6. Organizing Icons

You may wish to re-order the location of the application icons on the screens. To organize application icons:
1. Touch an icon and hold it until all of the icons begin to shake (about two seconds). The icons can now be moved around the screen. Touch additional icons while holding the first to move multiple icons at once.
2. Move the icons to the desired location and let go of the screen. The icons are relocated and the surrounding icons are re-ordered accordingly. If an icon that used to be on the screen is gone, then it has been moved to a different Home screen in the process.
3. To move an icon to another screen, move the icon to the edge of the current one and hold it there. The adjacent screen appears. Drop the icon in the desired location.
4. Touch **Done** at the top of the screen or touch the bottom of the screen and slide your finger up. The icons are placed.

7. Creating an Icon Folder

When there are many icons on the Home screens, you may wish to organize the icons into folders. Each folder can have a meaningful name to enable you to find the icons easily. To create a folder:
1. Touch an icon and hold it until all of the icons begin to shake. The icons can now be moved.
2. Move one icon on top of another and let go of the screen. A folder with the selected icons is created, as shown in **Figure 6**. Touch the folder and then touch and hold its name to enter a name for the folder.
3. Enter a name for the folder, and touch **Done**. The new name is saved.
4. To exit the folder, touch the bottom of the screen. The folder is closed.
5. Touch **Done** at the top of the screen or touch the bottom of the screen and slide your finger up. The icons stop shaking.

Note: To add more icons to a folder, just touch an icon while it is shaking and move it onto the folder.

Getting Started

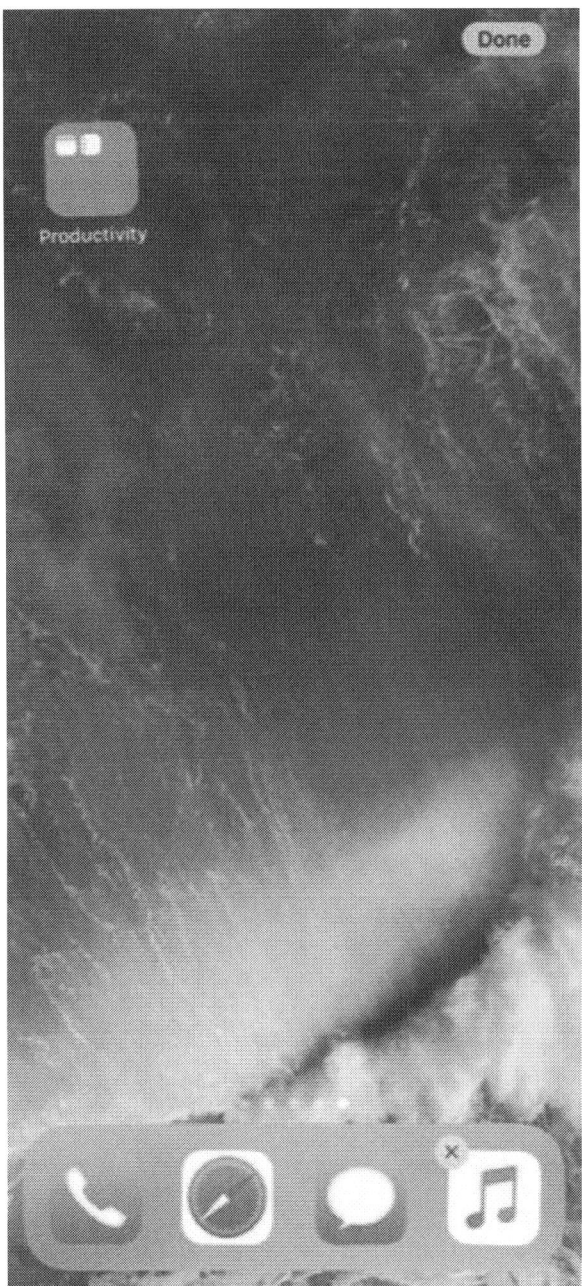

Figure 6: A New Folder

25

8. Using Wi-Fi

Use a nearby Wi-Fi hotspot or a home router to avoid having to use data. Wi-Fi is required to download large applications. To turn on Wi-Fi:

1. Touch the ![icon] icon. The Settings screen appears, as shown in **Figure 7**.
2. Touch **Wi-Fi**. The Wi-Fi Networks screen appears, as shown in **Figure 8**.
3. Touch the ![switch] switch next to 'Wi-Fi'. Wi-Fi turns on and a list of available networks appears, as shown in **Figure 9**. If the network has an ![lock] icon next to it, a password is needed to connect to it.
4. Touch the network to which you would like to connect. The Wi-Fi Password prompt appears if the network is protected, as shown in **Figure 10**.
5. Enter the network password. Touch **Join**. Provided that you entered the correct password, a check mark appears next to the network name and the ![wifi] icon appears at the top of the screen. You are connected to the Wi-Fi network.

Note: If you enter an incorrect password, the message "Unable to join the network >Network Name<" appears, where '>Network Name<' is the name of your network. The network password is usually written on the modem given to you by your internet service provider. It is sometimes called a WEP Key.

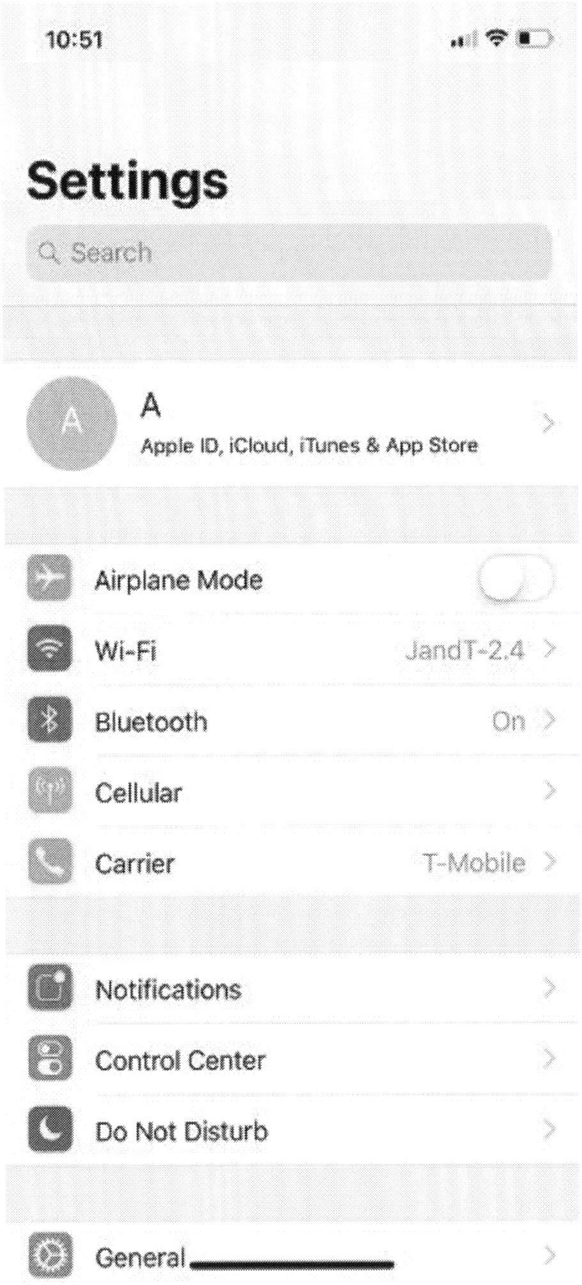

Figure 7: Settings Screen

Help Me! Guide to the iPhone X

Figure 8: Wi-Fi Networks Screen

28

Getting Started

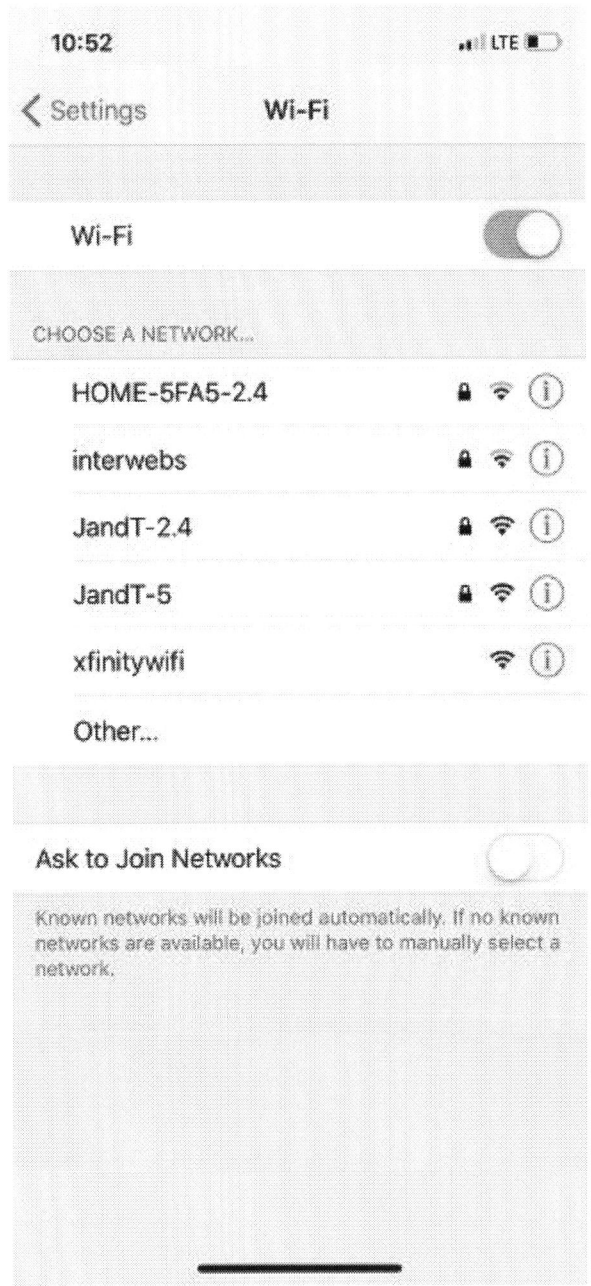

Figure 9: List of Available Wi-Fi Networks

29

Help Me! Guide to the iPhone X

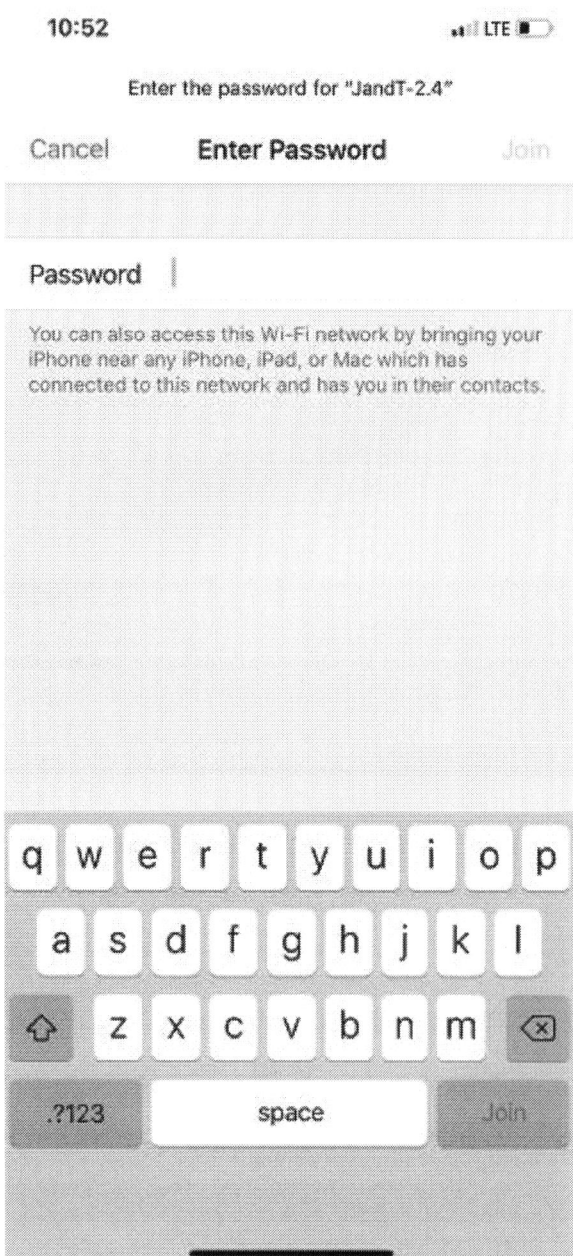

Figure 10: Wi-Fi Password Prompt

9. Accessing Quick Settings through the Control Center

There are various settings that you can access without opening the Settings screen by using the Control Center. To use the Control Center:
1. Touch the upper right-hand corner of the screen at any time and slide your finger down. The Control Center appears, as shown in **Figure 11**.
2. Touch one of the following icons to turn the corresponding function on or off:

 - Turns Airplane mode on or off.

 - Turns Cellular Data on or off.

 - Turns Wi-Fi on or off.

 - Turns Bluetooth on or off.

 - Turns 'Do not disturb' on or off.

 - Turns automatic screen rotation on or off.

 - Turns the flashlight on or off.

 - Opens the timer application.

 - Opens the calculator application.

 - Turns on the camera.

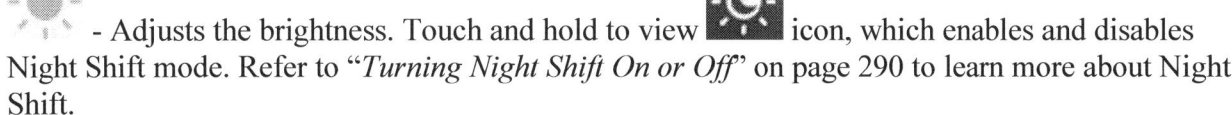

- Adjusts the brightness. Touch and hold to view icon, which enables and disables Night Shift mode. Refer to "*Turning Night Shift On or Off*" on page 290 to learn more about Night Shift.
You can also force touch (3D Touch) an icon for additional options.

 - Adjusts the volume.

Help Me! Guide to the iPhone X

Figure 11: Control Center Main Screen

10. Using the Cover Sheet

The Cover Sheet replaced the Notification Center in iOS 11. This screen looks the same whether your phone is locked or unlocked.

The Cover Sheet shows event reminders and all types of alerts, such as calendar events, received texts, and missed calls. You can also search the iPhone, App Store, the web, or even content within applications from this screen.

To open the Cover Sheet, touch the upper left-hand corner of the screen at any time (even while using an application) and move your finger down. Touch a notification to open the corresponding application. For instance, touch a calendar event to open the calendar.

11. Accessing Application Shortcuts Using 3D Touch

Some applications that support 3D Touch let you press down firmly on the application icon on the Home screen. You can then slide your finger to the option of your choice, and let go of the screen to confirm your selection.

Here are several examples of the menus that appear when using 3D Touch with application icons:

Safari

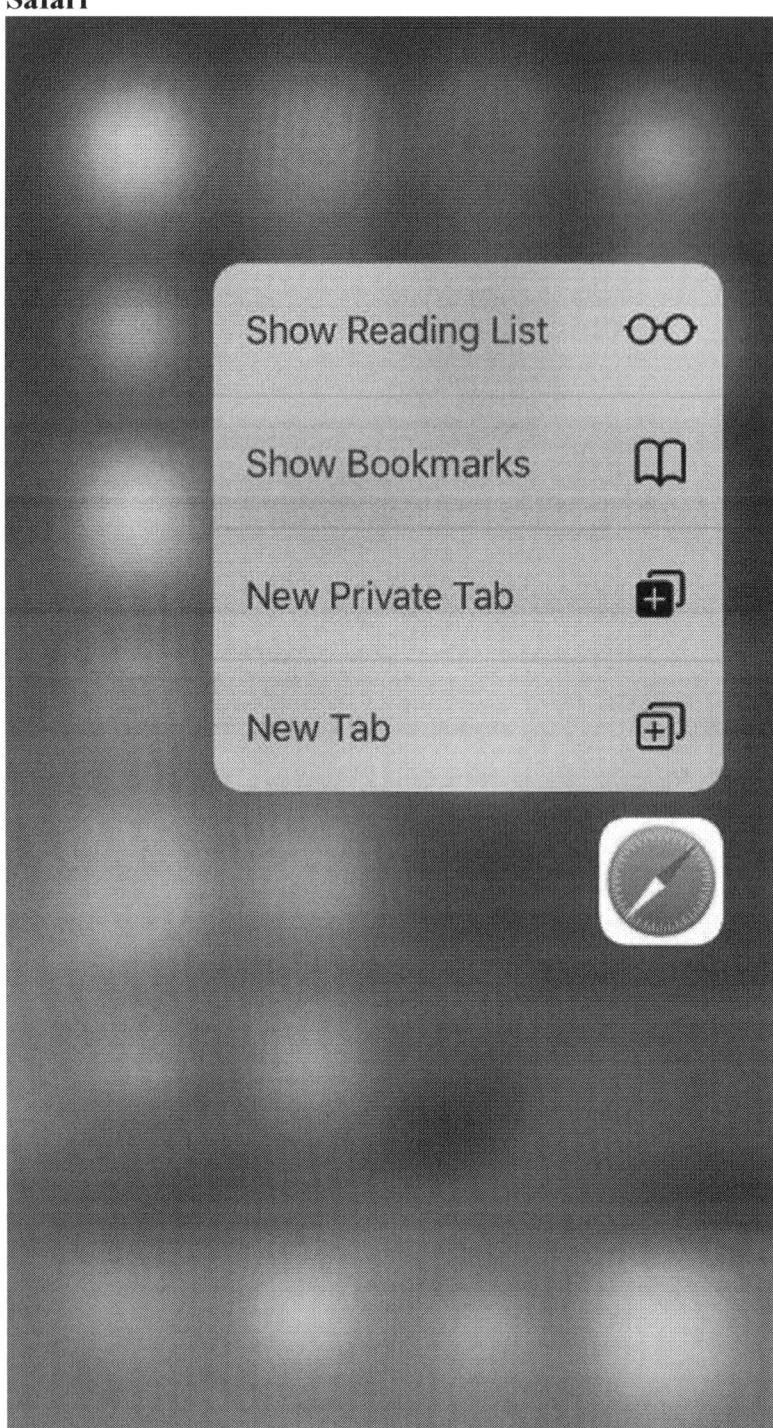

Camera

Help Me! Guide to the iPhone X

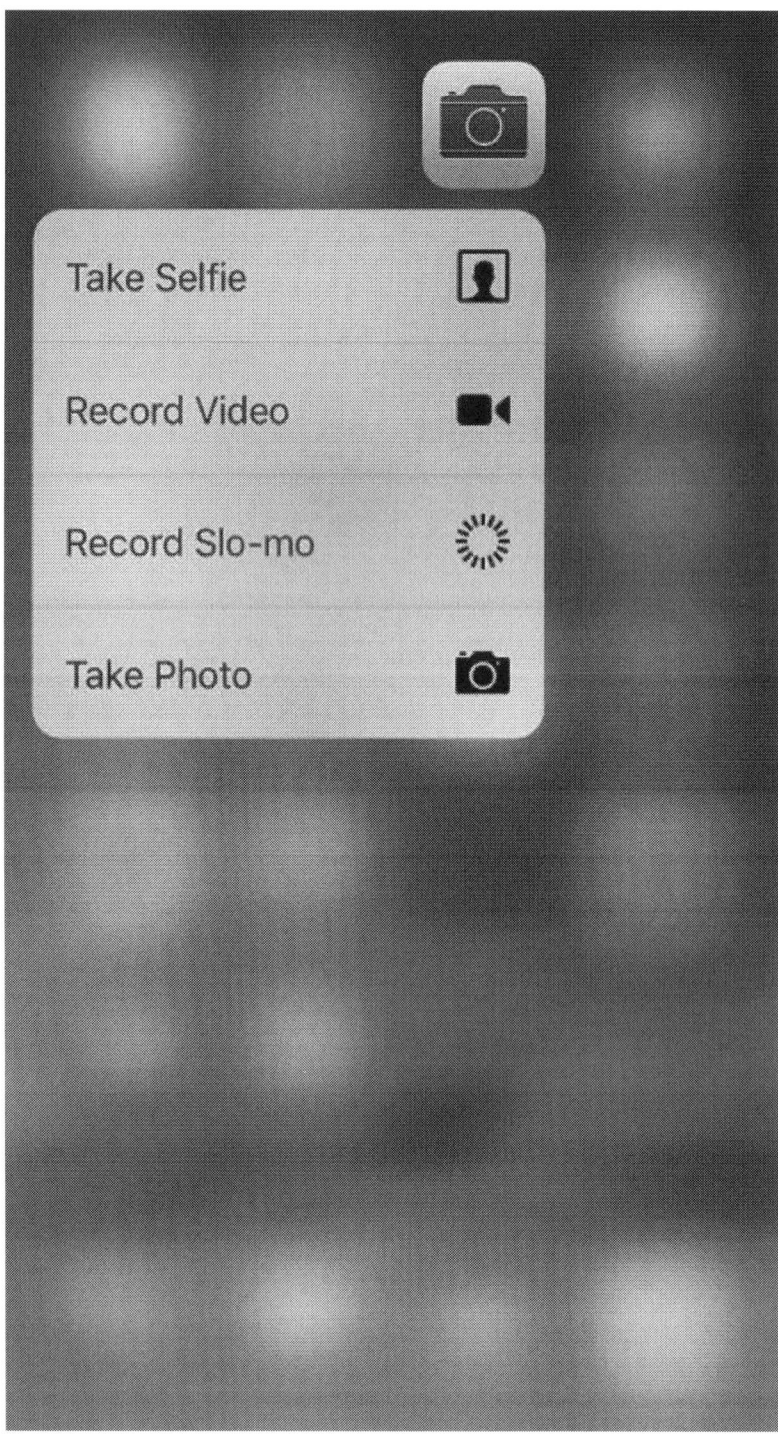

Mail

Getting Started

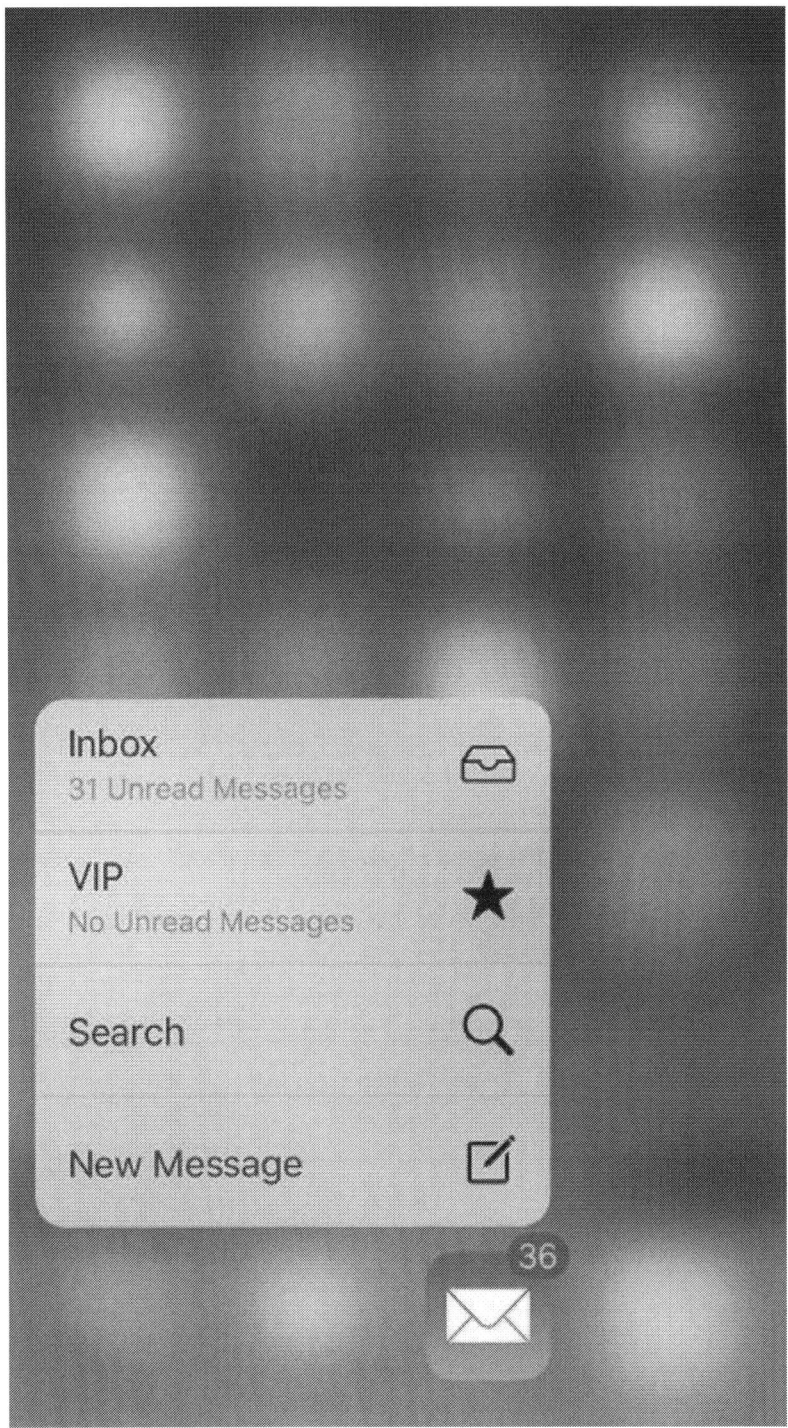

Music

Help Me! Guide to the iPhone X

Maps

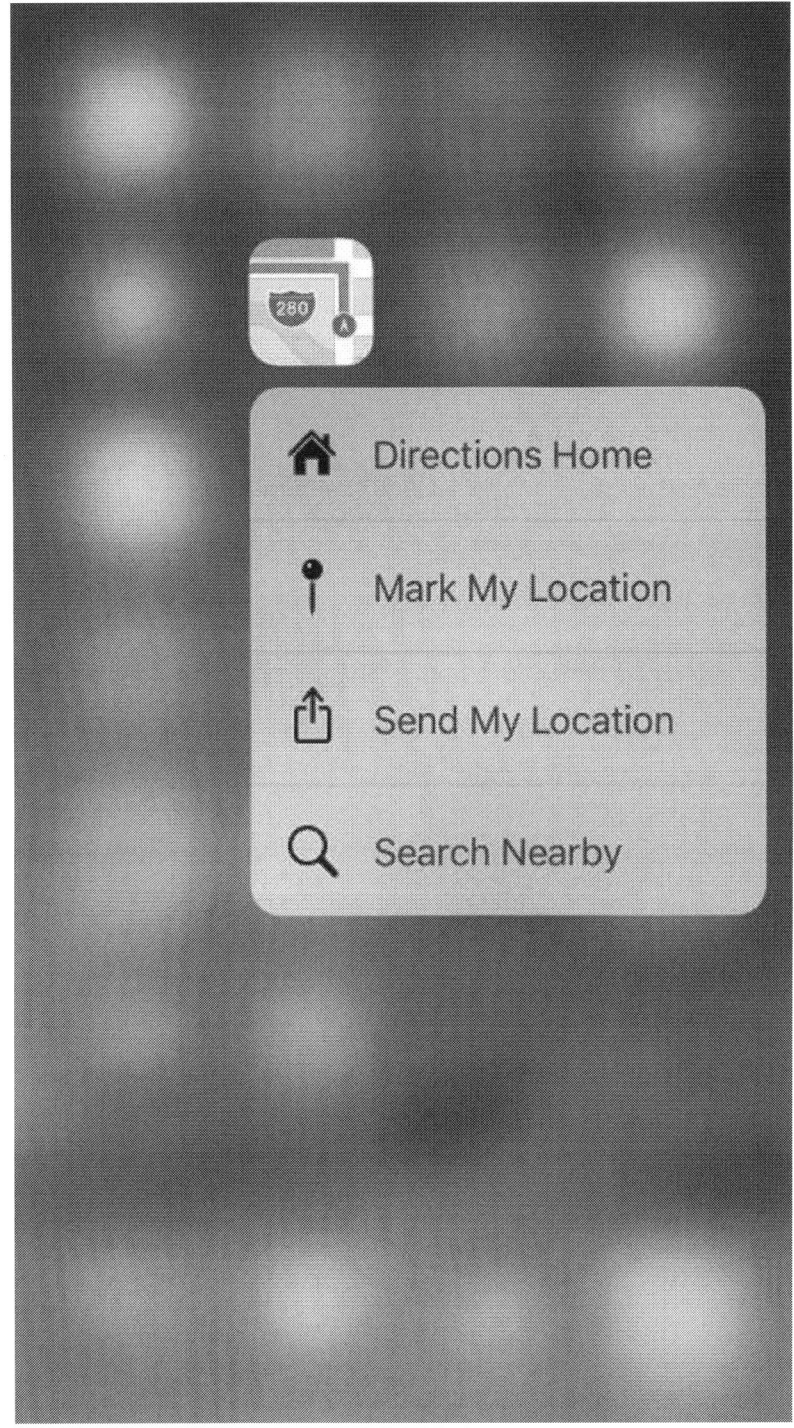

12. Searching the Phone or Web for Content

To find an application, email, contact, event, or other item on your phone or on the web, use the Spotlight Search. To use Spotlight Search, touch the center of any home screen, and slide your finger down. The Spotlight Search screen appears. Search results appear as you type. You can also call or message contacts directly from the search results.

13. Managing and Using Widgets

You can use widgets on your iPhone. A widget is a tool that you can use to quickly find content within applications, such as calendar events, email, and photos. You can access widgets from the Cover Sheet.

To use a widget, open the Cover Sheet and slide your finger to the right. The Widget screen appears, as shown in **Figure 12**.

To manage widgets:
1. Scroll down and touch **Edit**. The Add Widgets screen appears, as shown in **Figure 13**.
2. Touch the ![−] icon next to a widget, and then touch **Remove** to remove a widget from the Widget screen.
3. Touch the ![+] icon next to a widget to add it to the Widget screen.
4. Touch **Done**. The updated Widget screen appears.

Getting Started

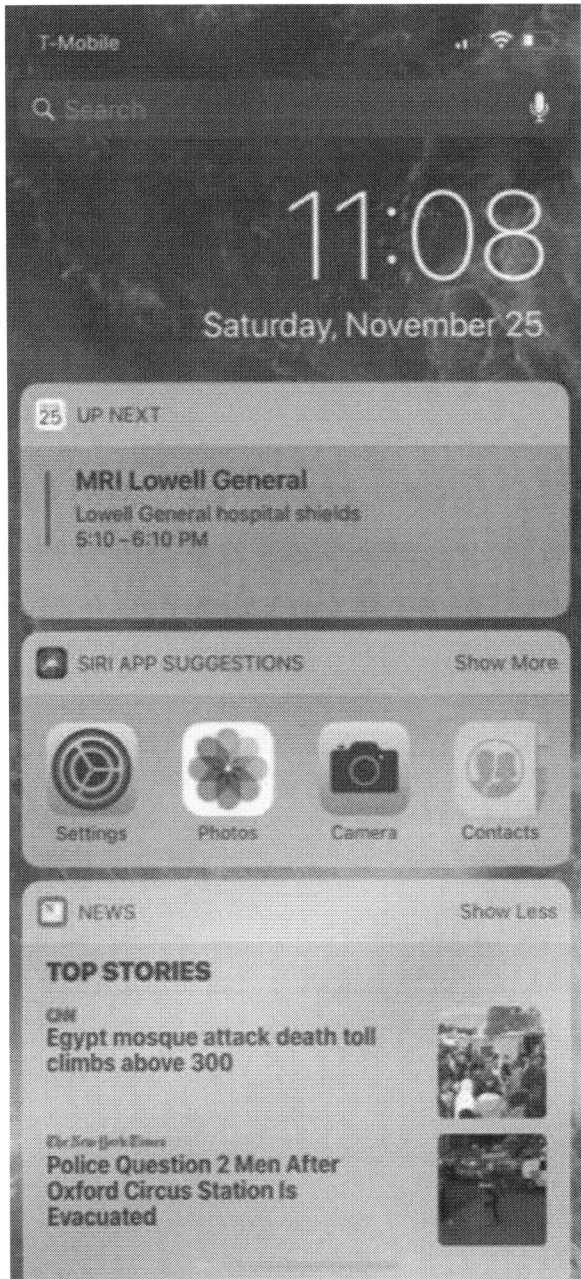

Figure 12: Widget Screen on the Cover Sheet

41

Help Me! Guide to the iPhone X

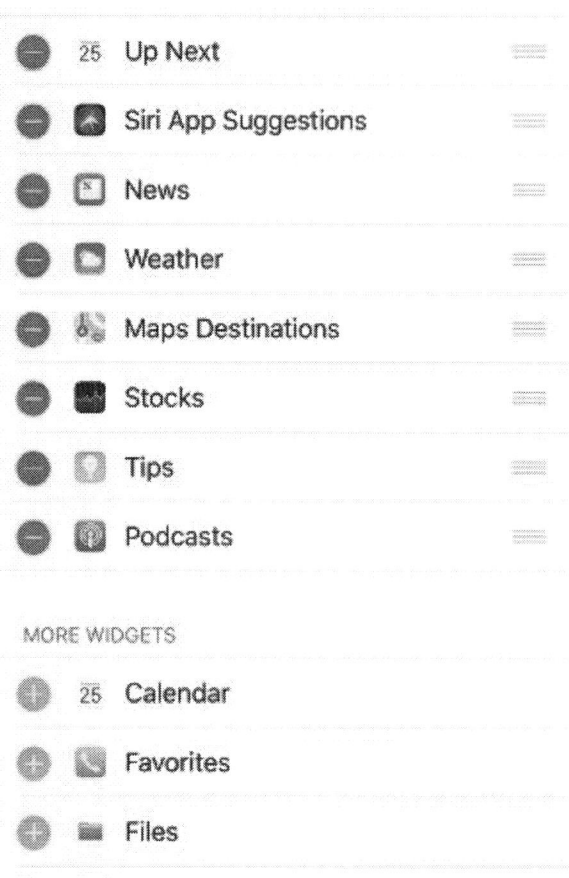

Figure 13: Add Widgets Screen

42

14. Using Interactive Notifications

When a notification arrives on the Cover Sheet, you can view it or clear it immediately. When a message notification arrives while the phone is unlocked, you can reply to the message from the notification and attach images or audio. Use the following tips with interactive notifications:
- Slide your finger to the left to view the notification options. Touch **Clear** or **View** to perform the associated action.
- Slide your finger to the right to view the notification. Sliding your finger to the right on a Missed Call notification immediately returns the call.
- 3D Touch the Missed Call notification to return the call.
- 3D Touch the text message notification to quickly reply to the text.

Making Voice and Video Calls

Table of Contents

1. Dialing a Number
2. Calling a Contact
3. Calling a Favorite
4. Returning a Recent Phone Call
5. Receiving a Voice Call
6. Replying to an Incoming Call with a Text Message
7. Setting a Reminder to Return an Incoming Call
8. Using the Speakerphone During a Voice Call
9. Using the Keypad During a Voice Call
10. Using the Mute Function During a Voice Call
11. Putting a Caller on Hold (hidden button)
12. Starting a Conference Call (Adding a Call)
13. Making a Call Over Wi-Fi
14. Making an Emergency SOS Call
15. Blocking Phone Numbers
16. Starting a FaceTime Call

1. Dialing a Number

Numbers that are not in your Phonebook can be dialed on the keypad. To manually dial a phone number, touch the icon on the Home screen. The keypad appears, as shown in **Figure 1**. Touch the icon at the bottom of the screen if you do not see the keypad. Enter the desired phone number and then touch the at the bottom of the screen. The phone dials the number.

Making Voice and Video Calls

Figure 1: Keypad

45

2. Calling a Contact

If a number is stored in your Phonebook, you may touch the name of a contact to dial it. To call a contact already stored in your phone:

1. Touch the [icon] icon on the Home screen. The Phonebook appears, as shown in **Figure 2**.
2. Touch the name of a contact. The Contact Information screen appears, as shown in **Figure 3**.
3. Touch the desired phone number. The phone calls the contact's number. Refer to "*Managing Contacts*" on page 65 to learn more about adding or removing contacts.

Note: For some unexplained reason, Apple has decided to place the [icon] icon in the Extras folder by default. If you cannot find it, look in that folder.

Making Voice and Video Calls

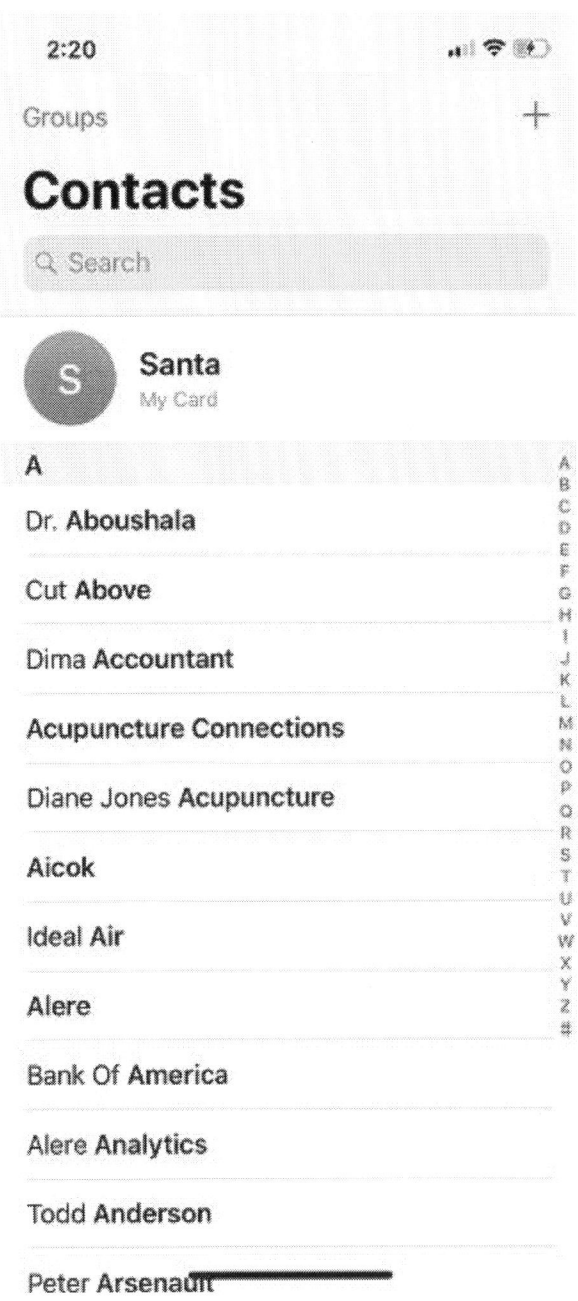

Figure 2: Phonebook

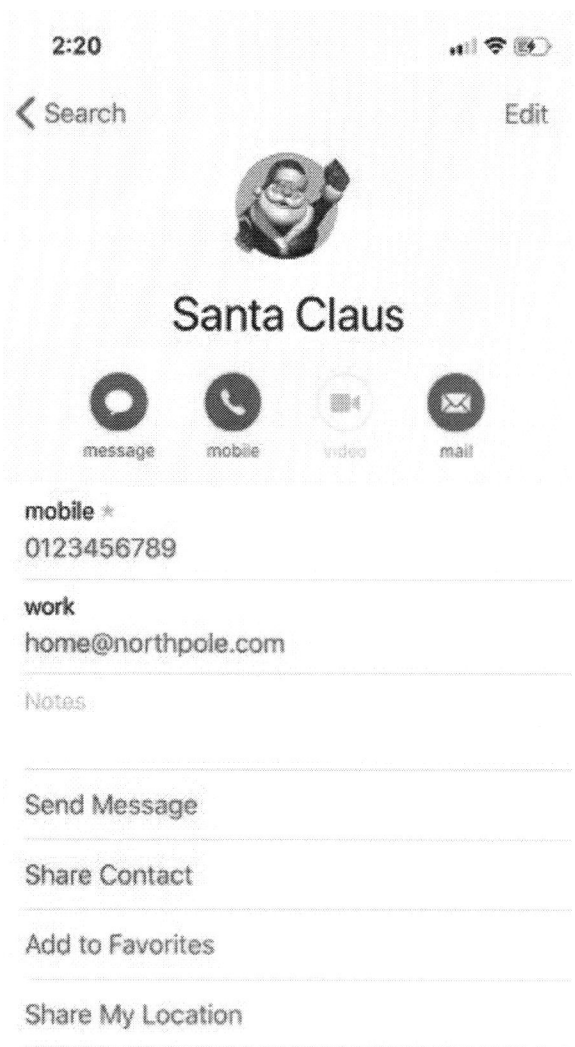

Figure 3: Contact Information Screen

Making Voice and Video Calls

3. Calling a Favorite

There is no Speed Dial feature on the iPhone X. Instead, frequently dialed numbers can be saved as Favorites, which can be accessed more quickly than other contacts. To call a number stored in Favorites:

1. Touch the ![phone] icon on the Home screen. The keypad screen appears.
2. Touch the ![star] icon at the bottom of the screen. The Favorites screen appears, as shown in **Figure 4**. If you wish to add a Favorite contact, touch the ![plus] button.
3. Touch the name of a Favorite. The phone calls the selected number. Refer to "*Managing Contacts*" on page 65 to learn more about managing Favorites.

Help Me! Guide to the iPhone X

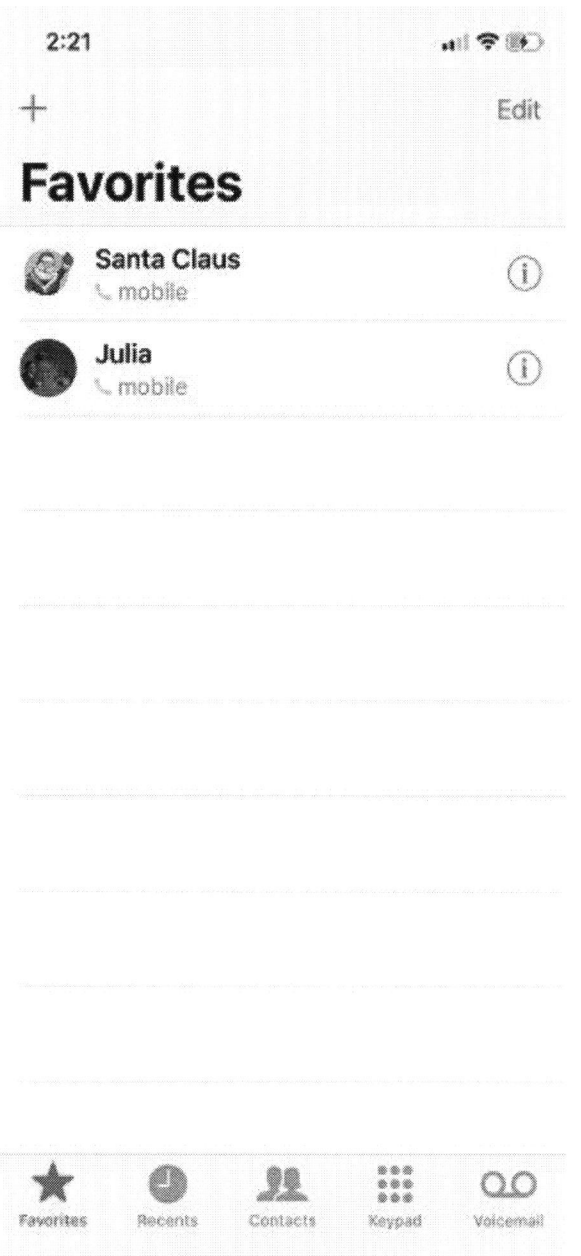

Figure 4: Favorites Screen

50

4. Returning a Recent Phone Call

After missing a call, your phone will notify you of who called and at what time. The phone also shows a history of all recently placed calls. To view and return a missed call or redial a recently entered number:

1. Touch the ![phone icon] icon on the Home screen. The Calling screen appears.
2. Touch the ![clock icon] icon at the bottom of the screen. The Recent Calls screen appears, with the most recent calls on top. Missed or declined calls are shown in red. The ![arrow icon] icon is shown next to a placed call, as shown in **Figure 5**.
3. Touch the name of a contact. The phone dials the contact.

You can also return a missed call by touching the notification on the Lock screen and sliding your finger to the right. Refer to "*Using Interactive Notifications*" on page 43 to learn more.

Note: To view only missed calls, touch **Missed** *at the top of the Recent Calls screen.*

Help Me! Guide to the iPhone X

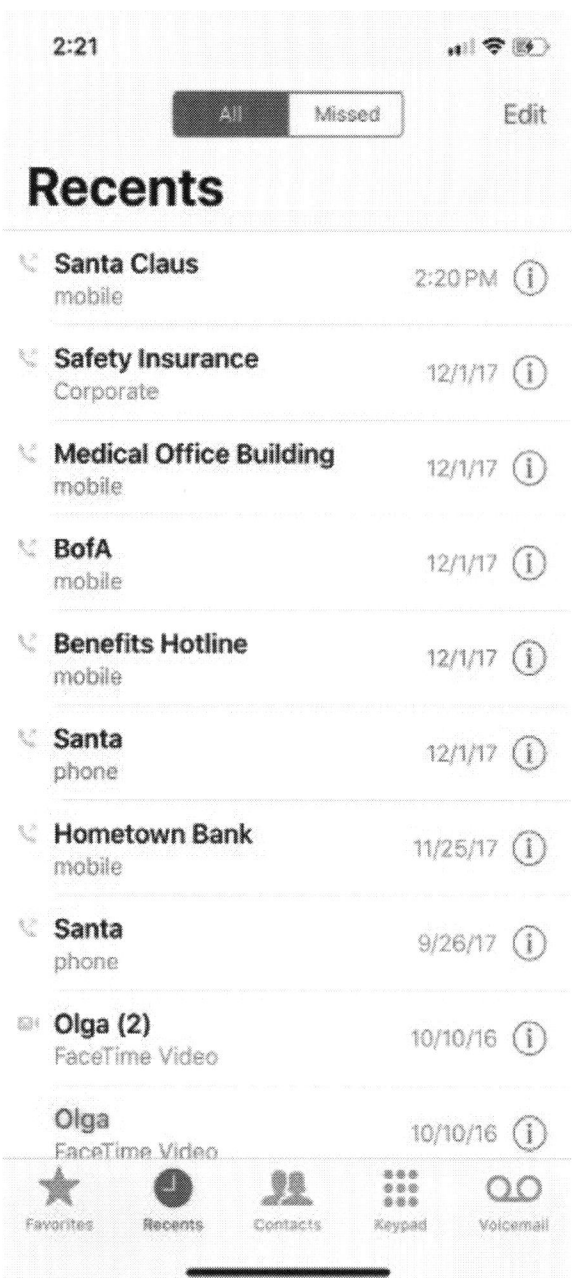

Figure 5: Recent Calls Screen

52

Making Voice and Video Calls

5. Receiving a Voice Call

There are several ways to accept or reject a voice call based on whether or not the screen is locked. Use the following tips when receiving a voice call:

- To pick up an incoming voice call while the phone is locked, touch and move the on the slider to the right. The call is answered.
- To mute the ringer, press the Sleep/Wake button. To reject the incoming call, press the Sleep/Wake button again.
- To receive an incoming call while using an application (or viewing a Home screen), touch the button. To reject the incoming call, touch the button. The call is declined. The number then appears in red in the list of recent calls, signifying that it is a missed call, and a notification appears above the icon on the Home screen.
- Touch **Message** or **Remind Me** to decline a call if you are currently busy but wish to address it later. Refer to "*Replying to an Incoming Call with a Text Message*" on page 53 or "*Setting a Reminder to Return an Incoming Call*" on page 53 to learn more about these options.

6. Replying to an Incoming Call with a Text Message

During an incoming call, you may reject it and automatically send a text message to the caller. To reply to an incoming call with a text message:
1. Touch **Message** during an incoming voice call. A list of pre-defined text messages appears.
2. Touch a message. The selected text message is sent to the caller. Alternatively, touch **Custom** to enter your own text message.
3. Touch **Send**. The phone sends the custom text message to the caller.

7. Setting a Reminder to Return an Incoming Call

During an incoming call, you may reject it and automatically set a reminder for yourself to return the call at a specified time or when you reach a specific location (such as work or home). To set a reminder to return an incoming call, touch **Remind Me** during an incoming voice call. The following reminder options appear: 'In 1 hour' and 'When I leave'. Touch **In 1 hour**. The phone displays a pop-up after one hour has passed reminding you to call back. Alternatively, touch **When I leave** to have the phone remind you when you leave your current location.

8. Using the Speakerphone During a Voice Call

The phone has a built-in Speakerphone, which is useful when calling from a car or when several people need to hear the conversation. To use the Speakerphone during a phone call:
1. Place a voice call. The Calling Screen appears.
2. Touch the ![icon] icon. The speakerphone is turned on. Adjust the volume of the speakerphone by using the Volume Controls. Refer to "*Button Layout*" on page 17 to locate the Volume Controls.
3. Touch the ![icon] icon. The Speakerphone is turned off.

Making Voice and Video Calls

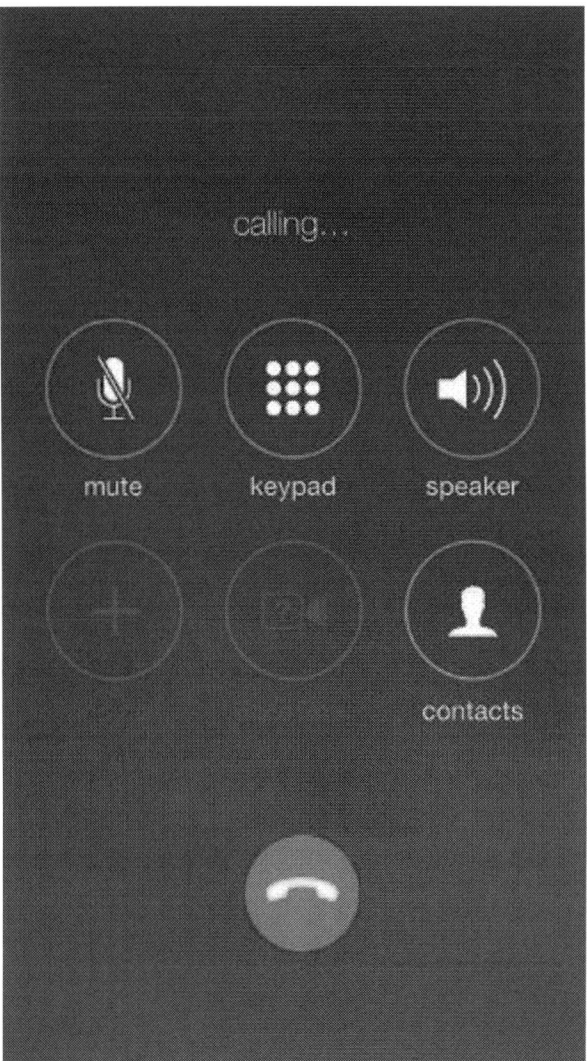

Figure 6: Calling Screen

9. Using the Keypad During a Voice Call

You may wish to use the keypad while on a call in order to input numbers in an automated menu or to enter an account number. To use the keypad during a phone call, place a voice call and touch the ▦ icon. The keypad appears. To hide the keypad again, touch **Hide**.

10. Using the Mute Function During a Voice Call

During a voice call, you may wish to mute your side of the conversation. When mute is turned on, the person on the other end of the line will not hear anything on your side. To use Mute during a call, place a voice call and touch the ![mute] icon. The phone mutes your voice and the caller(s) can no longer hear you, but you are still able to hear them. Touch the ![mute] icon. Mute is turned off.

11. Putting a Caller on Hold (hidden button)

Apple replaced the Hold button (![hold]) with the ![?] button on the iPhone 4 and later generations. However, the Hold function still exists. Press and hold the ![mute] button while on a call until the ![pause] button appears. Release the screen. The call is put on hold.

12. Starting a Conference Call (Adding a Call)

To talk to more than one person at a time, call another person while continuing the current call. To create a conference call, place a voice call and then touch the ![+] icon. The list of contacts or the keypad is shown. Dial a number or select a contact to call. The first contact is put on hold while the phone dials and connects to the second. Touch the ![merge] icon. A three-way conference call is created, as shown in **Figure 7**.

Note: Up to six lines may be included in a conference call.

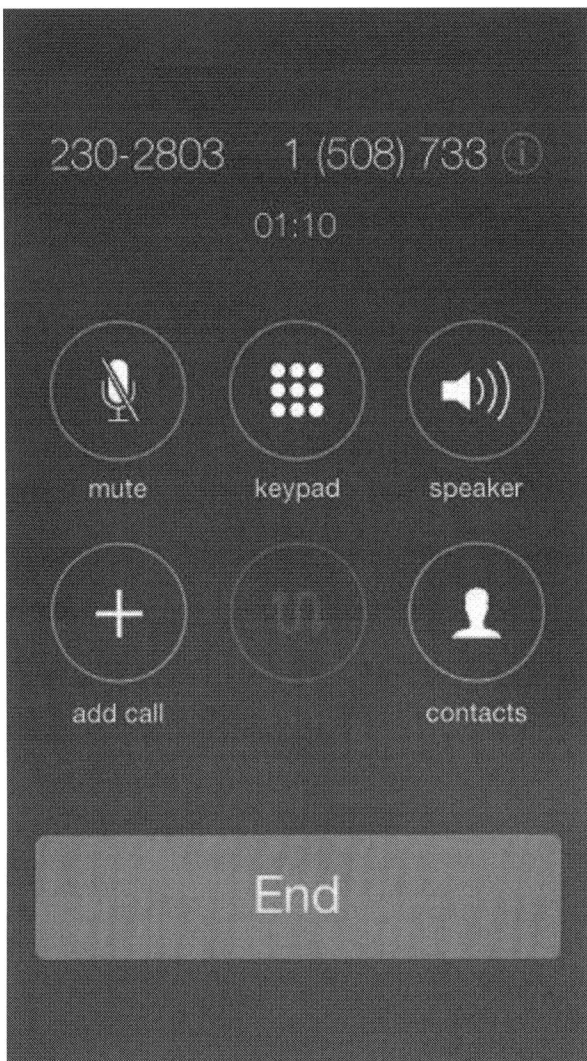
Figure 7: Three-Way Conference Call

13. Making a Call Over Wi-Fi

You can make calls using your Wi-Fi connection if you do not have any service, or to avoid using up your minutes. Calls over Wi-Fi connection will often be clearer and less prone to being dropped. To make a call using Wi-Fi, you must first turn on the feature. To turn on Wi-Fi Calling:

1. Touch the icon. The Settings screen appears, as shown in **Figure 8**.
2. Scroll down and touch **Phone**. The Phone Settings screen appears, as shown in **Figure 9**.
3. Touch **Wi-Fi Calling**. The Wi-Fi Calling settings appear, as shown in **Figure 10**.
4. Touch the switch next to **Wi-Fi Calling on This iPhone**. Wi-Fi Calling is turned on. To turn off Wi-Fi calling, touch the switch next to **Wi-Fi Calling on This iPhone**.

Figure 8: Settings Screen

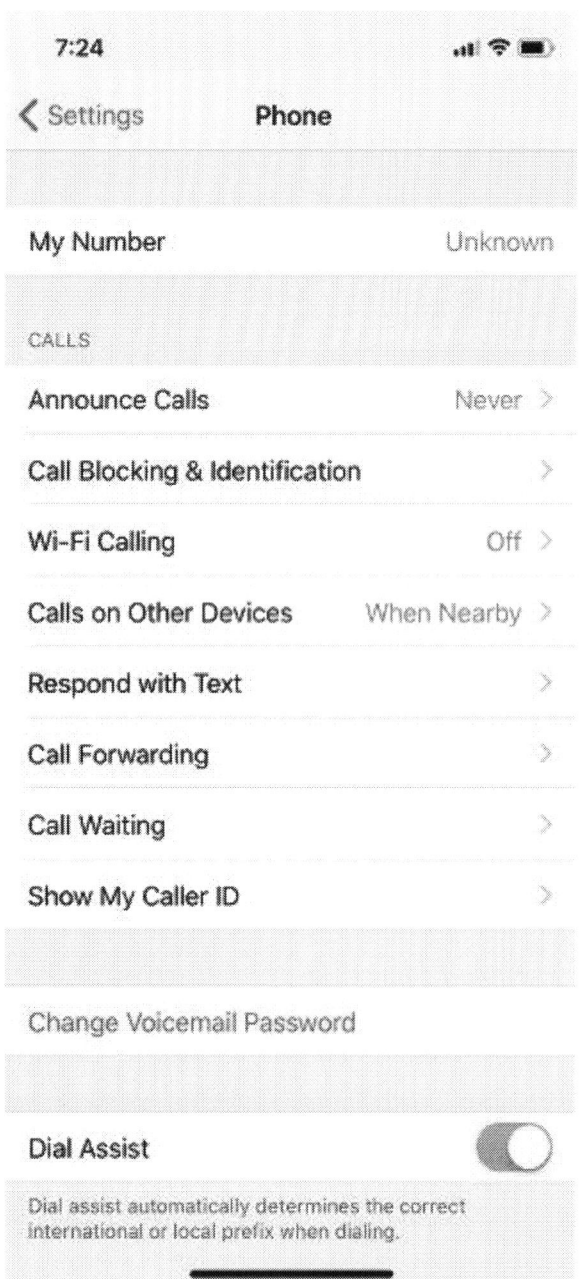

Figure 9: Phone Settings Screen

Making Voice and Video Calls

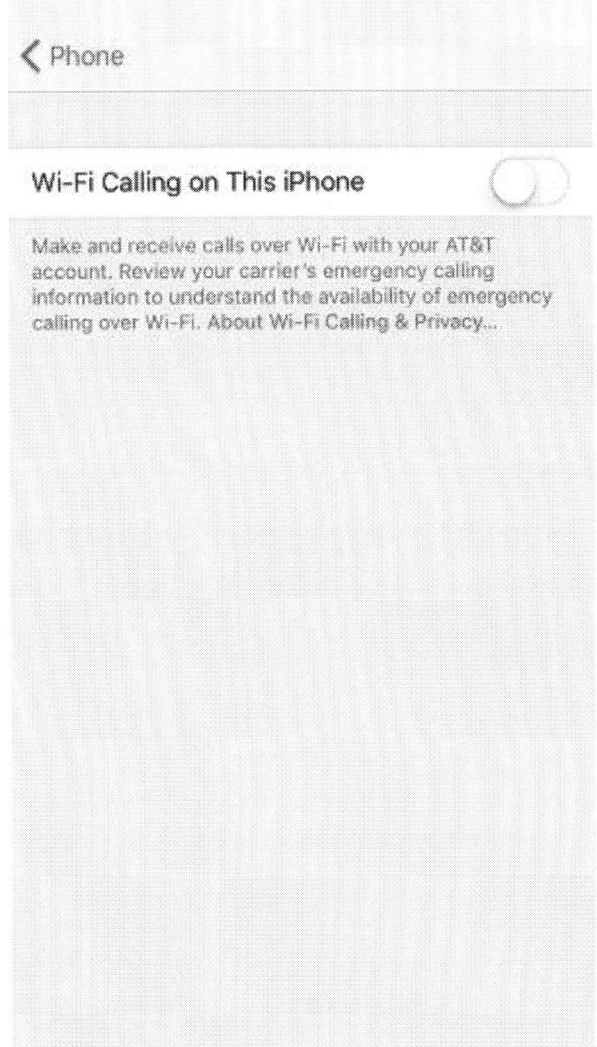

Figure 10: Wi-Fi Calling Settings

14. Making an Emergency SOS Call

The Emergency SOS feature is enabled by default starting in iOS 11 and cannot be turned off. To make an emergency SOS call if you are in trouble, press the Sleep/Wake button five times fast.

Touch the ![SOS] icon and slide it to the right to make the call.

15. Blocking Phone Numbers

If you do not wish to receive phone calls, text messages, or FaceTime calls from a specific number, you can block it. In order to block a number, you must first add it to your Phonebook. Refer to "*Adding a New Contact*" on page 65 to learn how. To block a number:

1. Touch the ![icon] icon. The Settings screen appears.
2. Scroll down and touch **Phone**. The Phone Settings screen appears.
3. Touch **Call Blocking & Identification**. The Call Blocking & Identification screen appears, as shown in **Figure 11**.
4. Touch **Block Contact**. The Phonebook appears.
5. Touch the contact whom you wish to block. The contact is added to the list and will be blocked.

To remove a contact from the list, touch the name of the contact, slide your finger to the left, then touch **Unblock**.

Making Voice and Video Calls

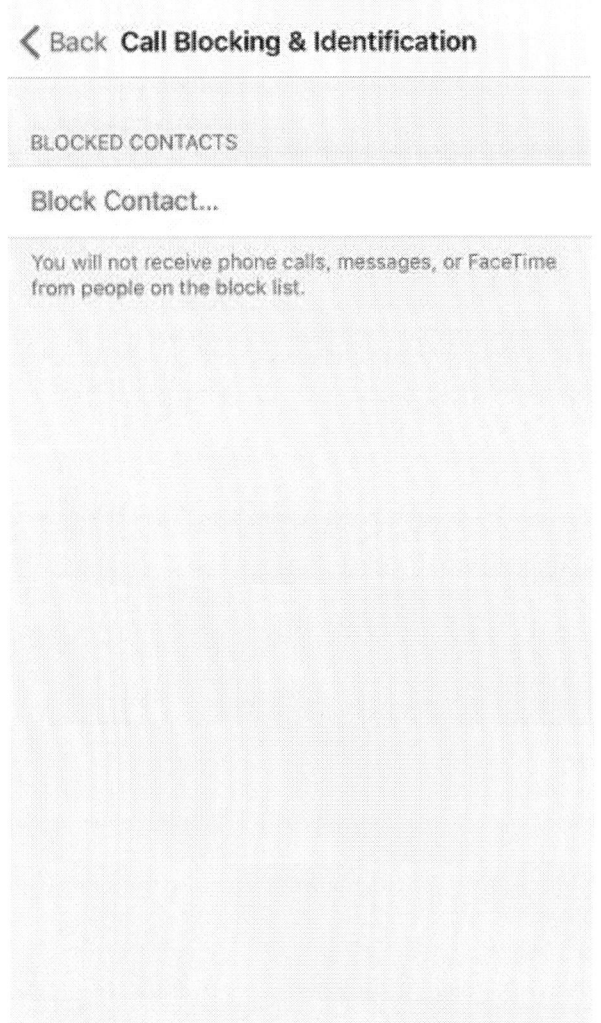

Figure 11: Call Blocking & Identification Screen

16. Starting a FaceTime Call

The iPhone X has the ability to place video calls to other phones, such as iPads, Macs, or iPods (third generation and higher). FaceTime does not require a Wi-Fi connection. You can place and receive FaceTime calls using a 4G connection (provided that you have at least one bar of service). However, using Wi-Fi may still provide a better video calling experience. Refer to "*Using Wi-Fi*" on page 26 to learn how to turn it on. You may also place a FaceTime voice call if you do not wish to use the camera. To place a Facetime call:

1. Touch the icon on the Home screen. The Phonebook appears.

Help Me! Guide to the iPhone X

2. Touch the name of a contact. The Contact Information screen appears.
3. Touch the 🎥 icon to place a FaceTime call. A Facetime call is placed. A high-pitched beeping sound plays until the call connects.
4. Touch the 📷 button at any time to switch cameras, as outlined in **Figure 12**. Using this feature, you can either show your contact what you are seeing or show them your face.

iOS 11 phones can also receive FaceTime calls. To receive an incoming FaceTime call, touch **Accept** or touch and move the 📞 on the slider to the right.

Note: You cannot place a FaceTime call to a phone that is not compatible with FaceTime. The 🎥 icon does not appear on the Contact Information screen if the contact's phone cannot use FaceTime.

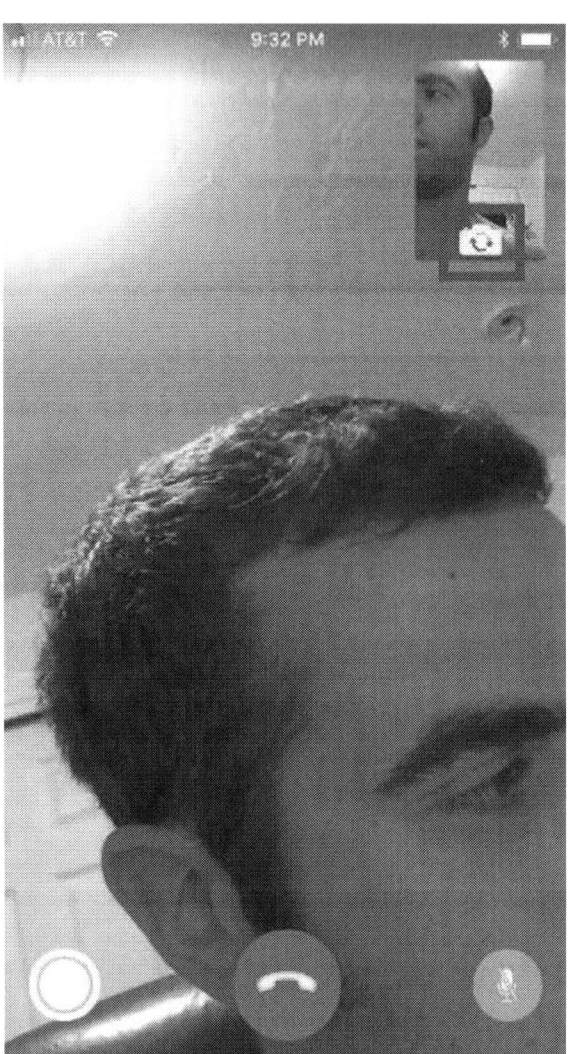

Figure 12: Switch Camera Icon

64

Managing Contacts

Table of Contents

1. Adding a New Contact
2. Finding a Contact
3. Deleting a Contact
4. Editing Contact Information
5. Sharing a Contact's Information
6. Changing the Contact Sort Order

1. Adding a New Contact

You can store phone numbers, email addresses, and other contact information in the phonebook. To add a new contact to the phonebook:

Note: For some unexplained reason, Apple has decided to place the Contacts icon in the Extras folder by default. If you cannot find it, look in that folder.

1. Touch the  icon on the Home screen. The phonebook appears.
2. Touch the ✚ button at the top of the screen. The New Contact screen appears, as shown in **Figure 1**.
3. Touch **First name**. The keyboard appears. Enter the first name of the contact.
4. Touch **Last name**. Enter the last name of the contact.
5. Touch any empty field to enter the desired information, and then touch **Done** in the upper right-hand corner of the screen. The contact's information is stored.

Note: Refer to "Tips and Tricks" on page 348 to learn how to add an extension after the contact's phone number.

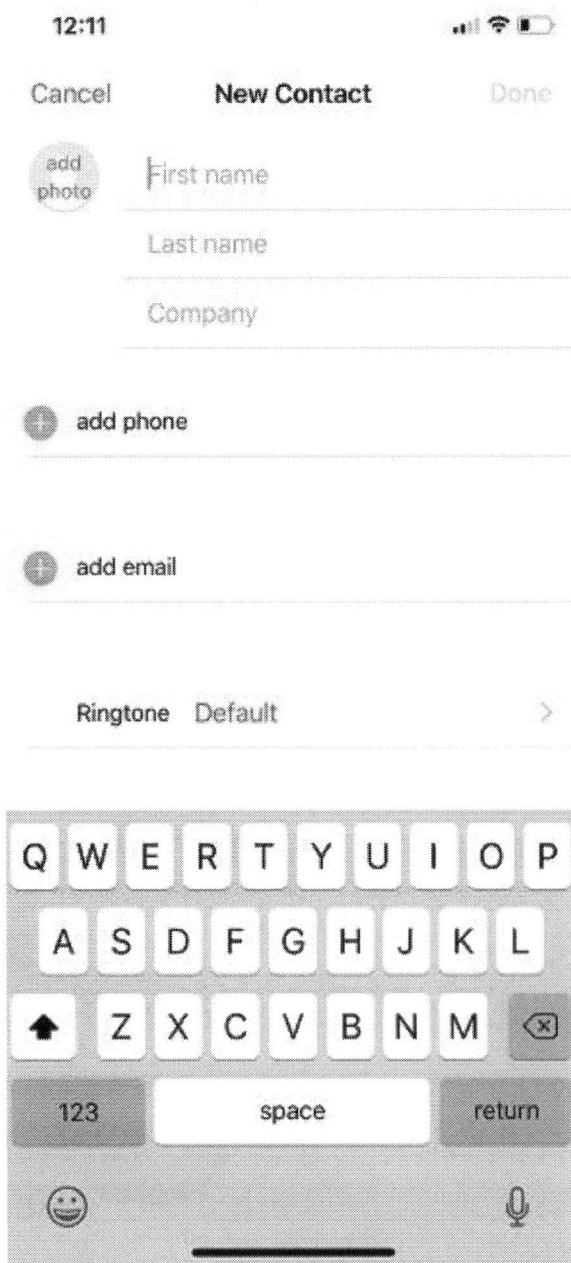

Figure 1: New Contact Screen

2. Finding a Contact

After adding contacts to your phone's phonebook, you may search for them. To find a stored contact:

1. Touch the ![icon] icon on the Home screen. The phonebook appears.
2. Touch **Search** at the top of the screen. The keyboard appears.
3. Start typing the name of a contact. Contact matches appear as you type, as shown in **Figure 2**.
4. Touch a match. The Contact Info screen appears, as shown in **Figure 3**.

Help Me! Guide to the iPhone X

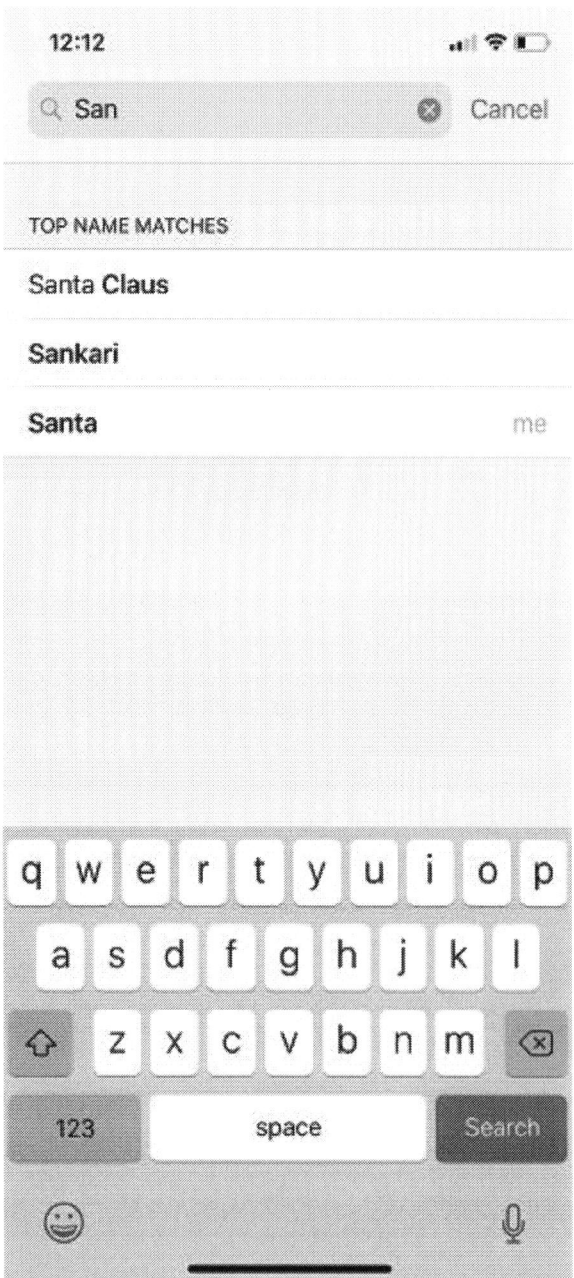

Figure 2: Contact Matches

Figure 3: Contact Info Screen

3. Deleting a Contact

You may delete contact information from your phonebook in order to free up space. To delete unwanted contact information:

Warning: There is no way to restore contact information after it has been deleted.

1. Touch the icon on the Home screen. The phonebook appears. If a list of all contacts does not appear, touch **All Contacts** in the upper left-hand corner of the screen to view the list.
2. Find and touch the name of the contact that you wish to delete. The Contact Info screen appears. Refer to *"Finding a Contact"* on page 67 to learn how to search for a contact.
3. Touch **Edit** at the top of the screen. The Contact Information Editing screen appears.
4. Scroll down and touch **Delete Contact** at the bottom of the screen, as shown in **Figure 4**. A Confirmation dialog appears.
5. Touch **Delete Contact** again. The contact's information is deleted and will no longer appear in your phonebook.

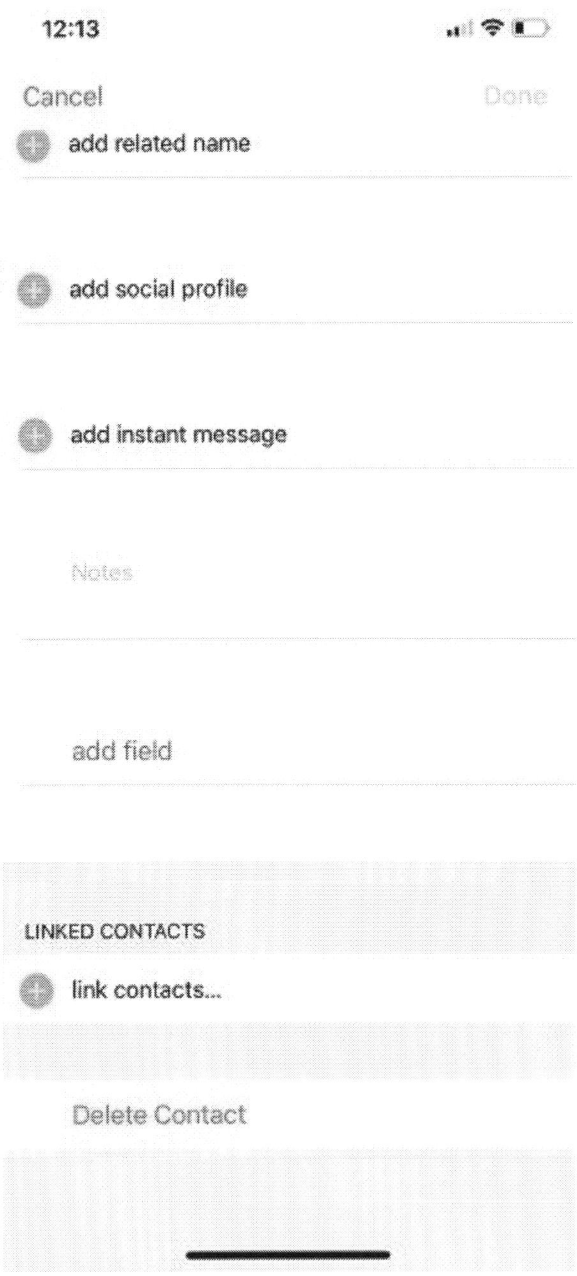

Figure 4: Delete Contact

4. Editing Contact Information

After adding contacts to your phonebook, you may edit them at any time. To edit an existing contact's information:

1. Touch the [icon] icon on the Home screen. The phonebook appears. If a list of all contacts does not appear, touch **All Contacts** in the upper left-hand corner of the screen to view the list.
2. Find and touch a contact's name. The Contact Info screen appears. Refer to *"Finding a Contact"* on page 67 to learn how to search for a contact.
3. Touch **Edit** at the top of the screen. The Contact Editing screen appears.
4. Touch a field to edit the corresponding information. Touch **Done** at the top of the screen when you are finished. The contact's information is updated.

5. Sharing a Contact's Information

You can share a contact's information, including their phone number, email and street addresses, and more. To share a contact's information with someone else:

1. Touch the [icon] icon. The phonebook appears. If a list of all contacts does not appear, touch **All Contacts** in the upper left-hand corner of the screen to view the list.
2. Find and touch a contact's name. The Contact Info screen appears. Refer to *"Finding a Contact"* on page 67 to learn how.
3. Touch **Share Contact** at the bottom of the contact's information. The Sharing Options menu appears at the bottom of the screen, as shown in **Figure 5**.
4. Follow the steps in the appropriate section below to email or text the contact's information:

To send contact information via email:

1. Touch the [icon] icon in the Sharing Options menu. The New Email screen appears, as shown in **Figure 6**. Choose one of the following options for entering the email address:
   - Start typing the name of the contact with whom you wish to share the information. The matching contacts appear. Touch the contact's name. The contact's email address is added.
   - Enter the email address from scratch. To use a number, touch the **.?123** button at the bottom left of the screen. When done, touch the **return** button. Enter more addresses if needed.

- Touch the ⊕ icon to select contacts from your phonebook, or enter as many email addresses as you wish.
2. Enter an optional subject by touching **Subject**, and touch **CC** to add other addresses to which to send the information.
3. Touch **Send** at the top of the screen. The contact's information is sent to the selected email addresses.

To send contact information via multimedia message, touch the ⬤ icon in the Sharing Options menu. The New Message screen appears, as shown in **Figure 7**. Enter the phone number or phone numbers, and touch **Send**. The contact's information is sent. There are three methods for entering the phone number:

- Start typing the name of the contact with whom you wish to share the information. Matching contacts appear. Touch the contact's name. The contact's number is added.
- Type the phone number from scratch. To use numbers, touch the **.?123** button at the bottom left of the screen. When done, touch the `return` button in the lower right-hand corner of the screen.
- Touch the ⊕ icon to select one or more contacts from the phonebook.

Help Me! Guide to the iPhone X

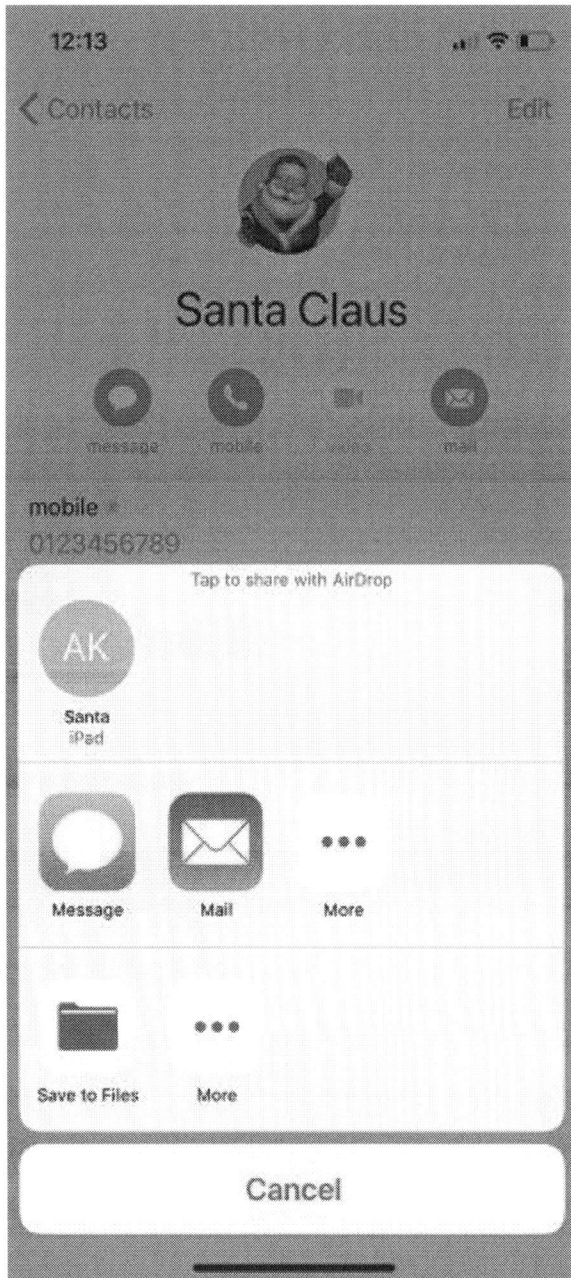

Figure 5: Sharing Options Menu

Managing Contacts

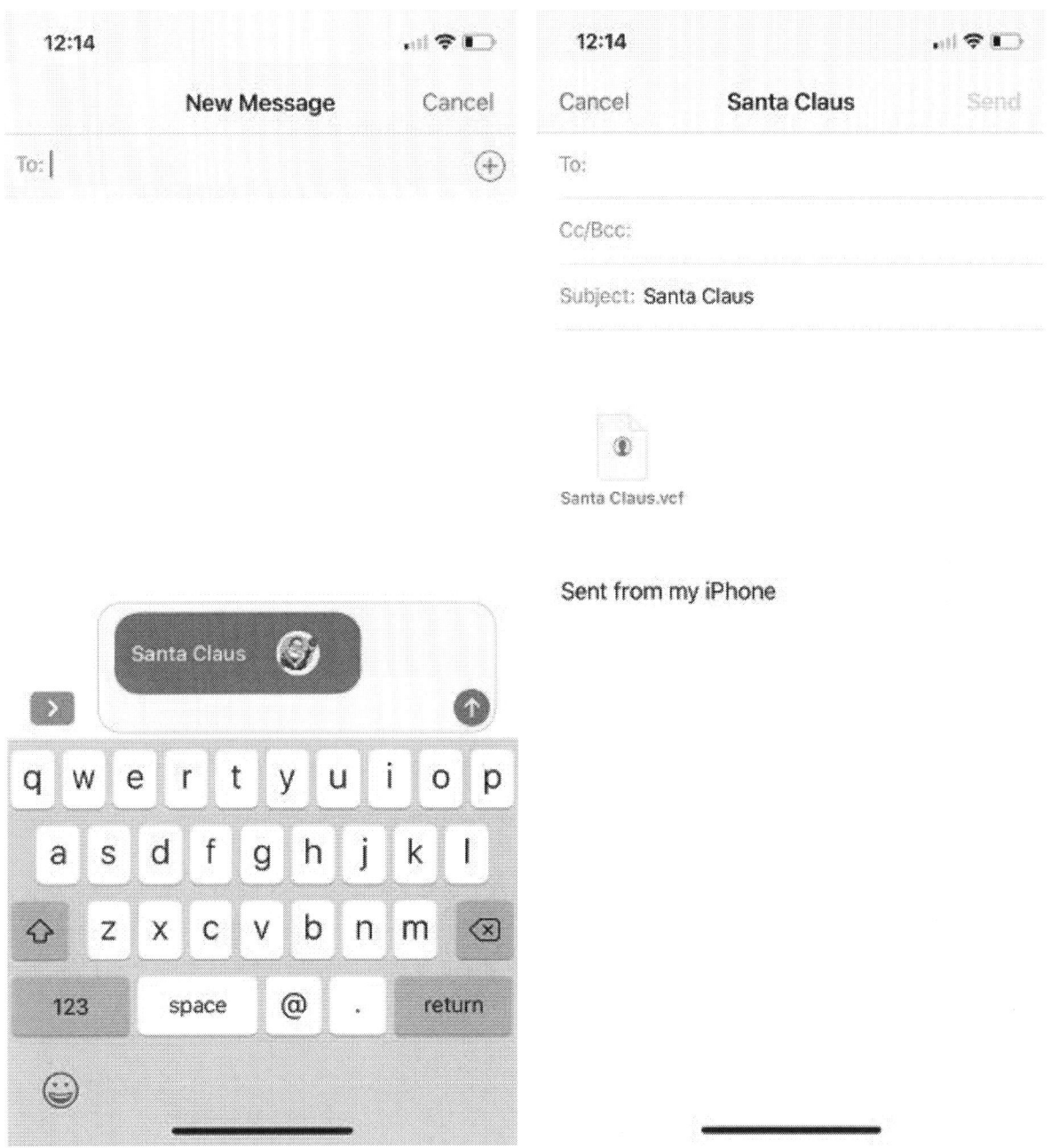

Figure 6: New Email Screen

Figure 7: New Message Screen

75

6. Changing the Contact Sort Order

By default, the phone sorts the contacts in the phonebook by last name. For instance, if the names Jane Doe and John Johnson are in the phonebook, John Johnson would come after Jane Doe because 'J' comes after 'D' in the English alphabet. To change the sort order:

1. Touch the icon. The Settings screen appears, as shown in **Figure 8**.
2. Scroll down and touch **Contacts**. The Contacts Settings screen appears, as shown in **Figure 9**.
3. Touch **Sort Order**. The Sort Order screen appears, as shown in **Figure 10**.
4. Touch **First, Last**. A check mark appears to the right of the option, and the contacts will be sorted by first name.
5. Touch **Last, First**. A check mark appears to the right of the option, and the contacts will be sorted by last name.

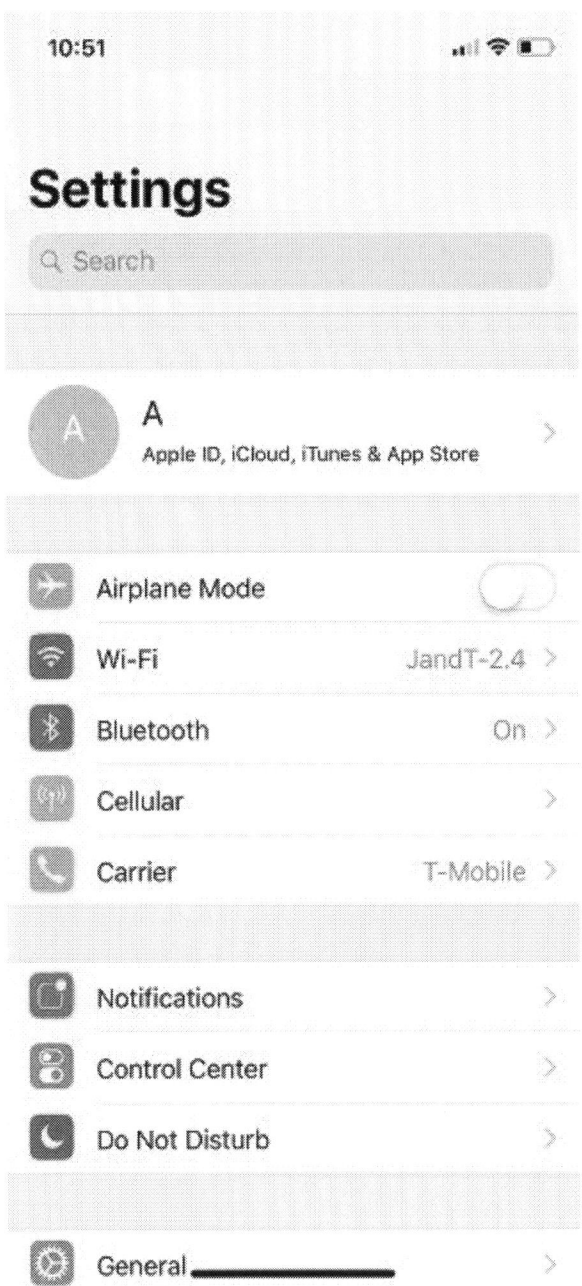

Figure 8: Settings Screen

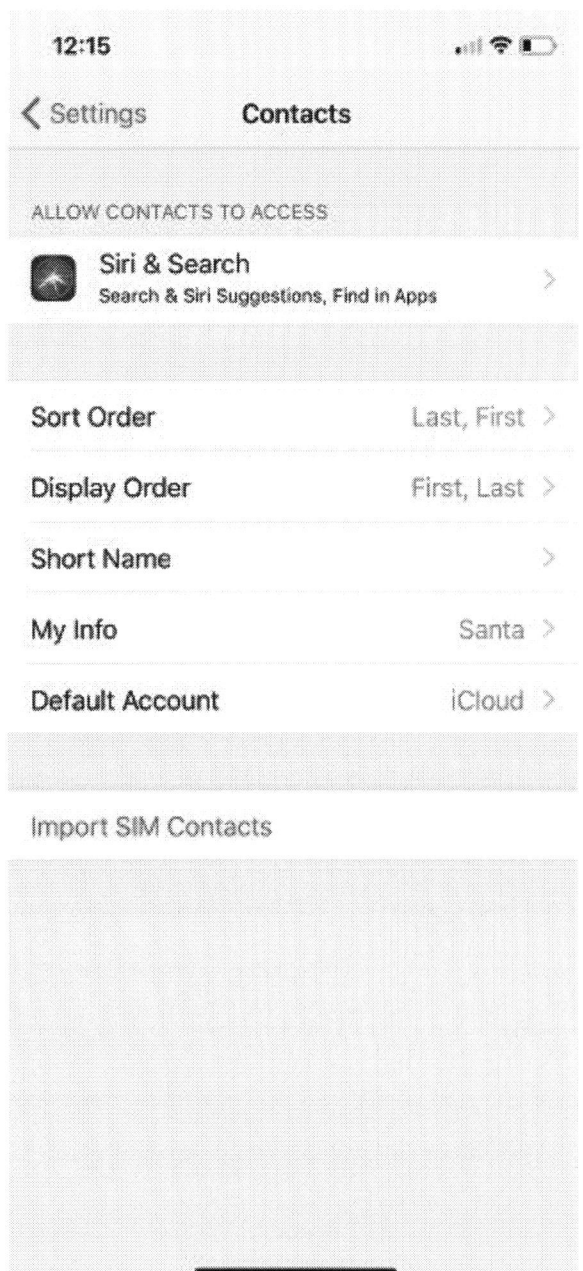

Figure 9: Contacts Settings Screen

Figure 10: Sort Order Screen

Text Messaging

Table of Contents

1. Composing a New Text Message
2. Copying, Cutting, and Pasting Text
3. Using the Spell Check Feature
4. Receiving a Text Message
5. Reading a Stored Text Message
6. Forwarding a Text Message
7. Calling the Sender from within a Text
8. Viewing Sender Information from within a Text
9. Deleting a Text Message
10. Adding Texted Phone Numbers to the Phonebook
11. Sending a Picture Message
12. Leaving a Group Conversation
13. Naming a Conversation
14. Adding a Voice Message to a Conversation (iMessage Only)
15. Sharing Your Location in a Conversation
16. Viewing All Attachments in a Conversation
17. Handwriting a Message
18. Sending a Digital Touch
19. Sending an Animoji
20. Using Tapback in a Message
21. Turning Read Receipts for a Single Conversation On or Off
22. Using iMessage Applications

1. Composing a New Text Message

You can send text messages to other mobile phones, tablets, and Macs. To compose a new message:

- Touch the icon on the Home screen. The Messages screen appears, as shown in **Figure 1**.
- Touch the icon. The New Message screen appears, as shown in **Figure 2**.
- Enter the phone number of the recipient. There are three options for entering this information:

- Start typing the name of the contact. Matching contacts appear as you type. Touch the contact's name. The contact's number is added.
- Enter the phone number from scratch.
- Touch the ⊕ button to select a contact from the Phonebook. Add as many numbers as desired.
- Touch the text field. The cursor starts flashing at the beginning of the field.
- Enter your message. If you begin to type a word incorrectly, the phone may give you a suggestion. Touch the suggestion to use it.
- Touch the ↑ button or the ↑ button when finished. The ↑ button appears if the recipient is using iMessage, in which case the text message is free to send. The message is sent. Your most recent message is shown in a gray bubble on the left side of the screen, as shown in **Figure 3**. All text messages are shown in conversation view.

To send a new message to someone you have already texted:

1. Touch the ▢ icon on the Home screen. The Messages screen appears.
2. Touch the name or number of the recipient. The Conversation screen appears. If the name is not in the list, try scrolling down by touching the screen and moving your finger up. If you cannot find the name, you may have deleted your conversation with that contact.
3. Touch the text field. The cursor starts flashing, and a keyboard is shown.
4. Enter the message and then touch the ↑ button or the ↑ button when finished. The message is sent. Touch the screen and move your finger down to scroll through older messages.

Figure 1: Messages Screen

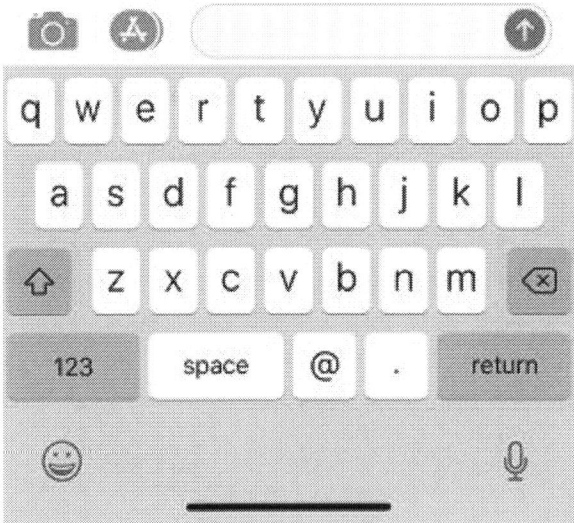

Figure 2: New Message Screen

Text Messaging

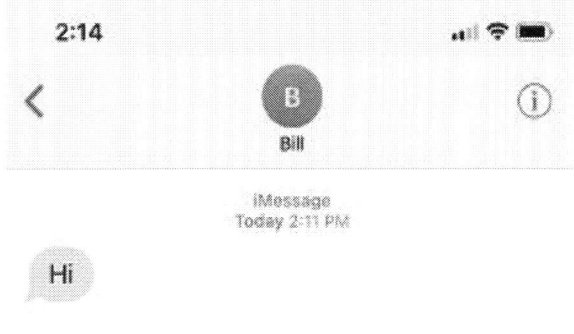

Figure 3: Your Message in a Gray Bubble

2. Copying, Cutting, and Pasting Text

The phone allows you to copy or cut text from one location and paste it to another. Copying leaves the text in its current location and allows you to paste it elsewhere. Cutting deletes the text from its current location and allows you to paste it elsewhere. To cut, copy, and paste text:

1. Touch and hold text in a text field or in a conversation. The Select menu appears above the text, as shown in **Figure 4**. Refer to *"Composing a New Text Message"* on page 80 to learn how to compose a text.
2. Touch **Select All**. All of the text is selected. To select a single word, touch **Select**. Blue dots appear around the word or phrase.
3. Touch and hold one of the blue dots and drag it in any direction. The text between the dots is highlighted and a text menu appears, as shown in **Figure 5**.
4. Touch **Cut** or **Copy**. The corresponding action is taken and the text is ready to be pasted.
5. Touch and hold any empty text field, and then touch **Paste**. The text is inserted.

Note: Refer to "Tips and Tricks" *on page 348 to learn more about editing text.*

Text Messaging

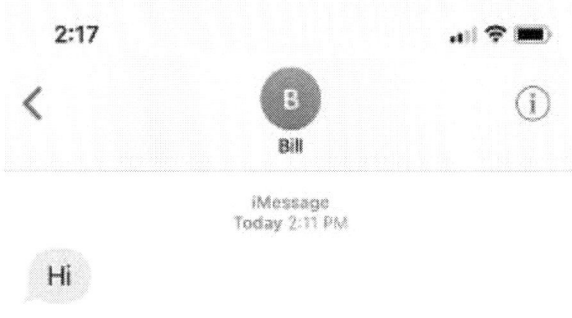

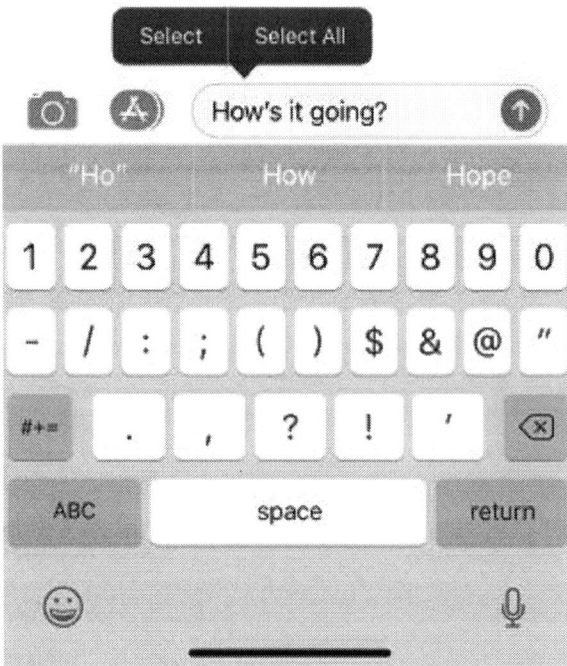

Figure 4: Select Menu

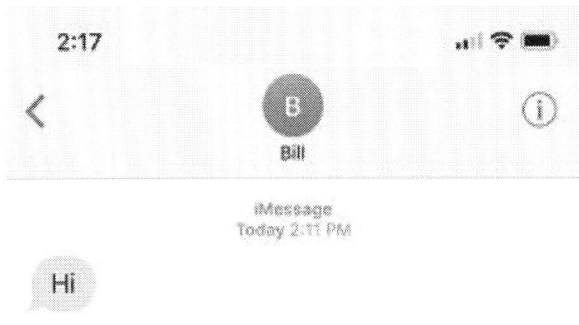

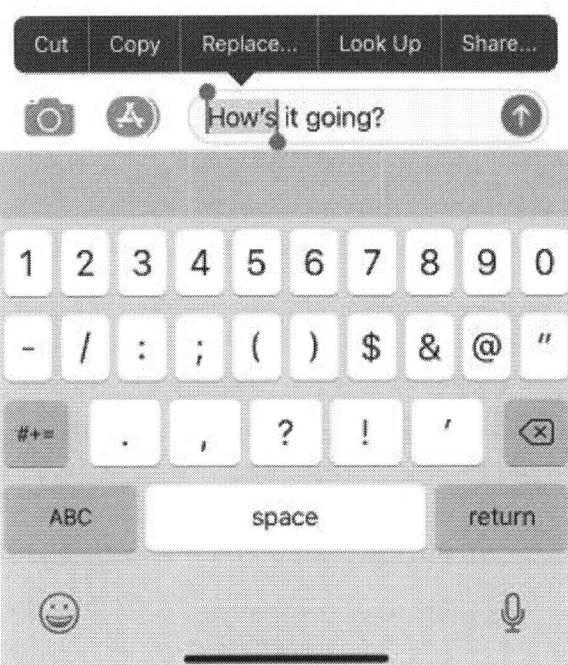

Figure 5: Text Menu

3. Using the Spell Check Feature

The phone will make suggestions for words that are spelled incorrectly. Touch a suggestion to substitute the word immediately. If auto-correction is enabled, the phone will automatically replace common typos. Over time, the phone will learn your most commonly typed words, even names and slang. Refer to *"Adjusting Language and Keyboard Settings"* on page 272 to learn more about auto-correction.

4. Receiving a Text Message

The phone can receive text messages from any other mobile phone. When the phone receives a text, it vibrates once or plays a sound, depending on the settings. The New Message notification appears on the Lock screen, as shown in **Figure 6**, or on the Home screen, as shown in **Figure 7**. Whether the notification appears in the Notification Bar or on the Home screen depends on your settings. Use the following tips when receiving text messages:

- Slide the text notification to the right on the Lock screen to open the text message.
- Touch the text message alert on the Home screen or while using an application to open the text message. Slide down on the alert to reply quickly. The Quick Reply window appears, as shown in **Figure 8**. Slide down again to close the Quick Reply window. To reply without opening the Messages application, enter a reply and touch **Send**.
- The ![icon] icon next to the ![icon] icon on the Home screen indicates that there is one unread message. This number changes depending on the number of unread messages. The number in the red circle will not disappear until the message is read. Touch the ![icon] icon to view the message.

Note: Refer to "Composing a New Text Message" *on page 80 to learn more about sending text messages.*

Figure 6: New Message Notification on the Lock Screen

Text Messaging

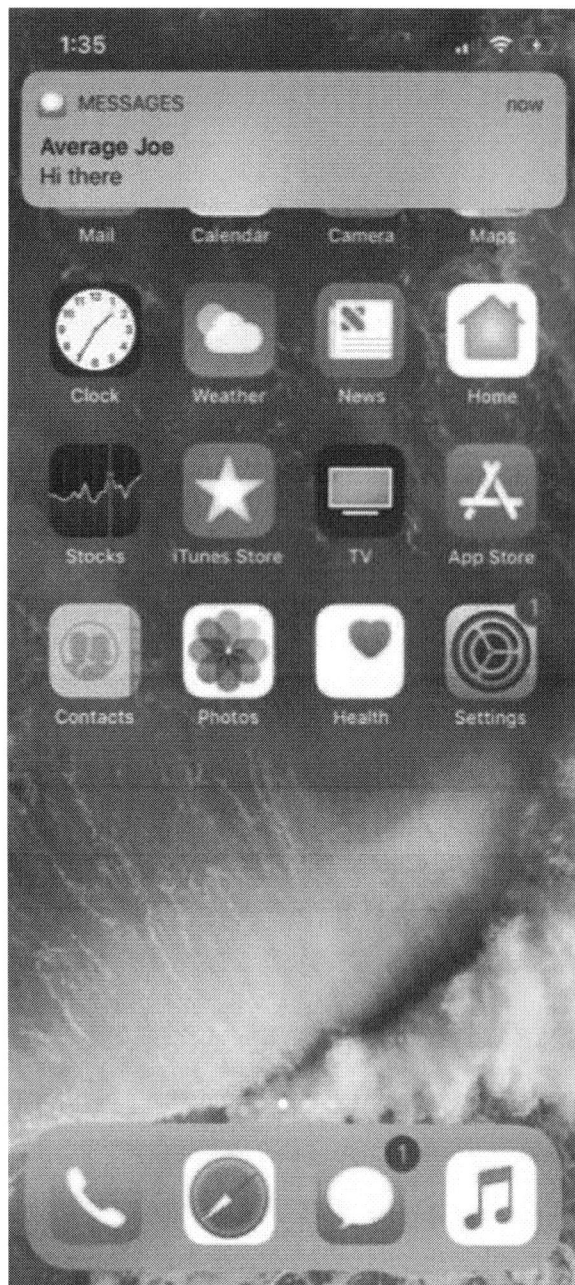

Figure 7: New Message Notification on the Home Screen

Figure 8: Quick Message Reply Window

Text Messaging

5. Reading a Stored Text Message

You may read any text messages that you have received, provided that you have not deleted them. To read stored text messages:

1. Touch the ⬜ icon on the Home screen. The Messages screen appears. The phone organizes conversations based on the date the last message in the conversation was sent or received, with the most recent conversation at the top of the list.
2. Touch the name of a contact to view the conversation. The Conversation screen appears.
3. Touch the screen, and move your finger up or down to scroll through the conversation. The most recent messages appear at the bottom.

6. Forwarding a Text Message

Forwarding a message copies the contents of the original message when you wish to send it to a new recipient. You may wish to forward a text message to save yourself some time entering the same message. To forward a text message:

1. Touch the ⬜ icon on the Home screen. The Messages screen appears, displaying each sender's name on the left and the date of the message on the right.
2. Touch the conversation that contains the message(s) that you wish to forward. The Conversation screen appears.
3. Touch and hold a message in the conversation. The Message menu appears above the message, as shown in **Figure 9**.
4. Touch **More**. A blue check mark appears next to the message, as shown in **Figure 10**.
5. Touch the ↪ button at the bottom of the screen. The New Message screen appears, with the selected message copied into the text field.
6. Start typing the name of a contact or touch the ⊕ icon to select a number from the Phonebook. The contact is added to the Addressee list.
7. Touch the ⬆ button or the ⬆ button. The message is forwarded to the contacts in the 'To:' field.

92

Figure 9: Message Menu

Text Messaging

Figure 10: Selected Messages

7. Calling the Sender from within a Text

After receiving a text message from a contact, you may call that person without ever exiting the text message. To call someone from whom you have received a text message:

1. Touch the ![icon] icon on the Home screen. The Messages screen appears. The phone organizes conversations based on the date the last message in the conversation was sent or received, with the most recent conversation at the top of the list.
2. Touch the conversation that contains the message(s) from the sender that you wish to call. The Conversation screen appears.
3. Touch the ![i button] button at the top of the screen. The Conversation Details screen appears, as shown in **Figure 11**.
4. Touch the ![phone icon] icon. The iPhone places the call.

You can also call a contact from the Messages screen. Press down firmly on the contact's picture or initials, then slide your finger to **Call**.

Text Messaging

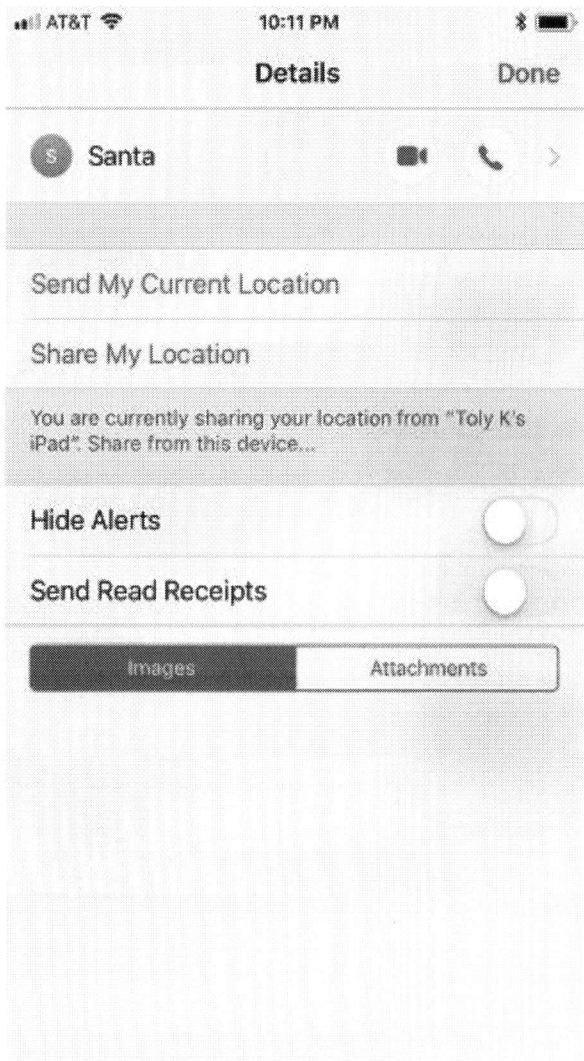

Figure 11: Conversation Details Screen

8. Viewing Sender Information from within a Text

If you have stored a contact's information in the Phonebook, you may view it at any time without leaving a text conversation between the two of you. To view the information of a contact who sent you a message:

1. Touch the ![icon] icon on the Home screen. The Messages screen appears.
2. Touch a conversation. The Conversation screen appears.
3. Touch the screen and move your finger down until the top of the conversation appears.
4. Touch the contact's name at the top of the screen. The Contact Information screen appears.

Help Me! Guide to the iPhone X

9. Deleting a Text Message

The phone can delete separate text messages or an entire conversation, which is a series of text messages between you and a contact.

Warning: Once deleted, text messages cannot be restored.

To delete an entire conversation:

1. Touch the ![] icon on the Home screen. The Messages screen appears.
2. Touch and hold a message in a conversation, and slide your finger to the left. 'Delete' appears.
3. Touch **Delete**. The entire conversation is deleted.

To delete a separate text message:

1. Touch the ![] icon on the Home screen. The Messages screen appears.
2. Touch a conversation. The conversation opens.
3. Touch and hold a message in a conversation. The message menu appears.
4. Touch **More**. Touch any other messages that you wish to delete. A ![] mark appears next to each selected message.
5. Touch the ![] icon at the bottom of the screen. A confirmation dialog appears.
6. Touch **Delete Message**. The selected messages are deleted.

10. Adding Texted Phone Numbers to the Phonebook

A phone number sent via text message can be added to your Phonebook immediately. To add a texted phone number to your Phonebook:

1. Touch the ![] icon on the Home screen. The Messages screen appears.
2. Touch a conversation. The Conversation screen appears.
3. Touch and hold the phone number in the conversation. The Phone Number menu appears, as shown in **Figure 12**.
4. Touch **Add to Contacts**. The Info screen appears.
5. Touch **Create New Contact** or **Add to Existing Contact**. The New Contact screen appears, with the phone number field filled in, as shown in **Figure 13**. If you touched 'Add to Existing Contact', the Phonebook appears, and you may choose the contact that you want to modify.
6. Enter the contact's information, then touch **Done.** The contact is added to your Phonebook.

Text Messaging

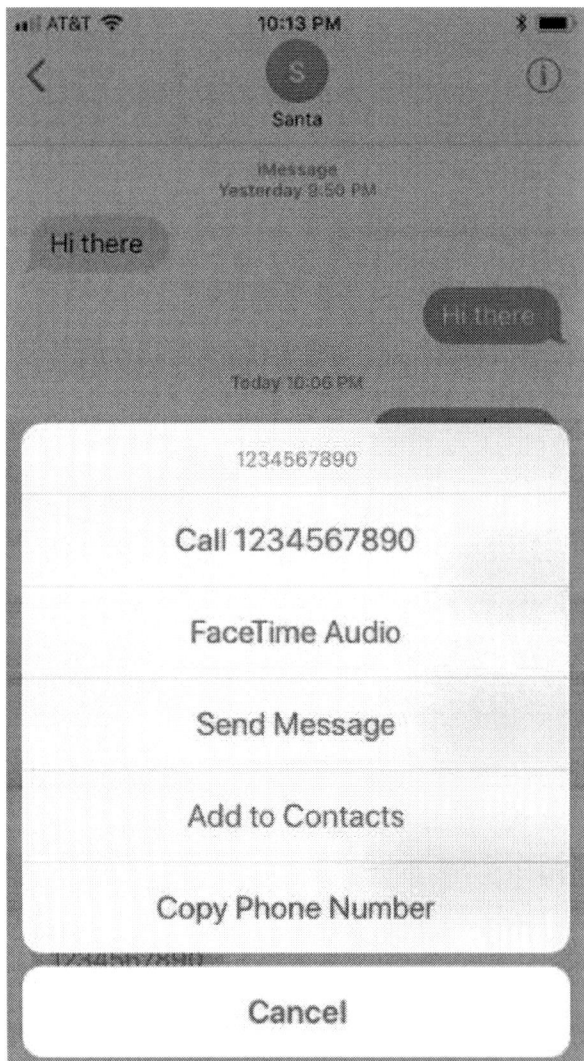

Figure 12: Phone Number Menu

Help Me! Guide to the iPhone X

Figure 13: New Contact Screen

99

Text Messaging

11. Sending a Picture Message

You may attach a picture to any text message that you send.

To send a picture message:

1. Touch the ![icon] icon on the Home screen. The Messages screen appears.
2. Touch the ![icon] icon. The New Message screen appears.
3. Touch the ![icon] button to the left of the text field. The Photo Attachment menu appears and the camera turns on, as shown in **Figure 14**. If you do not see the ![icon] button touch the ![icon] button first.
4. Follow the steps in one of the sections below to either attach an existing picture or take a picture to send:

To attach an existing picture to the text message:

1. Touch **Photos**. A list of Photo Albums appears, as shown in **Figure 15**.
2. Touch a photo album. The photo album opens.
3. Touch a photo. The preview of the photo appears.
4. Touch **Choose**. The photo is attached to the text message. Alternatively, touch **Cancel** to select a different photo.
5. Touch the ![icon] button or the ![icon] button. The picture message is sent.

To take a picture and attach it to the text message:

1. Touch **Camera**. The camera turns on, as shown in **Figure 16**. You can also capture a photo immediately by touching the ![icon] button in the Photo Attachment menu.
2. Touch the ![icon] button at the bottom of the screen. The photo is captured and a preview of the photo appears.
3. Touch **Done** to use the photo in the message, or touch **Retake** to discard the picture and take another one. You can also touch **Markup** to draw on the photo before attaching it. The photo is attached. Alternatively, touch **Cancel** while the camera is turned on to return to the conversation without taking a picture.
4. Touch the ![icon] button or the ![icon] button. The picture message is sent.

Note: Up to nine photos may be sent in a picture message.

Figure 14: Photo Attachment Menu

Text Messaging

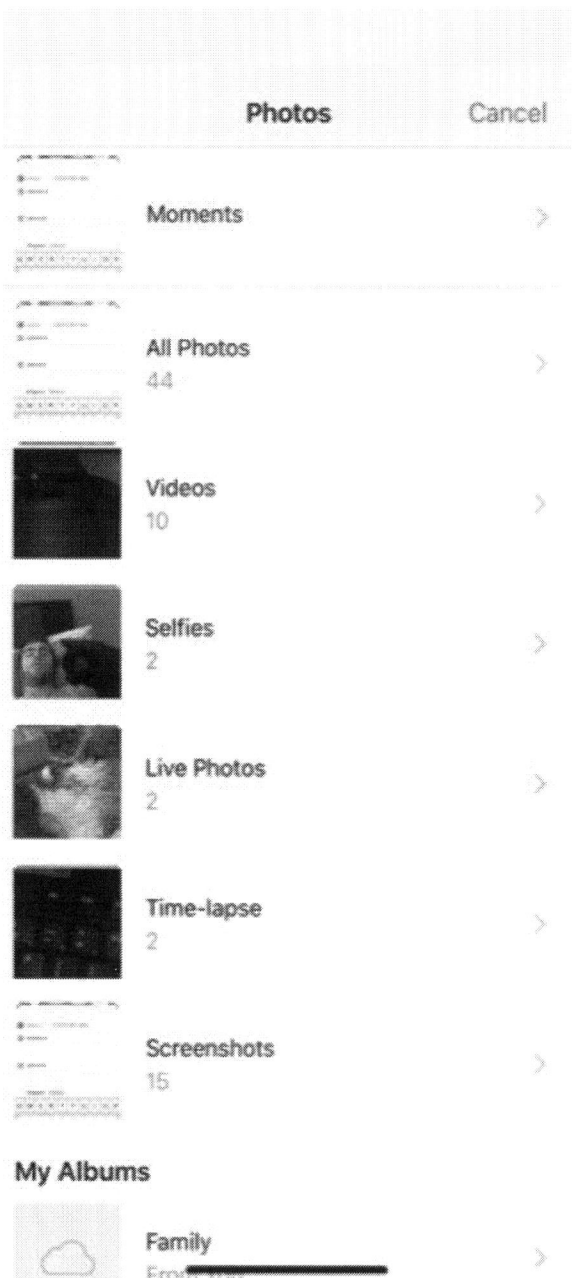

Figure 15: List of Photo Albums

Figure 16: Camera Turned On

Text Messaging

12. Leaving a Group Conversation

You may remove yourself from a group conversation if you no longer wish to participate. Once removed, you will not receive any further messages in that conversation. To leave a group conversation:

1. Touch the (i) button at the top of the conversation. The Conversation details appear.
2. Touch **Leave this Conversation**. A confirmation dialog appears.
3. Touch **Leave this Conversation** again. You are removed from the conversation.

13. Naming a Conversation

In order to find it more quickly and easily, you may name a conversation with a group. The title of the conversation will show up on the phone of everyone involved in the conversation. To name a conversation:

1. Touch **Details** at the top of the conversation. The Conversation details appear.
2. Touch the (i) button at the top of the screen. The Conversation Details screen appears.
3. Touch **Enter a Group Name**, then enter the title of the conversation. The conversation is renamed.

14. Adding a Voice Message to a Conversation (iMessage Only)

You may add a short voice message to a text message or conversation. This feature only works when using iMessage. If you send a text message to someone who does not use an iPhone, or has not registered for iMessage, this feature will not work. To add a voice message to an iMessage:

1. Touch and hold the 🎤 button to the right of the text field. The microphone turns on.
2. Speak the voice message that you would like to attach. When you are finished, release the 🎤 button. The voice message is recorded, as shown in **Figure 17**.

104

Help Me! Guide to the iPhone X

3. Touch the ⬆ button. The voice message is sent. You can also slide your finger up to the ⬆ button without letting go of the screen to immediately send the voice message. Alternatively, let go of the screen, then touch the ▶ icon to preview the voice message. Touch the ✕ icon if you would like to discard the voice message.

Figure 17: Recorded Voice Message

105

15. Sharing Your Location in a Conversation

You may choose to share your location with a contact or a number of participants in a conversation. To share your location for a specified amount of time:

1. Touch the (i) button at the top of the screen. The Conversation Details screen appears.
2. Touch **Share My Location**. The Location Sharing menu appears, as shown in **Figure 18**.
3. Touch one of the following options to share your location for the corresponding amount of time: **Share for One Hour**, **Share Until End of Day**, or **Share Indefinitely**. You location is shared. The last option will allow you to share your location until you touch **Stop Sharing My Location** on the Conversation Details screen.

You can also touch **Send My Current Location** to share your location once immediately.

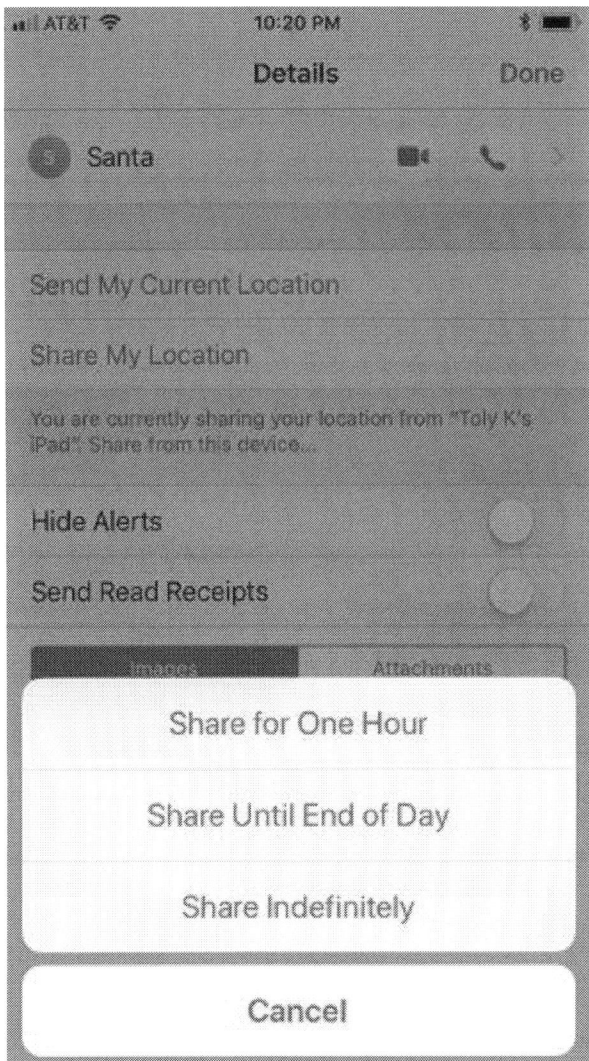
Figure 18: Location Sharing Menu

16. Viewing All Attachments in a Conversation

The Messaging application provides a convenient way to view all of the pictures, videos, and voice messages attached to a conversation in one neat list. To view all attachments in a conversation, touch the (i) button at the top of a conversation. The Conversation details appear and the list of attachments is shown at the bottom of the screen. To save one of the attachments in the list to a photo album:
1. Touch the attachment that you want to save. The attachment appears in full screen.
2. Touch the center of the screen. The Attachment menu appears, as shown in **Figure 19**.
3. Touch the icon. The Save Photo menu appears, as shown in **Figure 20**, or the Save Video menu appears, as shown in **Figure 21**.
4. Touch the icon. The attachment is saved to the Recently Added album on your phone.

Figure 19: Attachment Menu

Text Messaging

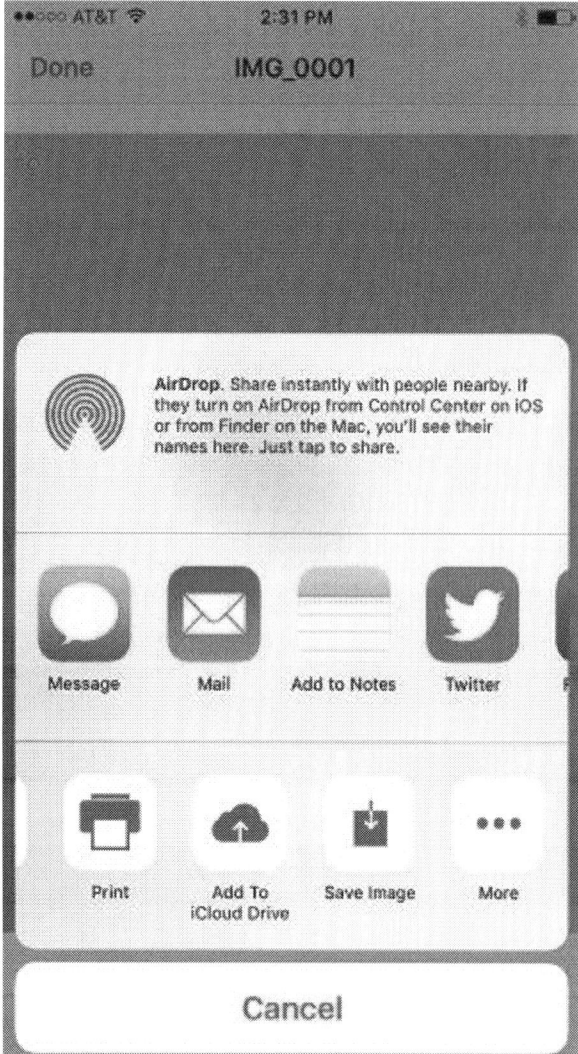

Figure 20: Save Photo Menu

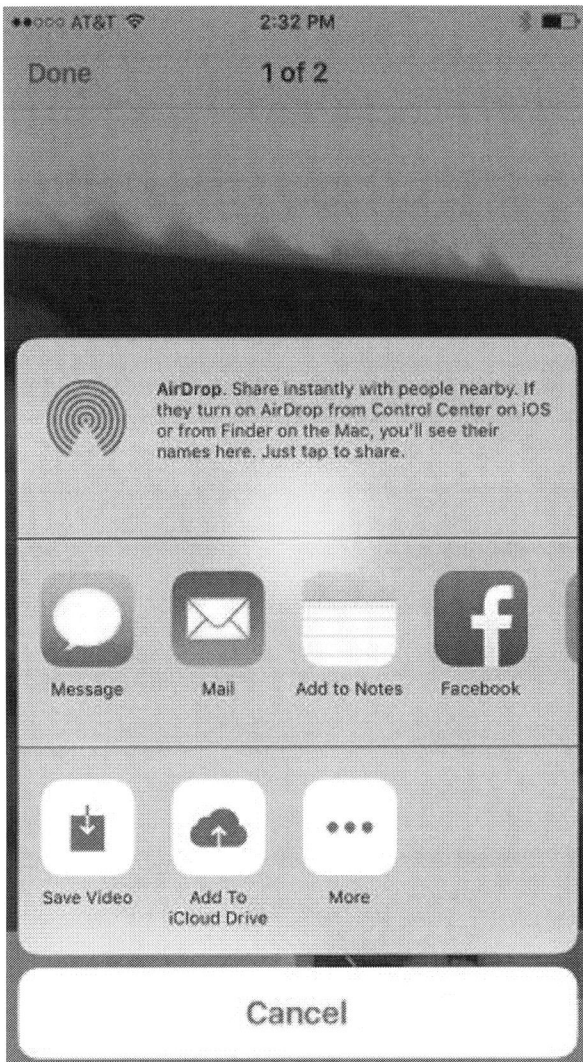

Figure 21: Save Video Menu

Text Messaging

17. Handwriting a Message

You can send a handwritten message when using iMessage, which plays animated handwriting on the recipient's screen. To send a handwritten message:

1. While viewing a text conversation, rotate the phone to view it in Landscape mode. The Handwriting screen appears, as shown in **Figure 22**. If you do not see the Handwriting screen, touch the button.
2. Write the message using your finger. Do NOT use a pen or stylus. If you do not have enough space, touch the right-facing arrow to move to the next area of the Handwriting screen.
3. Touch **Done**. The Conversation screen appears with the message entered.
4. Touch the button. The handwritten message is sent.

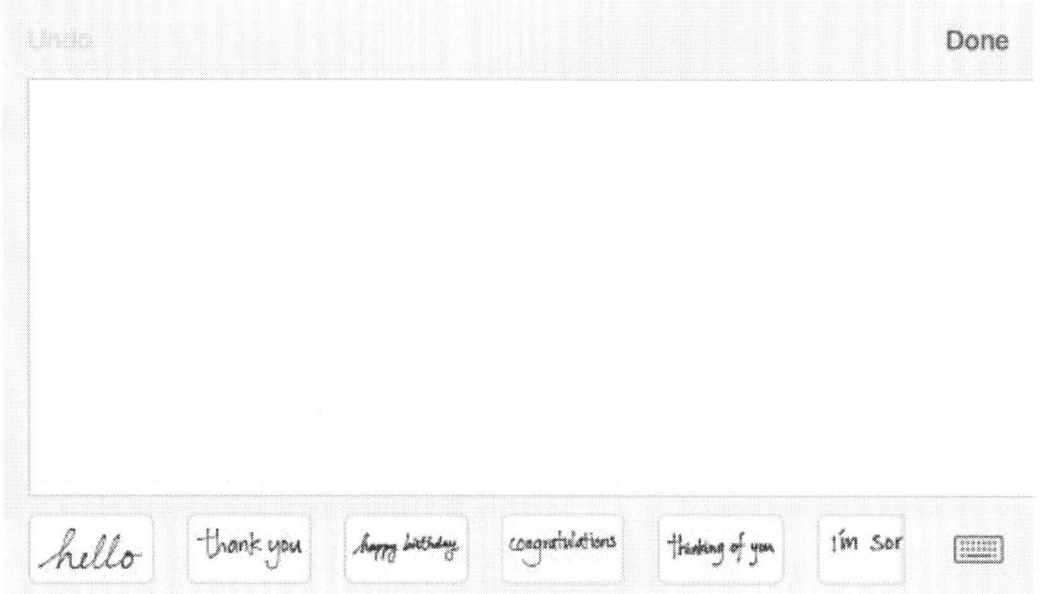

Figure 22: Handwriting Screen

18. Sending a Digital Touch

You can send a heartbeat or tap sequence in a message. This types of message is called Digital Touch. To send a Digital Touch, touch the [icon] icon and then touch the [icon] icon. Tap the screen in the preferred manner. Play around with it. You can touch one of the hand icons on the right side of the screen for more tips.

19. Sending an Animoji

You can send an animated emoji, dubbed by Apple as an animoji. To send an animoji, touch the [icon] icon and then touch the [icon] icon. Make a face and then touch the animoji to insert it into the text field.

20. Using Tapback in a Message

When you receive a message in iMessage, you can immediately respond with an emoji that appears directly on the person's original message. For example, you can send a thumbs up or a heart that appears on the original message. This feature is compatible with text and multimedia messages, such as pictures, videos, or Digital Touches. To send a Tapback, touch and hold the text message in the conversation. The Message menu appears. Touch a Tapback, such as a heart or thumbs up. The Tapback is immediately sent.

21. Turning Read Receipts for a Single Conversation On or Off

After receiving and opening a message from an iPhone, iPad, or iPod Touch, your phone can notify the sender that you have opened and read the message. These notifications are called Read Receipts, and appear under the original message on the sender's screen as "Read", followed by a time. Prior to iOS 11, you could turn read receipts off for the iMessage application. It is now possible to turn Read Receipts on or off for a single conversation. To turn Read Receipts on or off for a conversation:

1. Touch the [i] button at the top of a conversation. The Conversation Details screen appears.

113

Text Messaging

2. Touch switch next to 'Send Read Receipts'. The switch appears and Read Receipts are turned on.

3. Touch the switch next to 'Send Read Receipts'. The switch appears and Read Receipts are turned off.

22. Using iMessage Applications

There are certain applications that can now interact with iMessage. Each iMessage application in the App Store is indicated by the label "Offers iMessage App'. Download the application and access it from iMessage by touching the button. Then, touch the button. The list of installed iMessage applications appears, as shown in **Figure 23**. If you do not have any applications installed, touch **Store** to browse the available iMessage applications.

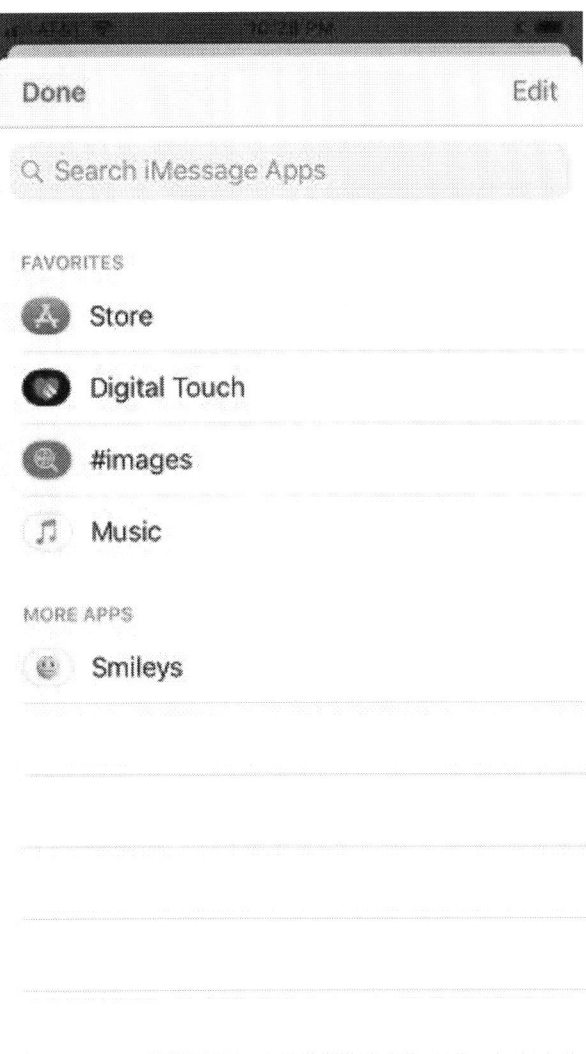

Figure 23: List of Installed iMessage Applications

Using the Safari Web Browser

Table of Contents

1. Navigating to a Website
2. Adding and Viewing Bookmarks
3. Adding a Bookmark to the Home Screen
4. Managing Open Browser Tabs
5. Blocking Pop-Up Windows
6. Changing the Search Engine
7. Clearing History and Browsing Data
8. Viewing an Article in Reader Mode
9. Turning Private Browsing On or Off
10. Setting Up the AutoFill Feature
11. Customizing the Smart Search Field
12. Viewing Recently Closed Tabs
13. Scanning a Credit Card Using the Phone's Camera

1. Navigating to a Website

You can surf the web using your phone. To navigate to a website using the web address:

1. Touch the ![icon] icon on the Home screen. The Safari Web browser opens.
2. Touch the Address bar at the top of the screen, as outlined in **Figure 1**. The keyboard appears. If you do not see the Address bar, touch the screen and move your finger down to scroll up.
3. Touch the web address at the top of the screen. The address field is erased.
4. Enter a web address and touch Go. Safari navigates to the website.
5. Touch the ![<] button. Safari navigates to the previous web page.
6. Touch the ![>] button. Safari navigates to the next web page.

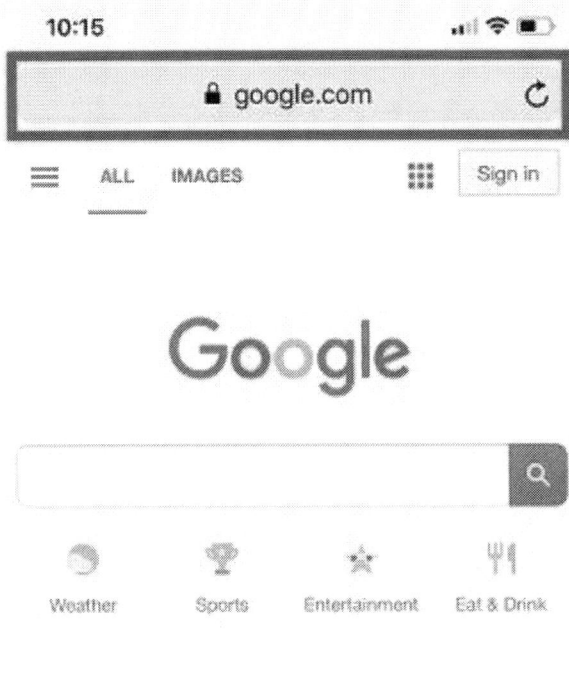

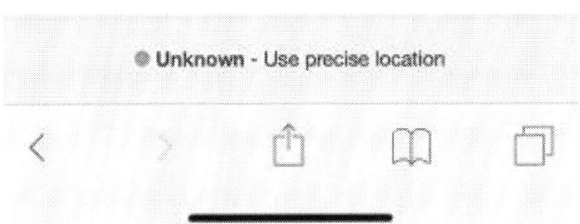

Figure 1: Address Bar in Safari

2. Adding and Viewing Bookmarks

The phone can store favorite websites as Bookmarks to allow you to access them faster in the future. To add a Bookmark in Safari:

1. Touch the ![] icon on the Home screen. The Safari browser opens.
2. Navigate to a website. Refer to *"Navigating to a Website"* on page 116 to learn how.
3. Touch the ![] button. The Bookmark menu appears, as shown in **Figure 2**.
4. Touch the ![] icon. The Add Bookmark window appears, as shown in **Figure 3**.
5. Enter a name for the bookmark and touch Save. The website is added to the Bookmarks.
6. To view saved Bookmarks, touch the ![] icon in the Safari browser. The Bookmarks screen appears, as shown in **Figure 4**. Touch a bookmark. Safari navigates to the indicated website.

Using the Safari Web Browser

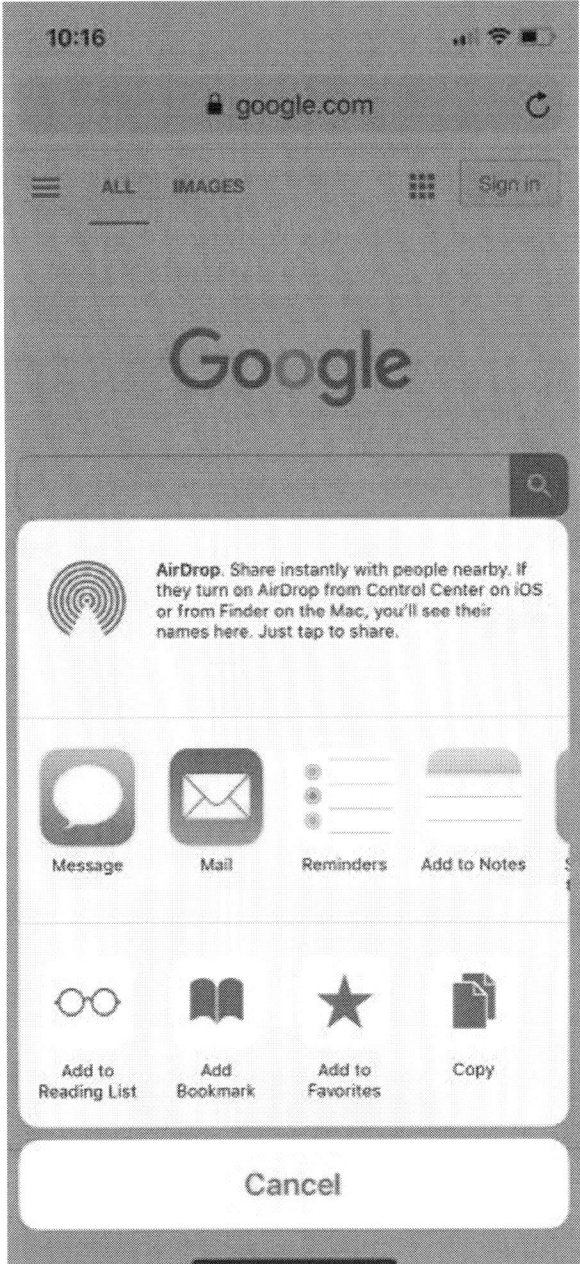

Figure 2: Bookmark Menu

119

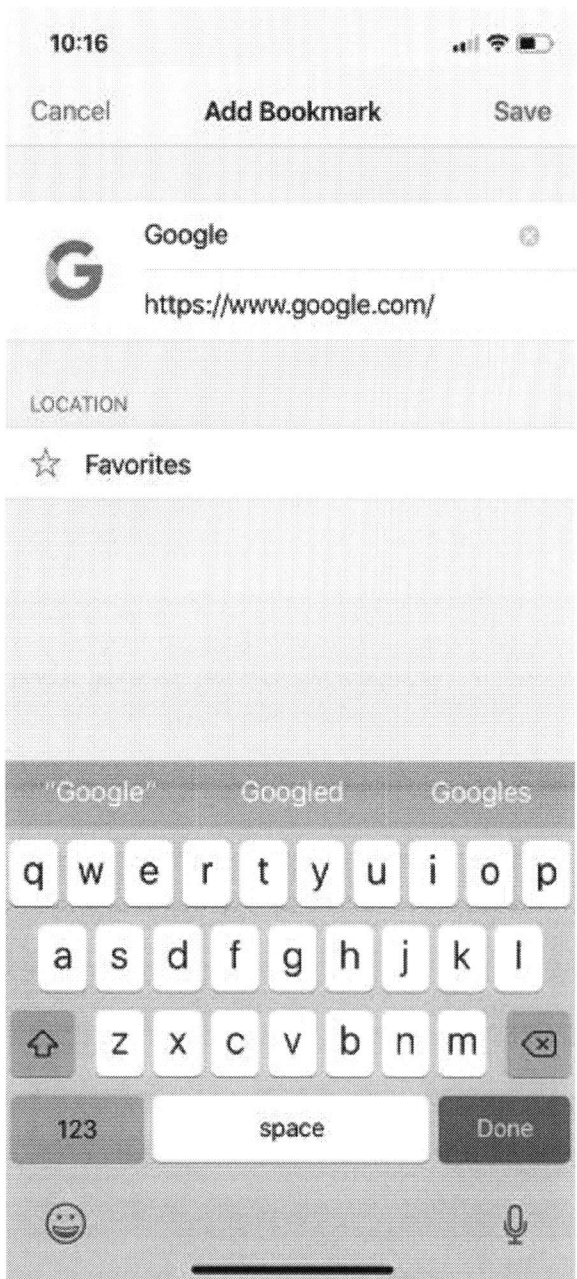

Figure 3: Add Bookmark Window

Using the Safari Web Browser

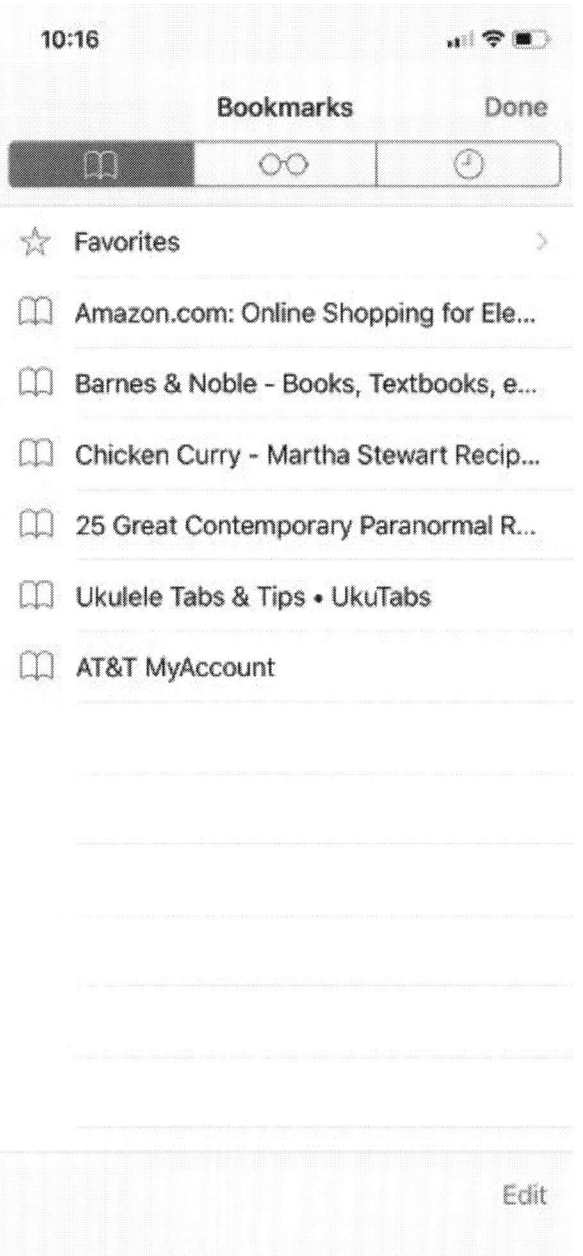

Figure 4: Bookmarks Screen

3. Adding a Bookmark to the Home Screen

On the phone, bookmarks can be added to the Home screen; they will then appear like application icons. To add a bookmark to the Home screen as an icon:

1. Touch the ![] icon on the Home screen. The Safari browser opens.
2. Navigate to a website. Refer to *"Navigating to a Website"* on page 116 to learn how.
3. Touch the ![] button. The Bookmark menu appears.
4. Touch the ![] icon. The Add to Home window appears, as shown in **Figure 5**.
5. Enter a name for the bookmark and touch Add. The bookmark is added to the Home screen.

Using the Safari Web Browser

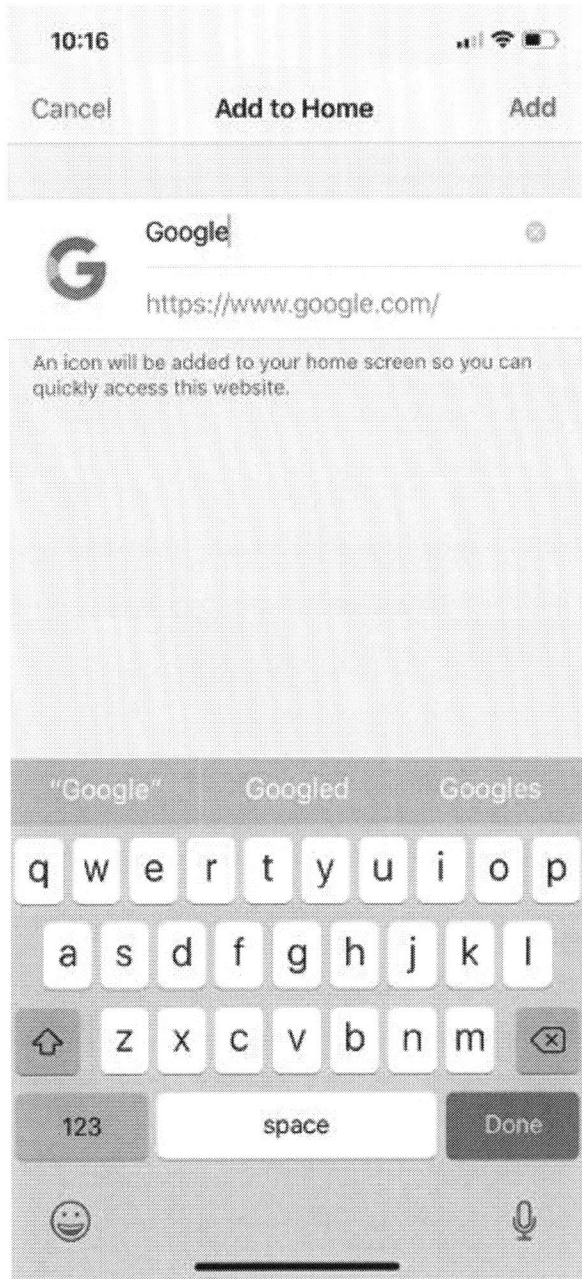

Figure 5: Add to Home Window

123

Help Me! Guide to the iPhone X

4. Managing Open Browser Tabs

The Safari Web browser supports an unlimited number of browser tabs. This feature is analogous to tabbed browsing in an internet browser like Firefox, Chrome, or Internet Explorer. Use the following tips when working with browser tabs:

- To view the open Safari tabs, touch the ⬜ button in Safari. The open Safari tabs appear, as shown in **Figure 6**. Touch the screen and flick your finger up or down to view other open tabs. While viewing the open Safari tabs:

- To open a new browser tab, touch the ＋ button.
- To close a tab, touch the X in the upper left corner of the tab. You can also touch Done to return to the tab that you were just viewing.
- To reorder the tabs, touch and hold a tab, and move it up or down.

- To close all tabs at once, touch and hold the ⬜ button, and then touch Close All # Tabs, where the # symbol represents the number of tabs that are currently open.

- To view two tabs at the same time in Split-Screen mode, touch and hold the ⬜ button, and then touch Open Split View. The screen is split and your currently open tabs appear on the left. A new tab opens on the right. You can open new tabs in the window on the right just as you would in a regular Safari session. To merge all tabs again, touch and hold the hold the ⬜ button, and then touch **Merge All Tabs**. You can also touch **Close Tab** to return to Full-Screen mode if you have only opened one tab in the window on the right.

Using the Safari Web Browser

Figure 6: Open Safari Tabs

125

5. Blocking Pop-Up Windows

Some websites may have pop-up windows that interfere with browsing the internet. By default, pop-ups are already blocked. To block pop-ups:

1. Touch the ![icon] icon on the Home screen. The Settings screen appears, as shown in **Figure 7**.
2. Scroll down and touch Safari. The Safari Settings screen appears, as shown in **Figure 8**.
3. Touch the ![switch] switch next to 'Block Pop-Ups'. Pop-ups will now be blocked.
4. Touch the ![switch] switch next to 'Block Pop-Ups'. Pop-ups will now be allowed.

Using the Safari Web Browser

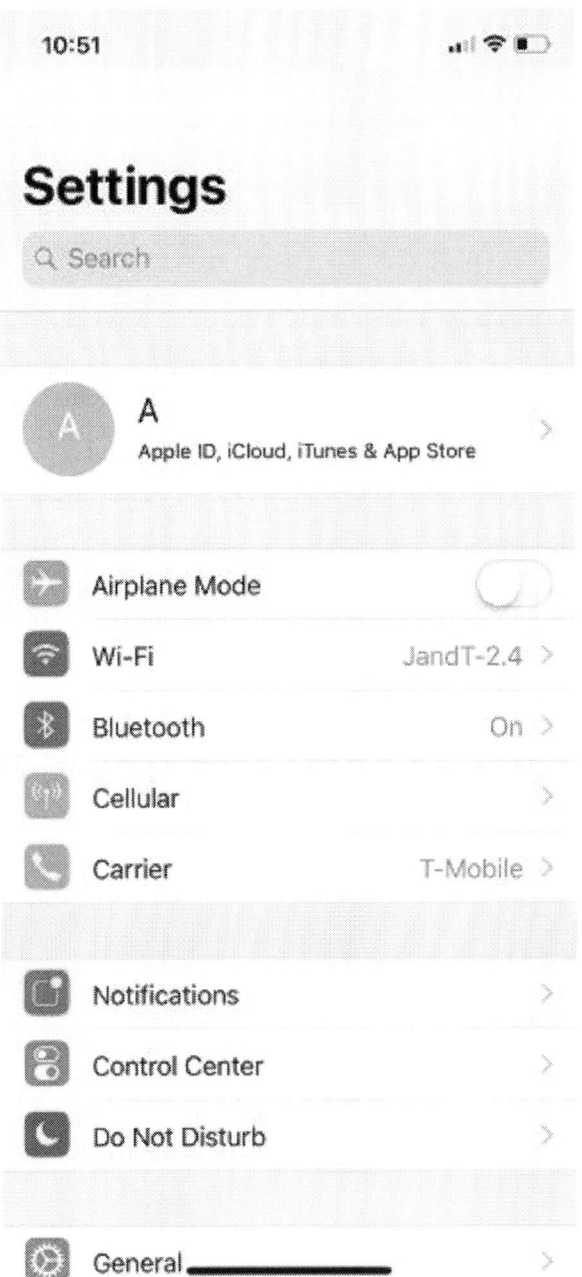
Figure 7: Settings Screen

Help Me! Guide to the iPhone X

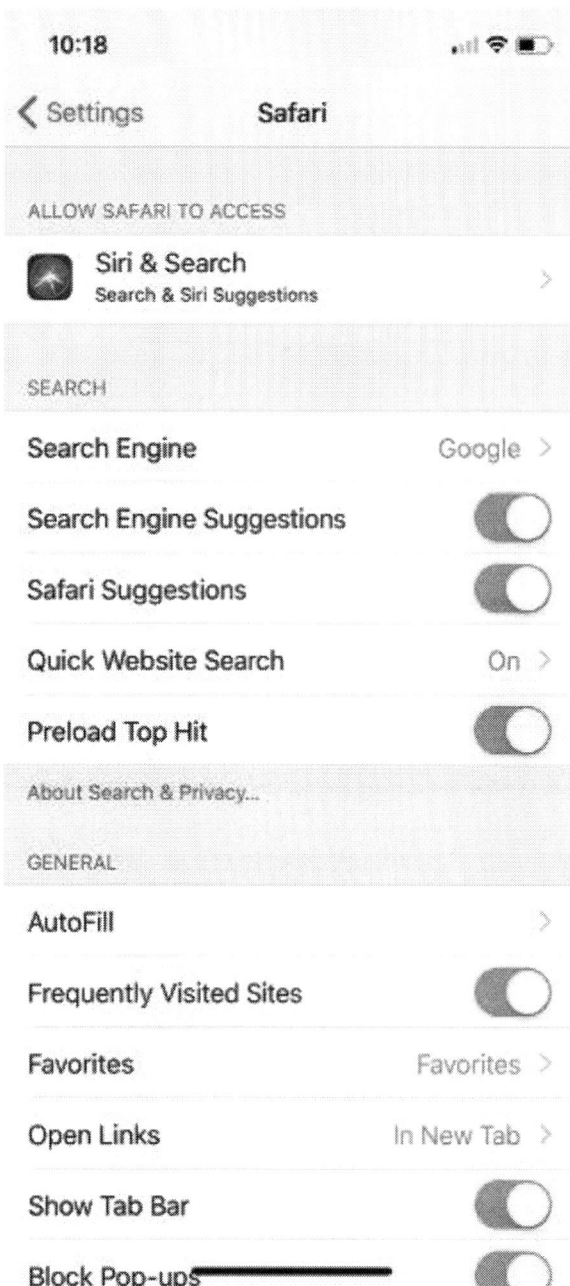

Figure 8: Safari Settings Screen

6. Changing the Search Engine

Google, Yahoo, or Bing can be set as the default search engine in Safari. When you get your new phone, the default search engine is set to Google. The Address bar at the top of the screen also acts as a search field in Safari. To change the default search engine:

1. Touch the ⚙ icon on the Home screen. The Settings screen appears.
2. Touch **Safari**. The Safari Settings screen appears.
3. Touch **Search Engine**. A list of search engines appears.
4. Touch the preferred search engine. The default search engine is set, and its name will now appear in the empty search field.

7. Clearing the History and Browsing Data

The phone can clear the list of recently visited websites, known as the History, as well as other data, such as saved passwords, known as Cookies. The phone can also delete data from previously visited websites, known as the Cache. To delete all of these items:

1. Touch the ⚙ icon on the Home screen. The Settings screen appears.
2. Touch **Safari**. The Safari Settings screen appears.
3. Touch **Clear History and Website Data**. A confirmation dialog appears.
4. Touch **Clear History and Data**. The selected data is deleted and the option is grayed out on the Safari Settings screen.

8. Viewing an Article in Reader Mode

The Safari browser can display certain news articles in Reader Mode, which allows you to read them like a book with no images or links. To view an article in Reader Mode, touch the ≡ button in the address bar (when available), as outlined in **Figure 9**. Reader Mode turns on, as shown in **Figure 10**. While in Reader Mode, you can customize the font by touching the ᴀA When Reader Mode is available, "Reader View Available" briefly appears in the address bar when the page has finished loading.

129

Help Me! Guide to the iPhone X

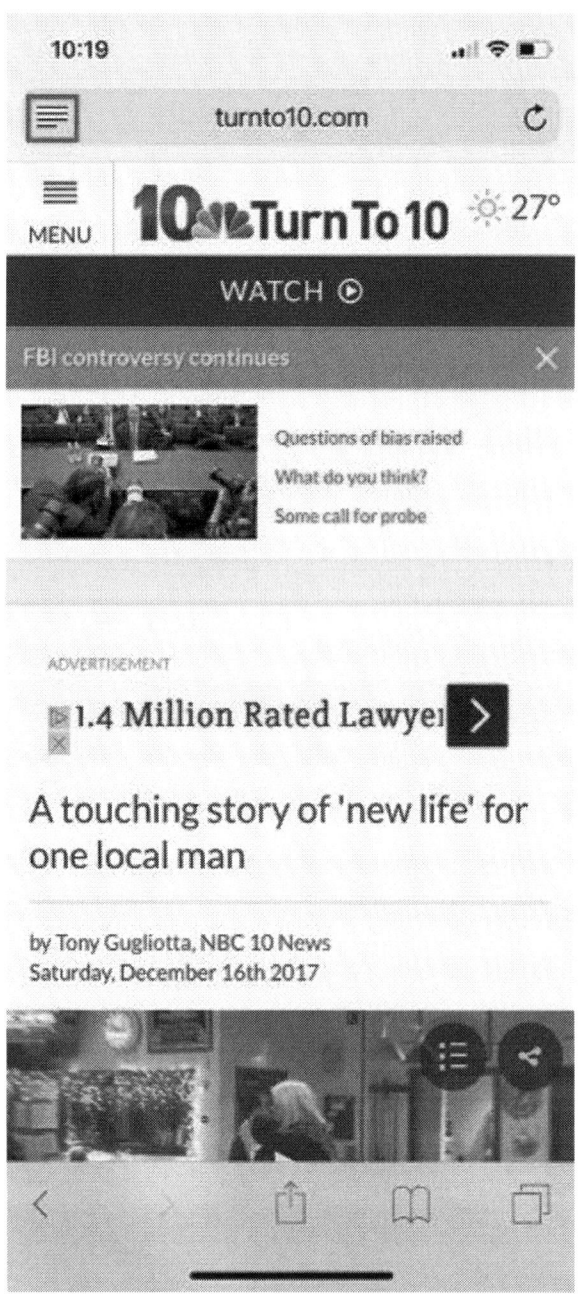

Figure 9: Reader Button in the Address Bar

Using the Safari Web Browser

Figure 10: Article in Reader Mode

Help Me! Guide to the iPhone X

9. Turning Private Browsing On or Off

In order to preserve privacy, the Safari Web browser allows you to surf the internet without saving the History or any other data showing that you have visited a particular website. To open a private tab:

1. Touch the ▢ button. The open browser tabs appear.
2. Touch Private. Private Mode is turned on.
3. Touch the ✚ icon to open a new private tab.
4. When you are ready to exit private mode, touch the ▢ button, and then touch Private again.

10. Setting Up the AutoFill Feature

Safari can automatically fill in personal information, such as passwords and credit card information, to save you time when filling forms or shopping online. To set up the AutoFill feature:

1. Touch the ⚙ icon on the Home screen. The Settings screen appears.
2. Touch **Safari**. The Safari Settings screen appears.
3. Touch **AutoFill**. The Autofill screen appears, as shown in **Figure 11**.
4. Touch one of the following ◯ switches turn on the corresponding AutoFill:

    - Use Contact Info - Enables the use of contact information when filling in forms. The Phonebook appears. Touch the name of a contact to use the contact information to fill in forms. It is recommended that you create a contact entry for yourself and use it for this feature.
    - Names and Passwords - Enables the use of saved names and passwords. You will be given the option to set up a security lock in order to keep your private information safe. Websites will give you the option to save your username and password. You can also touch the ◯ switch next to 'Always Allow' to save passwords even for websites that will never save your password otherwise.
    - Credit Cards - Enables the use of saved credit card information. You will be given the option to set up a security lock in order to keep your private information safe. Touch Saved Credit Cards, and then touch Add Credit Card to add a new credit card.

Using the Safari Web Browser

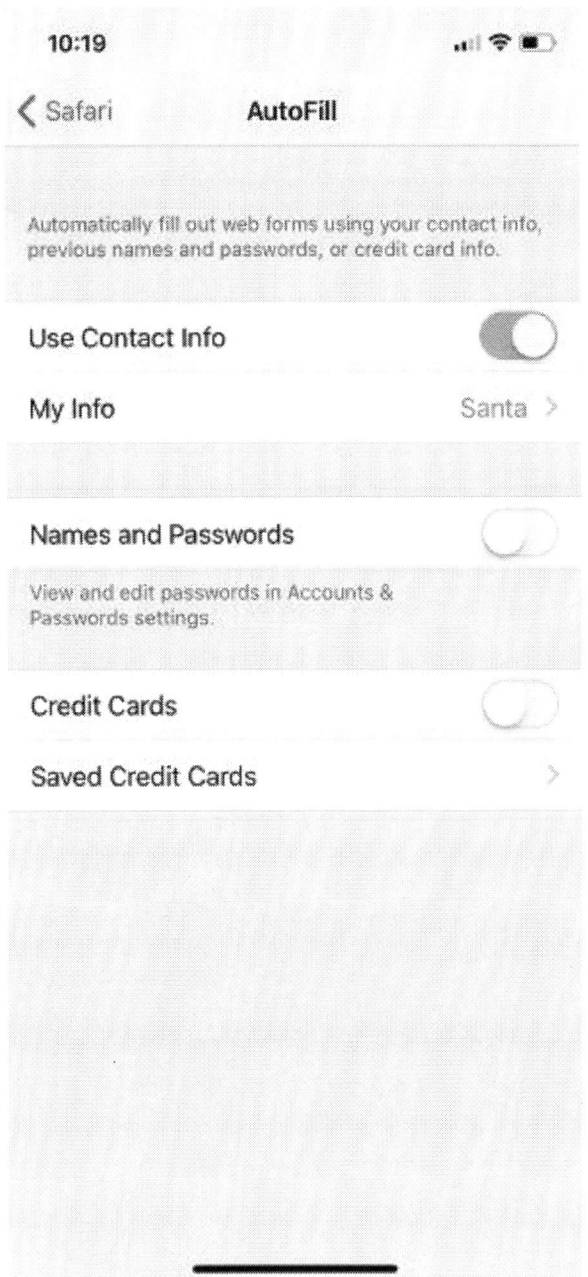

Figure 11: Autofill Screen

11. Customizing the Smart Search Field

The address bar in the Safari browser can act as a search field that assists you by matching your search terms while you type. To customize the smart search field:

1. Touch the icon on the Home screen. The Settings screen appears.
2. Touch Safari. The Safari Settings screen appears.
3. Touch one of the following switches to turn on the corresponding smart search feature:
   - Search Engine Suggestions - Enables search term matching to assist you when performing a search.
   - Preload Top Hit - Automatically loads the most popular search result when you perform a search. The web page is loaded in the background before you even touch the link.

12. Viewing Recently Closed Tabs

The Safari browser saves a history of all browser tabs that were recently closed. To view all recently closed browser tabs:

1. Touch the icon on the Home screen. The Safari Web browser opens.
2. Touch and hold the icon. A list of recently closed browser tabs appears, as shown in **Figure 12**.
3. Touch one of the websites in the list. The selected website opens in a new tab.

Using the Safari Web Browser

Figure 12: List of Recently Closed Tabs

13. Scanning a Credit Card Using the Phone's Camera

When you wish to use a credit card to purchase a product online, you have the option to use your phone's camera to scan the card. To scan a credit card using the camera:

1. Navigate to the website where you wish to enter the credit card number. Refer to *"Navigating to a Website"* on page 116 to learn how.
2. Touch the credit card field on the page. The virtual keyboard appears.
3. Touch Scan Credit Card above the keyboard. The camera turns on. If the Camera Access dialog appears, touch OK to allow Safari to use the camera.
4. Align the credit card with the white frame on the screen. The camera reads the credit card number, and enters it in the field.

Note: You will still need use the keyboard to enter the expiration date and security code (on the back of your card).

Managing Photos and Videos

Table of Contents

1. Taking a Picture
2. Capturing a Video
3. Using the Digital Zoom
4. Using the Flash
5. Focusing on a Part of the Screen
6. Browsing Photos
7. Editing a Photo
8. Deleting a Photo
9. Creating a Photo Album
10. Editing a Photo Album
11. Deleting a Photo Album
12. Browsing Photos by Date and Location
13. Searching for a Photo
14. Recording a Time-Lapse Video
15. Recovering Deleted Photos
16. Managing People in Photos
17. Managing Memories in Photos
18. Capturing and Viewing a Live Photo

1. Taking a Picture

The iPhone X have built-in rear-facing and front-facing cameras. To take a picture, touch the icon on the Home screen. The camera turns on, as shown in **Figure 1**. Use the following tips when taking a picture:

- Touch **Square** to take a square picture. Touch **Photo** to activate the default camera

- Touch the button to switch between the cameras.

- Touch the button to take a picture. The picture is captured, and is automatically stored on the phone. If the surroundings are too dark and you are using an iPhone, refer to *"Using the Flash"* on page 139 for help.

Managing Photos and Videos

Note: Refer to "Tips and Tricks" *on page 348 to learn how to take a picture directly from the Lock screen.*

Figure 1: Camera Turned On

2. Capturing a Video

The iPhone X has a built-in camcorder that can shoot HD video. To capture a video:

1. Touch the ⬛ icon. The camera turns on.
2. Touch **Video**. The camcorder turns on.
3. Touch the ⬤ button. The camera begins to record.
4. Touch the ⬤ button. The camera stops recording and the video is automatically saved to the 'Videos' album.

Note: Touch the thumbnail below the ⬤ or ⬤ button to preview the video.

3. Using the Digital and Optical Zoom

While taking pictures or capturing video, use the camera's built-in Digital Zoom feature if the subject of the photo is far away. To zoom in before taking a photo, touch the screen with two fingers and move them apart. The camera zooms in. To zoom out before taking a photo, touch the screen with two fingers apart and bring them together.
Note: Because of its digital nature, the zoom function will not provide the best resolution, and the image may look fuzzy. Try to be as close as possible to the subject of the photo.
You can also use the optical zoom without sacrificing quality. To use the optical zoom, touch the **1x** button above the ⬤ button. 2x appears and the iPhone zooms in.

4. Using the Flash

The iPhone X has a built-in LED flash that can be used along with the rear-facing camera. You cannot shoot a video with the flash turned on. To use the flash when taking a picture:

1. Make sure the camera is turned on and the rear camera is activated. Refer to *"Taking a Picture"* on page 137 to learn how.
2. Touch the ⚡ icon in the upper-left hand corner of the screen. The  menu appears.
3. Touch **On**. The flash is turned on and will be used when taking a picture.
4. Touch **Off.** The flash is turned off and will never be used.

Managing Photos and Videos

5. Touch **Auto**. The flash will be used as needed, as determined by the phone's light sensor.

5. Focusing on a Part of the Screen

While taking pictures, the camera can focus on a particular object or area on the screen. This will adjust the lighting and other elements to make the object or area stand out in the picture. To focus on a specific part of the screen, just touch that area. An orange box appears and the camera focuses.

6. Browsing Photos

After taking photos on your phone or transferring them from your computer, you may view them at any time. To view saved photos:

1. Touch the icon on the Home screen. The Photos application opens.
2. Touch **Albums** at the bottom of the screen. A list of photo albums appears, as shown in **Figure 2**.
3. Touch an album. The photos in the album appear.
4. Touch a photo. The photo appears in full screen.
5. Use the following tips when viewing photos:
   - Touch a photo with your thumb and forefinger and move the two fingers apart to zoom in on it. The zoom will center where your fingers were joined.
   - Touch the screen twice quickly to zoom out completely. Touch the photo with your thumb and forefinger spread apart and move the fingers together while touching the photo to zoom out gradually. Move your fingers apart to zoom in.
   - Touch the button at the top of the screen while viewing a photo to return to album view. If the button is not shown, touch the photo once to make the photo menus appear at the top and bottom of the screen. You can also touch the photo and slide your finger down to return to the album.
   - Touch and hold the photo ribbon at the bottom of the screen. Slide your finger to the left or right to preview each photo. Release the screen to leave the current photo on the screen.
   - Touch the screen and slide your finger up while viewing a photo to see related photos. Related photos may contain the same people (using facial recognition) or be captured in the same location.
   - Force touch (3D Touch) a photo in an album to preview it. Force touch again to open the photo to view it.

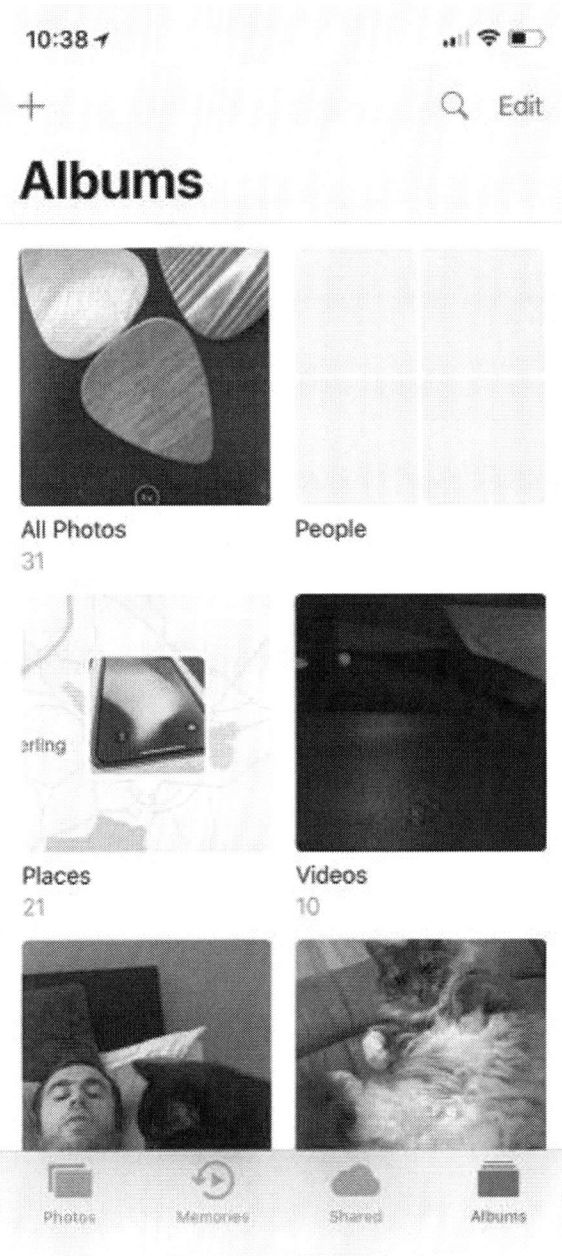

Figure 2: List of Photo Albums

Managing Photos and Videos

7. Editing a Photo

The iPhone X provides advanced photo-editing tools. To edit a photo:

1. Touch the ![icon] icon at the Home screen. The Photos application opens.
2. Touch **Albums**. A list of photo albums appears.
3. Touch an album. The photos in the album appear.
4. Touch a photo. The photo appears in full screen.
5. Touch **Edit** at the top of the screen. The Photo Editing menu appears, as shown in **Figure 3**.
6. Touch one of the following icons to edit the photo:

    ![icon] - Enhances the quality of the photo. Touch **Done** to save the changes.

    ![icon] - Allows you to crop or rotate the photo. Touch the corners of the photo and drag the selected portion, as shown in **Figure 4**. Touch **Done** at the bottom of the screen to save the crop. Repeat steps 1-6 above, and touch Revert to return the photo to its original appearance.

    ![icon] - Allows you to add a color effect, such as Mono (grayscale) or Instant (Polaroid) to the photo. Touch the color effect to view a preview of the photo with the effect applied. Touch the same effect again to return to viewing the original.

    ![icon] - Allows you to customize the appearance of the photo by adjusting the amount of light, color, and tone in the photo. These settings are for advanced users only.

    ![icon] (Available only when a photo contains a face) - Removes red-eye from the photo. Touch each red eye in the photo and then touch **Done** to save the changes.

    ![icon] - Allows you to draw on, magnify parts of, or add text to a photo. Touch this icon, and then touch Markup to use this feature. The Markup screen appears, as shown in **Figure 5**. On the Markup screen, touch one of the following icons to perform the corresponding markup:

    ![icon] - Magnify a portion of the photo. Touch the + to access this option.

    ![icon] - Add text to a photo. Touch the ₐA icon to change the font size and style. Touch the + to access this option.

142

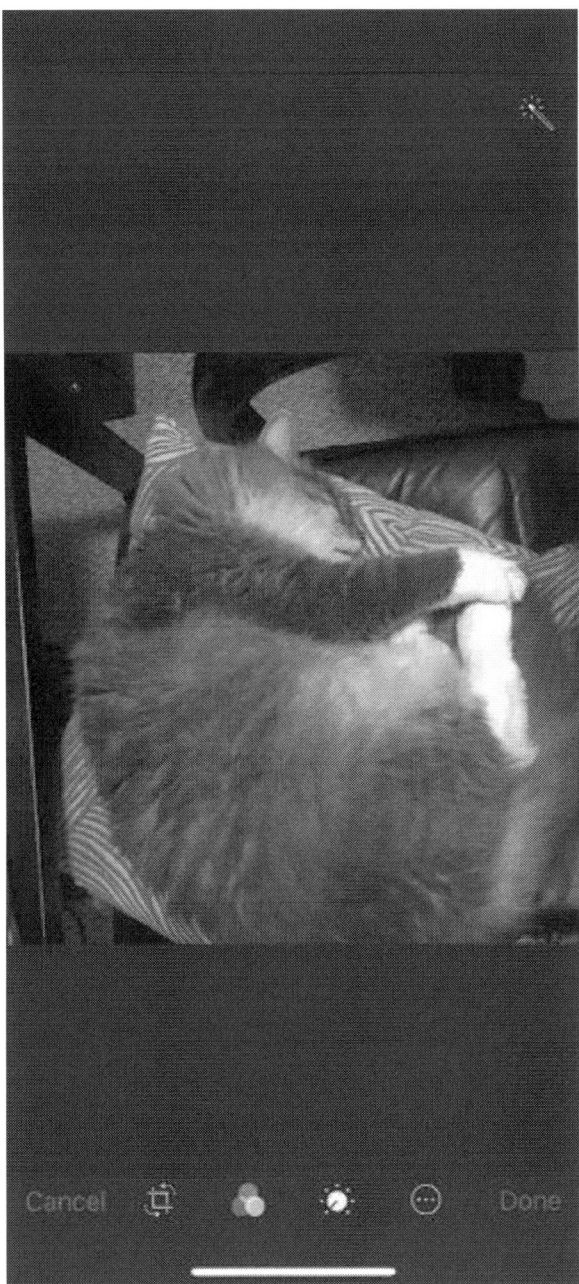

Figure 3: Photo Editing Menu

Managing Photos and Videos

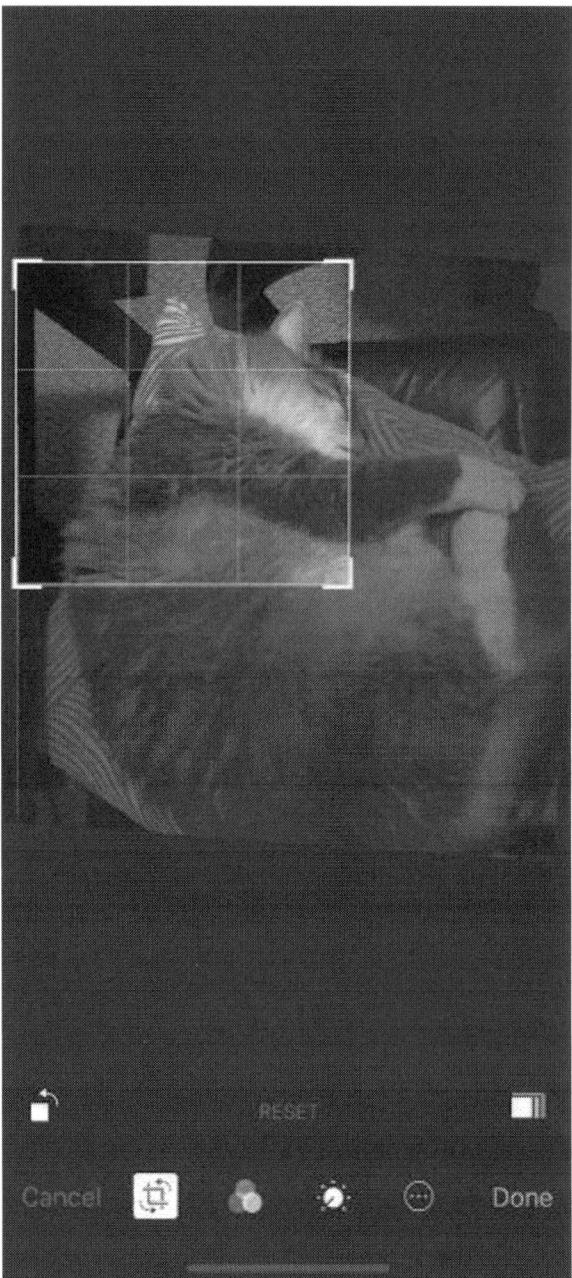

Figure 4: Cropping a Photo

144

Figure 5: Markup Screen

Managing Photos and Videos

8. Deleting a Photo

You may delete unwanted pictures from your phone to free up memory. To delete a photo:
Warning: Once a picture is deleted, there is no way to restore it unless you have backed it up in iTunes or iCloud. Deleting a picture removes it from all albums.

1. Touch the icon. The Photos application opens.
2. Touch **Albums** at the bottom of the screen. A list of photo albums appears.
3. Touch an album. The photos contained in the album appear.
4. Touch a photo. The photo appears in full screen view.
5. Touch the button. A confirmation dialog appears.
6. Touch **Delete Photo**. The photo is deleted from all albums on the phone. You may also delete several pictures at a time, by touching **Select** at the top of an album, and then selecting each photo that you wish to delete. Follow steps 5-6 to delete the selected photos.

Note: Refer to "Recovering Deleted Photos" on page 154 to learn how to recover deleted photos within 30 days of deleting them.

9. Creating a Photo Album

You can create a photo album right on your phone. To create a photo album:

1. Touch the icon. The Photos application opens.
2. Touch **Albums** at the bottom of the screen. A list of photo albums appears.
3. Touch the button at the top of the screen. The New Album window appears, as shown in **Figure 6**.
4. Enter a name for the album and touch **Save**. The new photo album is created, and you can now choose photos to add to it.
5. Touch a photo album, and then touch photos to add them. Touch a photo a second time to deselect it. Touch **Albums** at the bottom of the screen at any time to return to the album list.
6. Touch **Done** at the top of the screen. The selected photos are added to the new photo album.

Help Me! Guide to the iPhone X

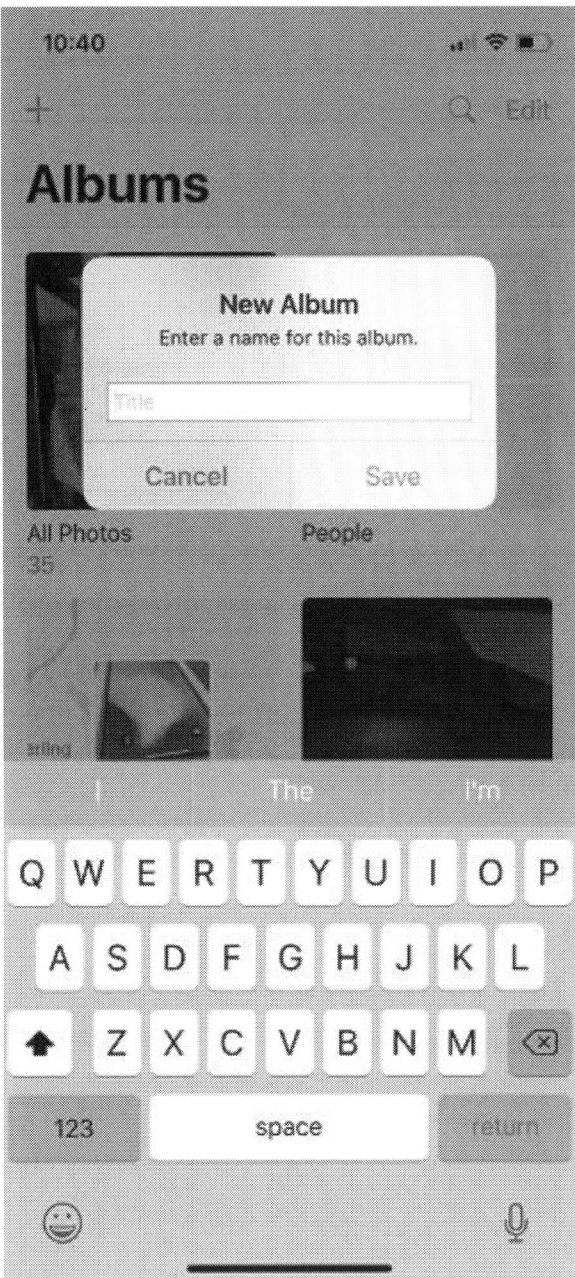

Figure 6: New Album Window

147

Managing Photos and Videos

10. Editing a Photo Album

Photo albums stored on the phone can be edited right from your phone. Refer to *"Creating a Photo Album"* on page 146 to learn how to make a new photo album using your phone.

To edit the name of a photo album:

1. Touch the ![icon] icon. The Photos application opens.
2. Touch **Albums** at the bottom of the screen. A list of photo albums appears.
3. Touch **Edit** at the top of the screen. A ![icon] icon appears next to each album that may be edited. Albums that are on your phone by default cannot be edited.
4. Touch the name of a photo album. The virtual keyboard appears.
5. Enter a new name for the album and touch **Done**. The album is renamed.

To add photos to an album:

1. Touch the ![icon] icon. The Photos application opens.
2. Touch **Albums** at the bottom of the screen. A list of photo albums appears.
3. Touch an album. The photos contained in the album appear.
4. Touch **Select** in the upper right-hand corner of the screen. Photos can now be selected.
5. Touch as many photos as desired. The photos are selected, and ![icon] icons appear on the thumbnails, as shown in **Figure 7**.
6. Touch **Add To**. A list of photo albums appears. You cannot add photos to any album that is grayed out.
7. Touch the name of a photo album. The selected photos are added to the album.

Note: Adding photos to an album does not remove them from the original album.

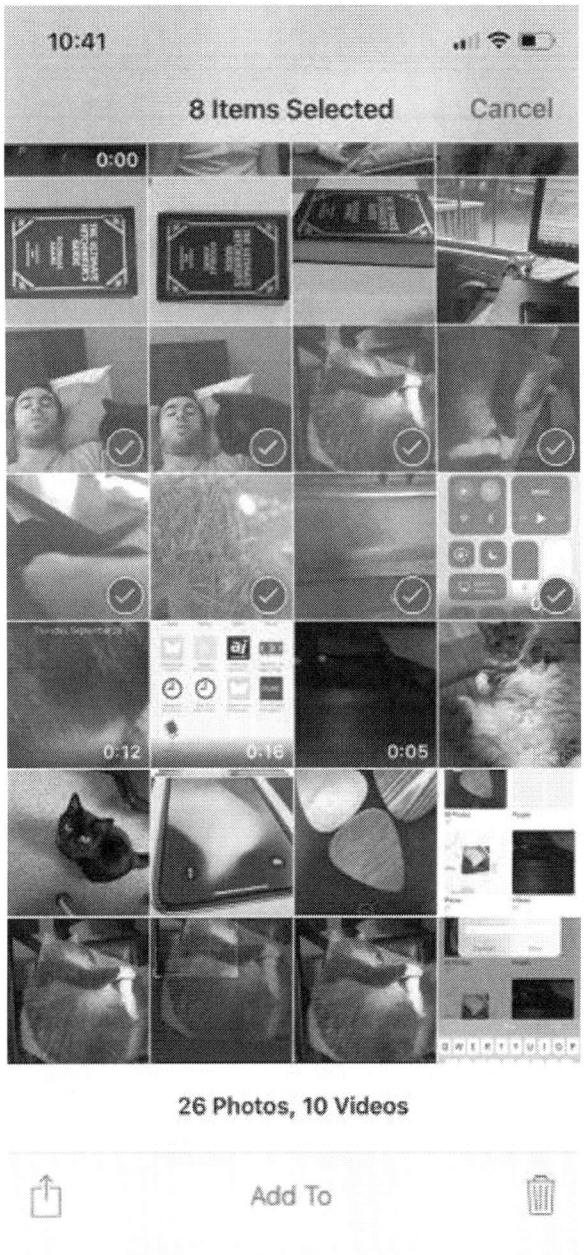

Figure 7: Selected Photos

Managing Photos and Videos

11. Deleting a Photo Album

Photo albums stored on the phone can be deleted right from your phone. To delete a photo album:

Warning: When an album is deleted from the phone, any photos that are stored in other albums will remain on the phone. Make sure any photos you wish to keep are stored in another album. Refer to "Editing a Photo Album" on page 148 to learn how to add photos to an album.

1. Touch the ![] icon. The Photos application opens.
2. Touch **Albums** at the bottom of the screen. A list of photo albums appears.
3. Touch **Edit** at the top of the screen. The ![] button appears next to each album that may be deleted.
4. Touch the ![] icon next to an album. A confirmation dialog appears.
5. Touch **Delete Album**. The photo album is deleted.

12. Browsing Photos by Date and Location

The phone can sort photos according to the physical locations where they were taken, as well as the dates on which they were captured. To browse photos by date and location:

1. Touch the ![] icon. The Photos application opens.
2. Touch **Photos** at the bottom of the screen. A list of albums appears, organized by date and location, as shown in **Figure 8**. If you do not see the list of albums, touch **Collections** at the top of the screen.
3. Touch an album in any location. The selected album opens.
4. Touch the name of a town. A map appears, showing the locations where photos were taken. Touch **Moments** to return to the photo list.

Note: You may only view pictures sorted by location if you have Location Services turned on. Refer to "Turning Location Services On or Off" on page 249 to learn more.

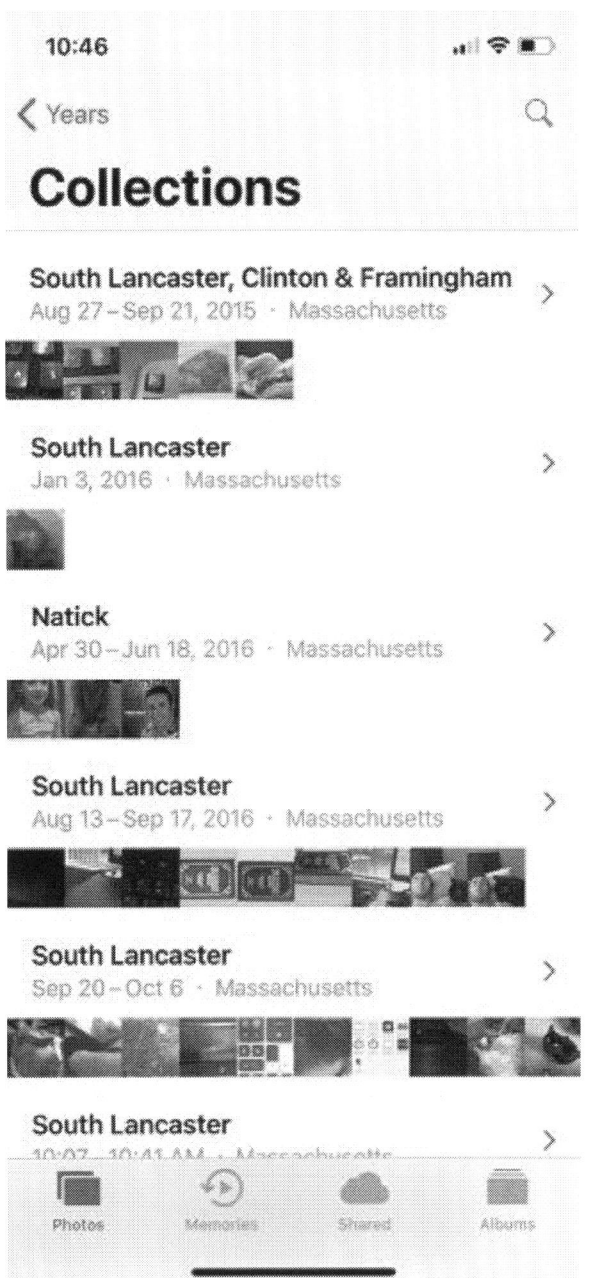

Figure 8: List of Albums Organized by Date and Location

13. Searching for a Photo

Use the Search feature to find a photo more quickly while viewing the Photos application. To search for a photo:

1. Touch the 🔍 icon at the top of the screen while using the Photos application. 'Search Photos' appears.
2. Enter the name of the album, or the location where the photo was taken. You may also search by date.
3. Touch **Search**. A list of matching results appears as you type, as shown in **Figure 9**.

Help Me! Guide to the iPhone X

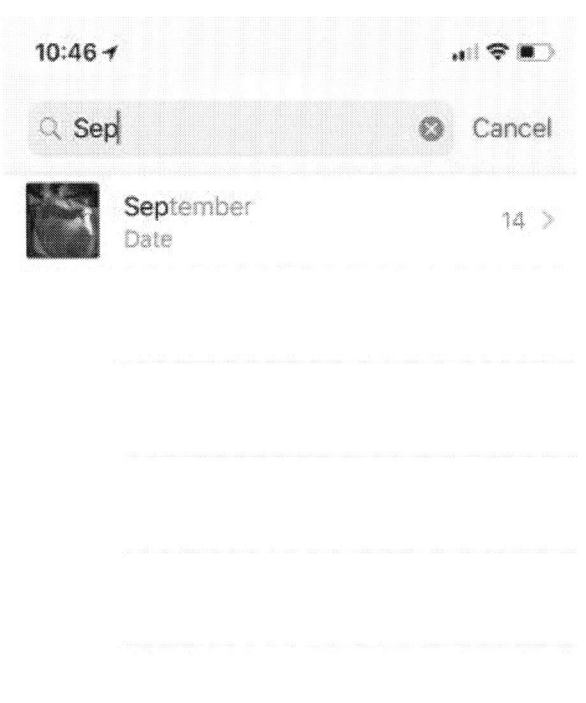

Figure 9: List of Matching Photo Results

153

Managing Photos and Videos

14. Recording a Time-Lapse Video

You can record a time-lapse video, which allows you to capture a short video of an event that takes place over a long period of time, such as the budding of a flower. To record a time-lapse video:

1. Touch the ![icon] icon. The camera turns on.
2. Touch the screen and slide your finger to the right. Continue to do this until 'Time-Lapse' appears above the ![icon] button.
3. Touch the ![icon] button. The camcorder begins to record the time-lapse video.
4. Touch the ![icon] button. The time-lapse video is captured and stored in the 'Time-lapse' album. The Photos application marks every time-lapse video with the ![icon] icon.

15. Recovering Deleted Photos

You may recover a deleted photo if fewer than 30 days have passed since you deleted it. To recover deleted photos:

1. Touch the ![icon] icon. The Photos application opens.
2. Touch **Albums** at the bottom of the screen. A list of photo albums appears.
3. Touch the **Recently Deleted** album. The recently deleted photos appear. The number of days on each photo shows the amount of time left before the photo will be permanently deleted.
4. Touch **Select**, and then touch each photo that you want to recover. The photos are selected, and ![icon] icons appear on the thumbnails.
5. Touch **Recover**. A confirmation dialog appears.
6. Touch **Recover Photo**. The selected photos are returned to their original albums.

16. Managing People in Photos

The Photos application recognizes faces to place groups of photos in the People album when they contain the same person. When you use your phone for the first time, it may take some time to process your photos, but it should pick up faces more quickly when you add them in the future. You can also manually add people to this list.

To manually add a person to the People list:
1. Open the photo that contains the person you wish to add.
2. Touch the photo and slide your finger up. The Photo Options menu appears, as shown in **Figure 10**.
3. Touch **People**. The Add Name screen appears.
4. Touch **Add Name** at the top of the screen. The Name screen appears, as shown in **Figure 11**.
5. Enter the name of the person and touch **Next**. The person is added to the People list.

To manage people in Photos:

1. Touch the icon. The Photos application opens.
2. Touch **Albums** at the bottom of the screen. A list of photo albums appears.
3. Touch the **People** album. The People album opens, as shown in **Figure 12**.
4. Use the following tips when managing the People album:

   - Touch the icon to add the person to your Favorites.
   - Touch a person's face, then touch **Confirm Additional Photos** to view all pictures that include that person.
   - While viewing a person's pictures, scroll down to the bottom, and then touch **Add to Memories** to include the person in your memories. Refer to *"Managing Memories in Photos"* on page 159 to learn more about Memories in Photos.
   - To remove a person from the list, touch **Select**, and then touch each person that you wish to hide. Touch **Remove**.

Managing Photos and Videos

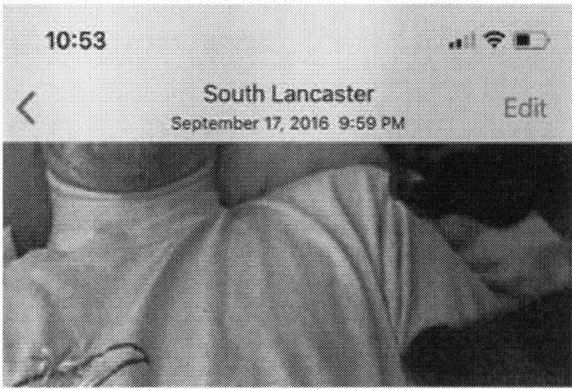

People

Places

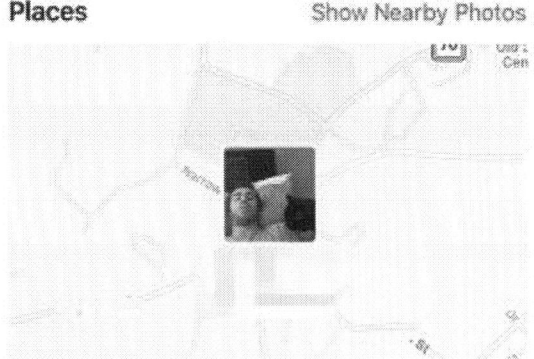

Figure 10: Photo Options Menu

156

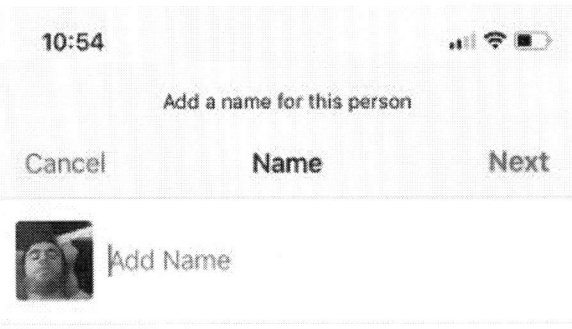

Figure 11: Name Screen

Managing Photos and Videos

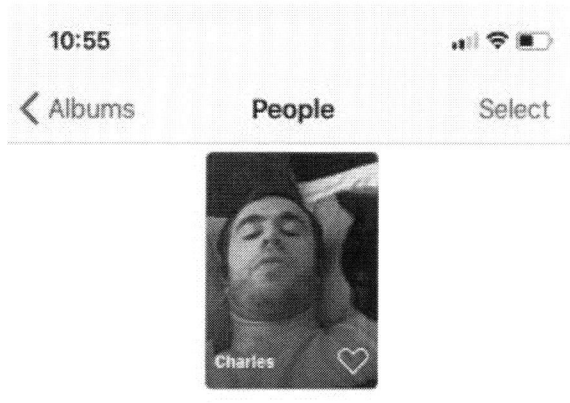

Figure 12: People Album

17. Managing Memories in Photos

The Memories folder also uses the facial recognition feature to create photo arrangements. After there are a sufficient number of pictures or videos on your phone, touch **Memories** at the bottom of the screen in the Photos application to view your memories.

18. Capturing and Viewing a Live Photo

The iPhone X can capture Live photos, which are animated photos that capture video several moments before and after the photo is captured. To capture a Live photo:

1. Make sure that the Live feature is turned on. Touch the ![icon] icon at the top of the screen. The ![icon] icon appears to indicate that Live is turned on, as outlined in **Figure 13**.
2. Touch the ![button] button. 'LIVE' appears at the top of the screen, and a Live photo is captured.
3. To view the Live photo, open the Photos application, and press the photo firmly. The animated photo plays.

Figure 13: Live Feature Turned On

Using iTunes

Table of Contents

1. Registering with Apple
2. Buying Music and Ringtones in iTunes
3. Buying or Renting Videos in iTunes
4. Searching for Media in iTunes
5. Sharing Your iTunes Account with Family
6. Adding Content to Your Wish List

1. Registering with Apple

In order to buy content, you will need to have an iTunes account. Refer to *"Signing In to an iTunes Account"* on page 218 to learn more.

2. Buying Music and Ringtones in iTunes

Music and ringtones can be purchased directly from the phone via iTunes. To buy music using the iTunes application:

1. Touch the ![star] icon. The iTunes application opens.
2. Touch the **Music** at the bottom of the screen. The iTunes Music Store opens and the new releases are shown.
3. Touch **Genres** at the top of the screen to browse music. A list of Genres appears. You may also search for a specific song or artist by touching the 🔍 button.
4. Touch an album. The Album description appears, as shown in **Figure 1**.
5. Touch the price of the album. The iTunes Store Music Purchase screen appears, as shown in **Figure 2**.
6. Touch **Purchase**. The album is purchased (you may need to enter your iTunes password). Touch the price of a song and then touch **Purchase** to buy a single song.

To purchase a ringtone, follow steps 1-3, and then touch the name of the ringtone.
Touch **Purchase** to purchase the ringtone. You will also need to set the ringtone as a default or assign it to a contact before purchasing it.

161

Using iTunes

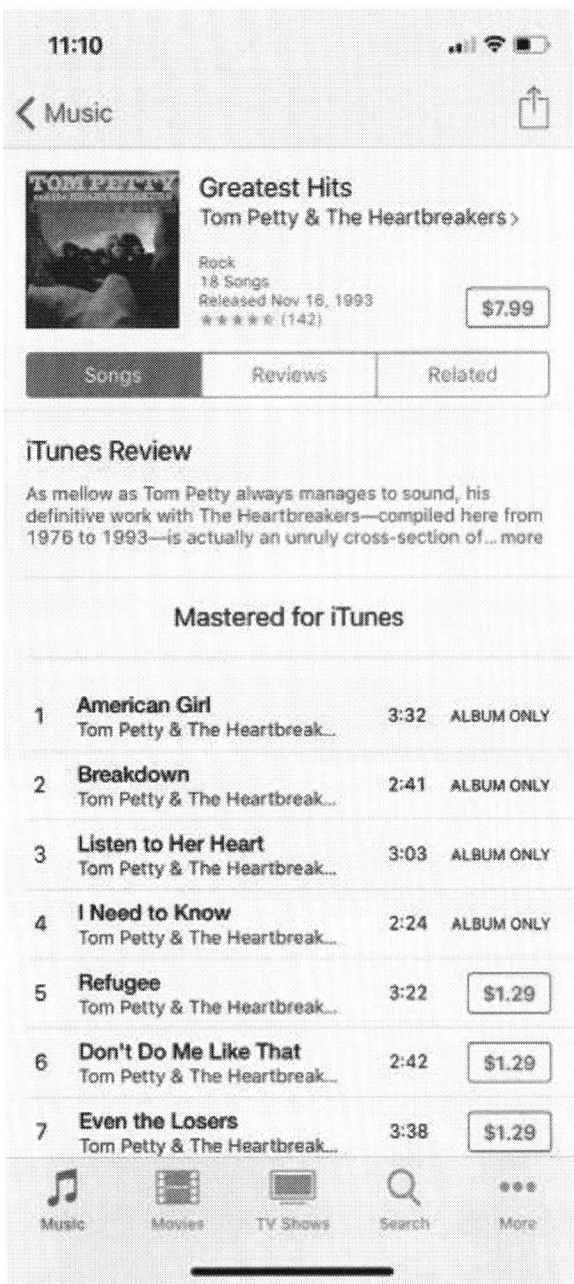

Figure 1: Album Description

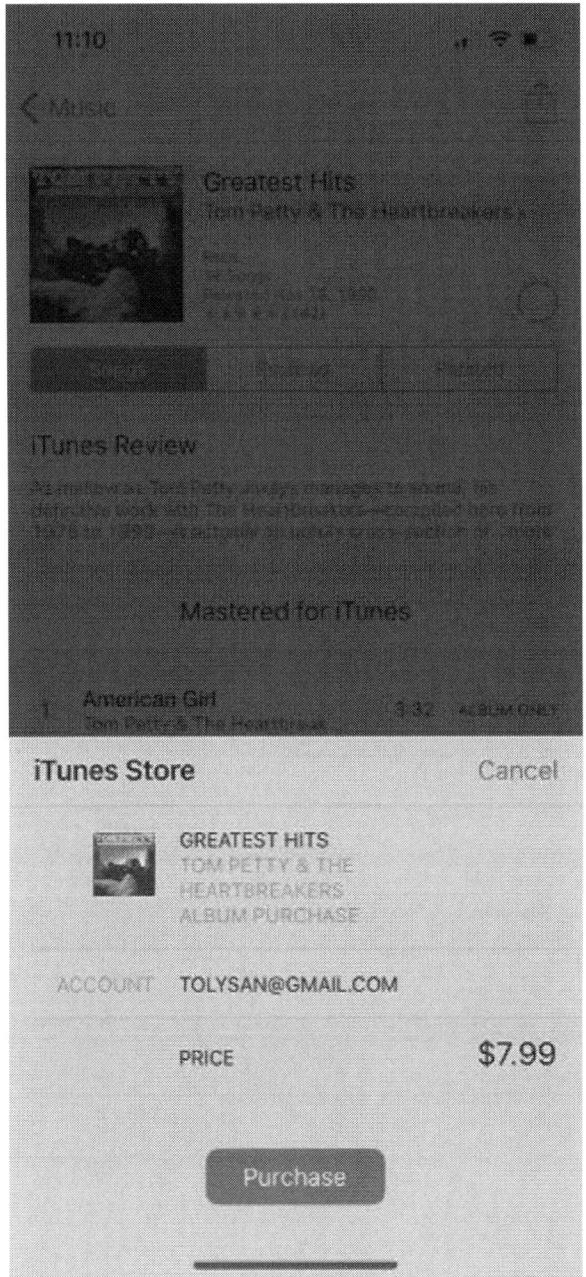

Figure 2: iTunes Store Music Purchase Screen

3. Buying or Renting Videos in iTunes

Videos can be purchased or rented directly from the phone and viewed using the Music application. To buy videos using the iTunes application:

1. Touch the ⭐ icon. The iTunes application opens.
2. Touch the **Movies** or **TV Shows** at the bottom of the screen. The iTunes Video Store opens, and the featured videos appear, as shown in **Figure 3** (Movie Store).
3. Touch a video. The Video description appears, as shown in **Figure 4**.
4. Touch the price of the video. The iTunes Store Video Purchase screen appears, as shown in **Figure 5**.
5. Touch **Buy NAME**, where NAME refers to the type of video that you are buying. The phone may ask for your iTunes password. The video is purchased or rented, and the download begins.

Note: When renting a video, the video is available for 24 hours once you start watching it. Once 24 hours has passed, you will not be able to resume the video if you pause it.

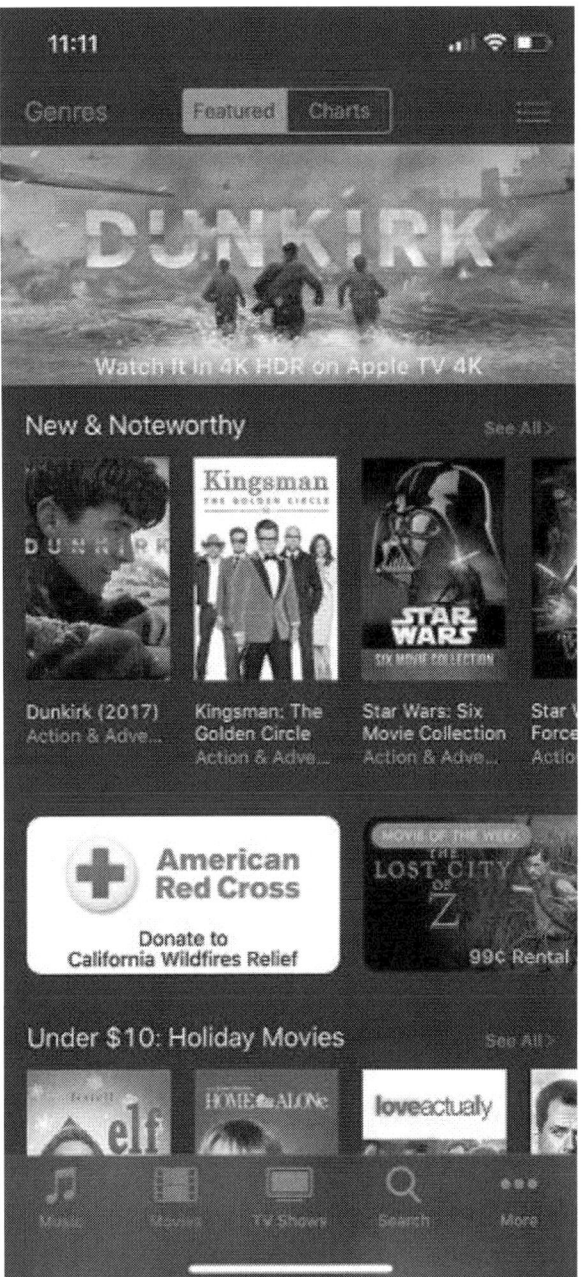

Figure 3: iTunes Video Store (Movies)

Using iTunes

Figure 4: Video Description

Help Me! Guide to the iPhone X

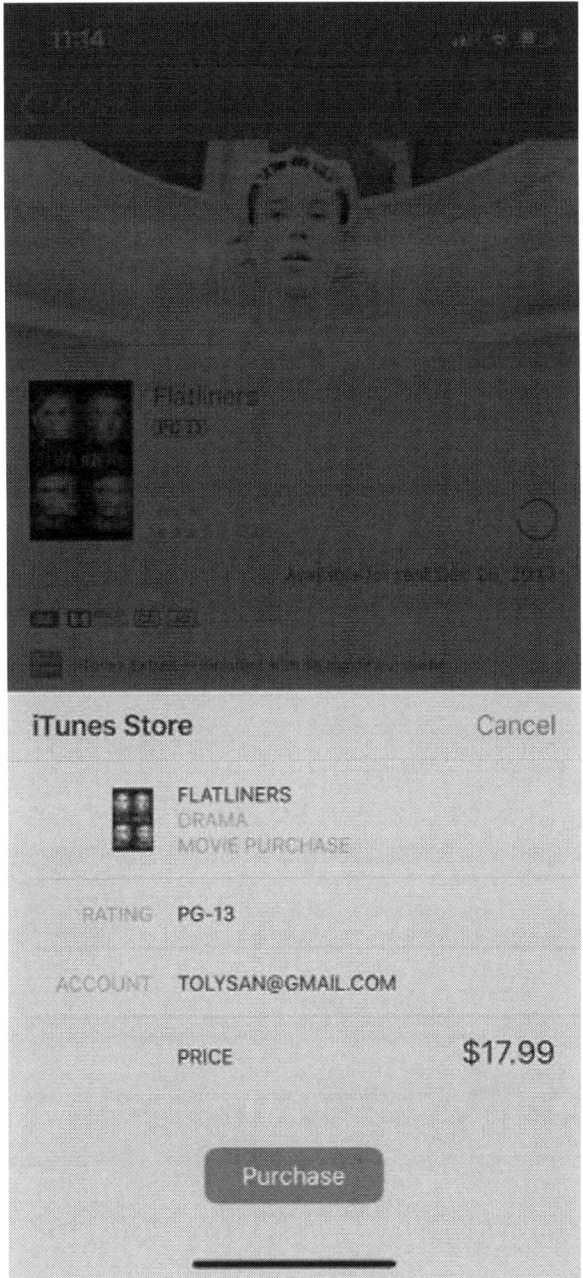

Figure 5: iTunes Store Video Purchase Screen

167

Using iTunes

4. Searching for Media in iTunes

The phone can search for any media in the iTunes Store. To search for media:

1. Touch the  icon. The iTunes application opens.

2. Touch the **Search** at the top of the screen. Touch the ⊗ button to clear the field, if necessary.
3. Enter the name of an artist, actor, song, or video that you wish to find. Touch **Search**. The matching results appear, organized by the type of media, as shown in **Figure 6**.
4. Touch a song, video, or ringtone. The media description appears.

Note: Refer to "Buying Music and Ringtones in iTunes" *on page 161 or* "Buying or Renting Videos in iTunes" *on page 164 to learn how to purchase media.*

Help Me! Guide to the iPhone X

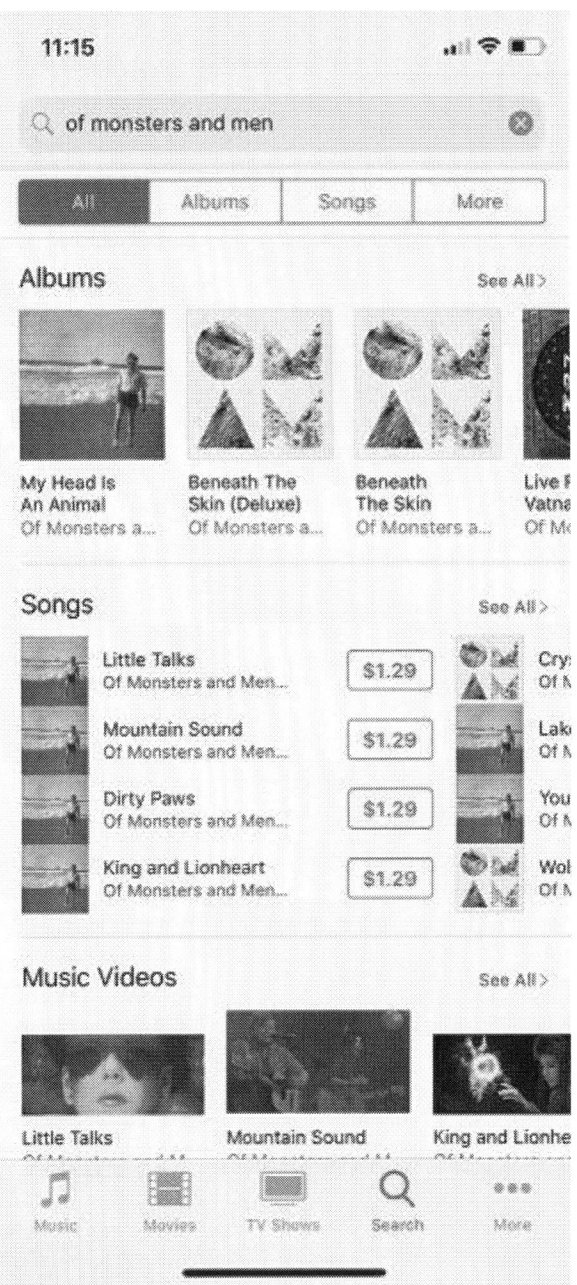

Figure 6: Available Media Results

169

5. Sharing Your iTunes Account with Family

You may allow your friends or family members to purchase content using your iTunes account. Make sure that you trust the people to whom you give access to your iTunes account. To share your iTunes account:

1. Touch the ![icon] icon. The Settings screen appears, as shown in **Figure 7**.
2. Scroll down and touch **Accounts & Passwords**. The Accounts & Passwords screen appears, as shown in **Figure 8**.
3. Touch **iCloud**. The iCloud settings appear, as shown in **Figure 9**.
4. Touch **Set Up Family Sharing**. The Family Sharing window appears.
5. Touch **Get Started**. The Family Setup begins.
6. Touch the feature that you would like to share with your family. Follow the rest of the screen prompts to share your media.

Help Me! Guide to the iPhone X

Figure 7: Settings Screen

Using iTunes

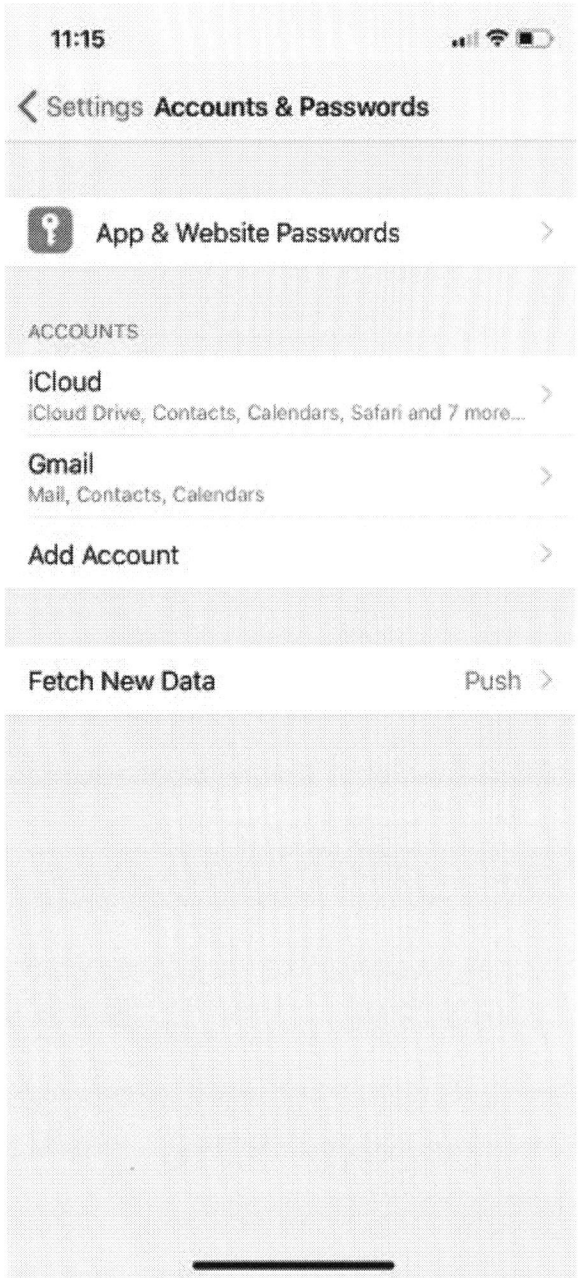

Figure 8: Accounts & Passwords Screen

Help Me! Guide to the iPhone X

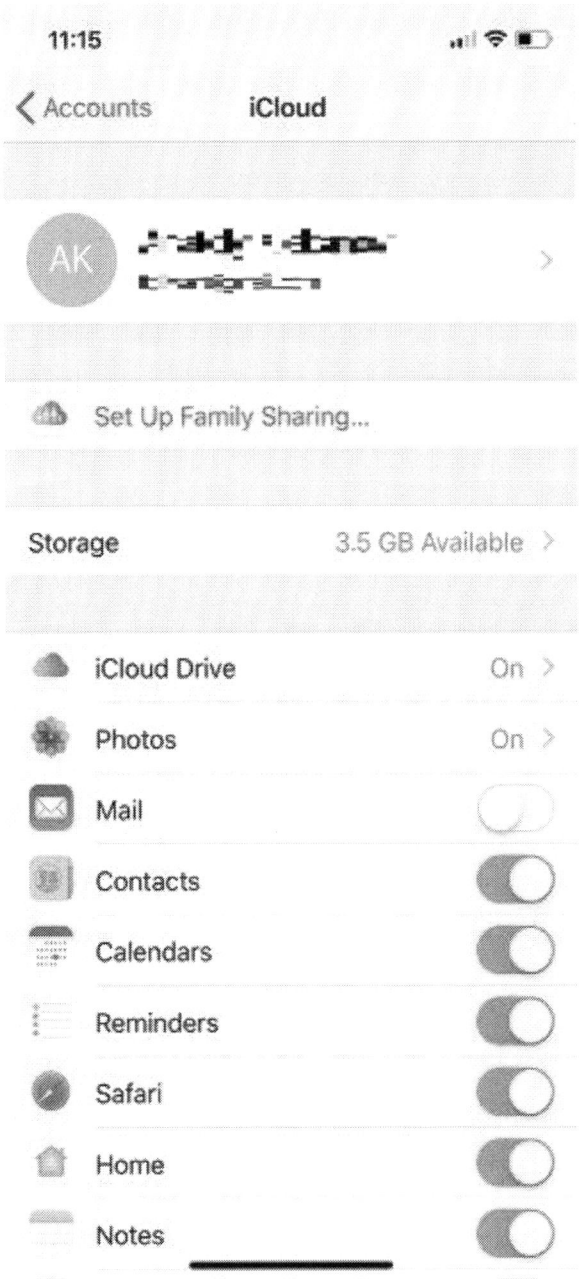

Figure 9: iCloud Settings

6. Adding Content to Your Wish List

While you are viewing a song or video, you can add it to your wish list to buy it later. To add content to your wish list, touch the 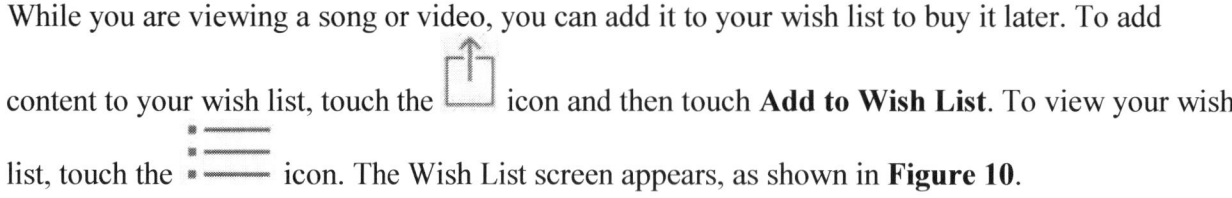 icon and then touch **Add to Wish List**. To view your wish list, touch the icon. The Wish List screen appears, as shown in **Figure 10**.

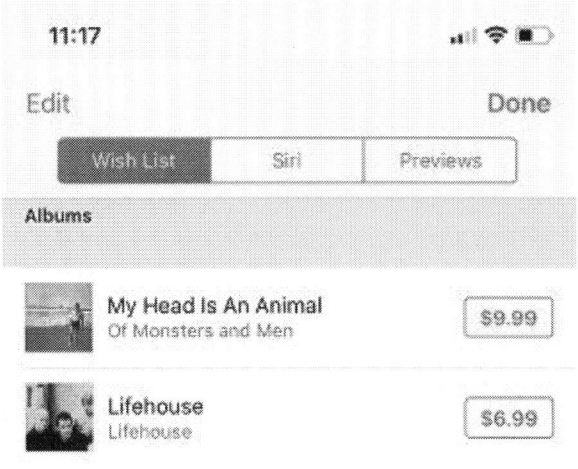

Figure 10: Wish List Screen

Using the Music Application

Table of Contents

1. Downloading Media
2. Playing Music
3. Using Additional Audio Control
4. Creating a Playlist
5. Using the iTunes Radio

1. Downloading Media

Use the iTunes Application to download media to the phone. Refer to *"Using iTunes"* on page 161 to learn how.

2. Playing Music

The Music application on the phone can be used to play music. To listen to your music:

1. Touch the icon. The Music application opens.
2. Touch **Library** at the bottom of the screen and then touch one of the following options to browse existing music:
   - **Recently Added**
   - **Playlists**
   - **Artists**
   - **Albums**
   - **Songs**
   - **Downloaded Music**
3. Use the following tips to navigate the Music Application:
   - Touch a playlist, artist, or album to view the songs contained in the category. Touch a song to play the item. The item is played, as shown in **Figure 1**.
   - After you have exited the Music application, touch the upper right-hand corner of the screen and slide your finger down. The music controls appear on the right-hand side of the screen, as outlined in **Figure 2**. Force touch the song name and then touch the album cover to return to the Music application at any time.

Using the Music Application

- The music controls also appear on the Cover sheet, as shown in **Figure 3**.

Figure 1: Music Playing

177

Figure 2: Music Controls

Using the Music Application

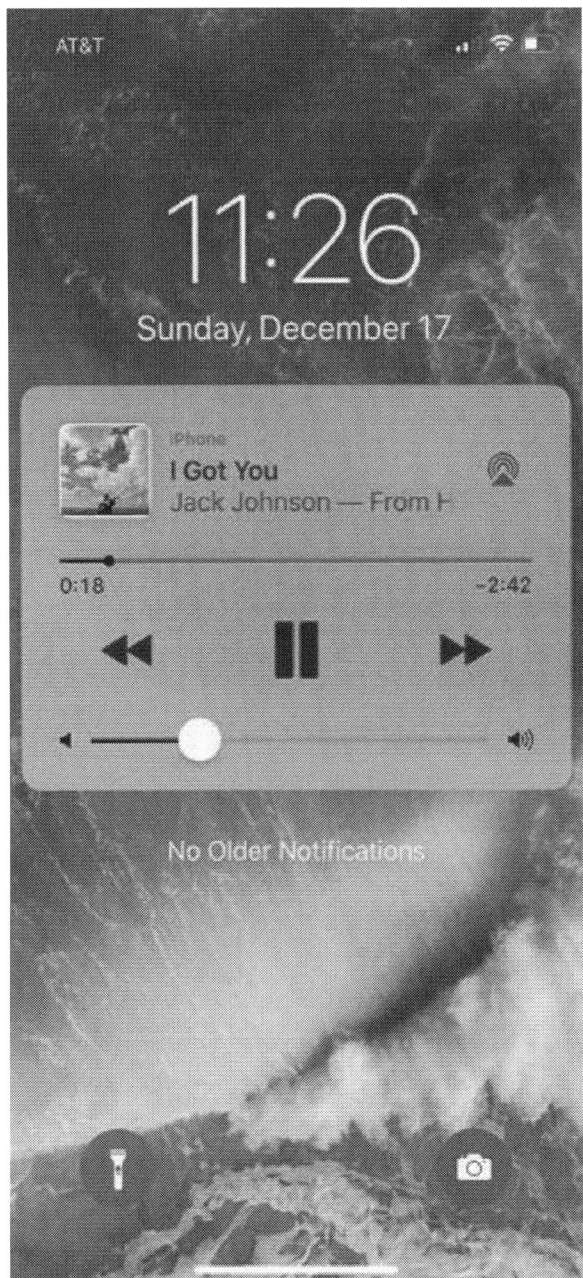

Figure 3: Music Controls on the Lock Screen

3. Using Additional Audio Controls

Use the Song Controls to control music while it is playing. Touch one of the following to perform the corresponding function:

⏮ - Skip to the beginning of the current song or skip to the previous song.

⏭ - Skip to the next song.

⏸ - Pause the current song.

▶ - Resume the current song when it is paused.

🔁 - Repeat the song or artist that is currently playing.

🔀 - Shuffle all songs in the playlist. Touch again to play the songs in order.

Note: Touch both **Repeat** *and* **Shuffle** *to play songs continuously in random order. To shuffle and play all songs on the phone, go to the song list and touch* **Shuffle**.

4. Creating a Playlist

Playlists can be created in iTunes. However, the Music application can perform the same function. To create a playlist using the Music application:
1. Touch **Library** and then touch **Playlists**. The existing playlists appear.
2. Touch **New Playlist**. The New Playlist screen appears, as shown in **Figure 4**.
3. Touch **Playlist Name**, then enter the name of the playlist.
4. Touch **Add Music**. A list of music categories on your phone appears, as shown in **Figure 5**.
5. Touch one of the categories to browse music to add to the new playlist.
6. Touch a song. A check mark appears next to each song that is added to the playlist.
7. Touch **Done**. The playlist is populated with the selected music.
8. Touch **Done**. The playlist is saved.

After creating a playlist, you can add or remove music from it. To edit a playlist:
1. Touch **Playlists** in the Music application. The existing playlists appear.
2. Touch a playlist. The Playlist screen appears, as shown in **Figure 6**.

3. Touch **Edit**. A ● button appears next to every song in the playlist.

4. Touch the ● button next to a song, then touch **Delete**. The song is removed from the playlist.

5. To add songs, touch **Add Music**, then repeat steps 4 and 5 from the instructions above. The selected songs are added to the playlist.
6. Touch **Done**. The changes to the playlist are saved.

Note: Removing a song from a playlist will not delete it from the Music library.

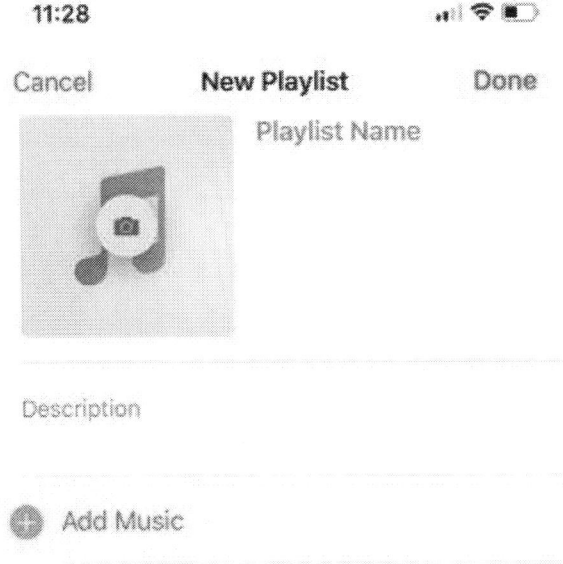

Figure 4: New Playlist Window

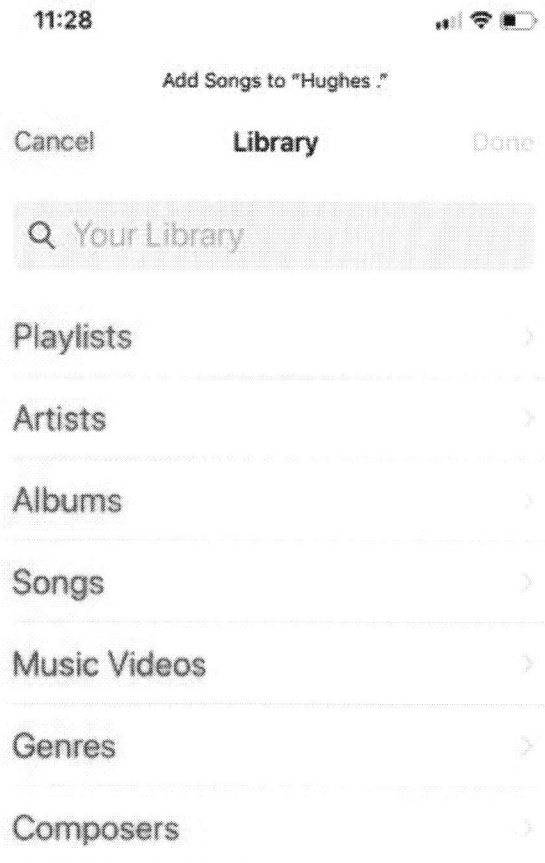
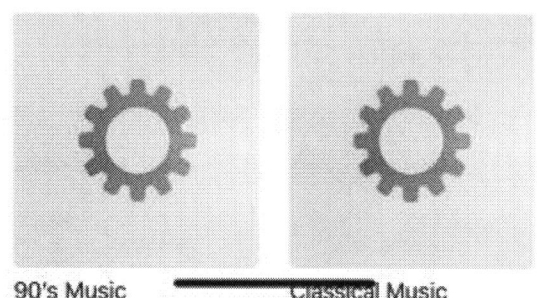

Figure 5: List of Music Categories on Your Phone

Using the Music Application

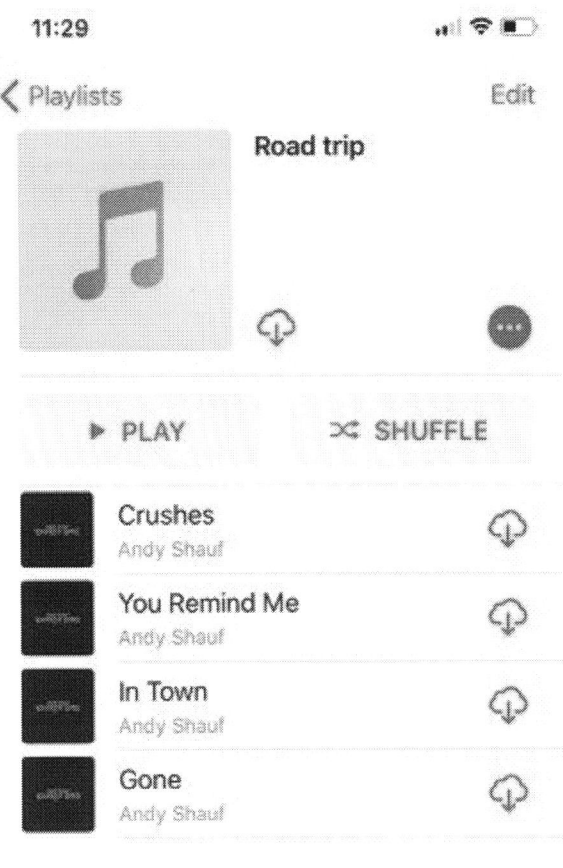

Figure 6: Playlist Screen

5. Using the iTunes Radio

The iTunes Radio is a free service that allows you to create personalized stations based on artists, songs, or genres.

To create a new iTunes Radio station, touch the ((•)) icon in the Music application. The iTunes Radio screen appears, as shown in **Figure 7**. Touch a genre in the list, or touch the search field at the top of the screen, and enter an artist, genre, or song. If you search for a station, touch the name of the artist, album, or song. The station begins to play, and is added to your list of stations automatically.

Using the Music Application

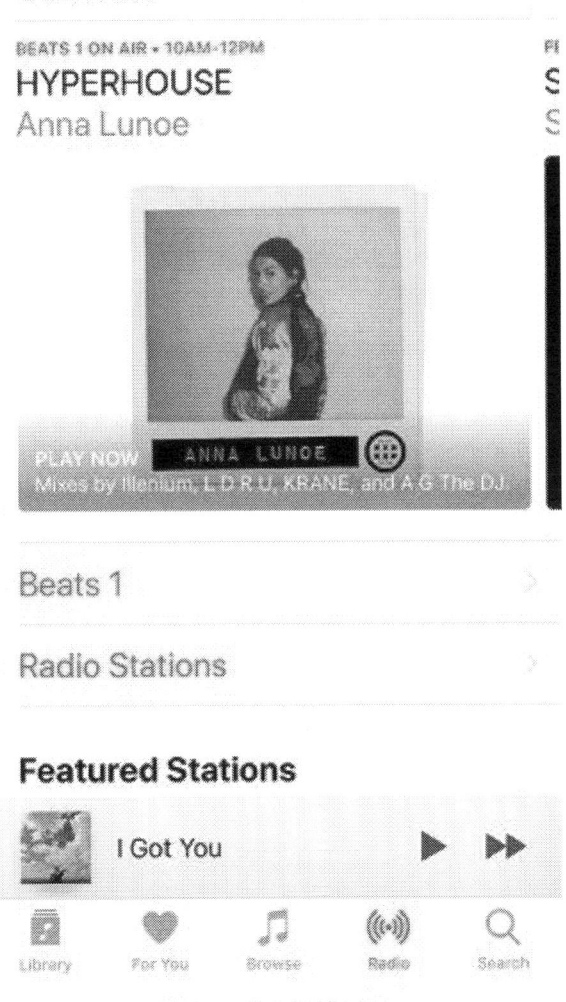

Figure 7: iTunes Radio Screen

Using the Mail Application

Table of Contents

1. Setting Up the Mail Application
2. Reading Email
3. Switching Accounts in the Mail Application
4. Writing an Email
5. Referring to Another Email while Composing a New Message
6. Formatting Text
7. Replying to and Forwarding Emails
8. Attaching a Picture or Video to an Email
9. Moving an Email in the Inbox to Another Folder
10. Flagging an Important Email
11. Archiving Emails
12. Changing the Default Signature
13. Changing Email Options
14. Unsubscribing from an Email List
15. Viewing Emails in Conversation View
16. Adding a Drawing in an Email

1. Setting Up the Mail application

Before the Mail application can be used, at least one account must be set up on your phone. To set up the Mail application:

1. Touch the ![icon] icon. The Settings screen appears, as shown in **Figure 1**.
2. Scroll down and touch **Accounts & Passwords**. The Accounts and Passwords screen appears, as shown in **Figure 2**.
3. Touch **Add Account**. The Account Type screen appears, as shown in **Figure 3**.
4. Touch one of the email services in the list to set up an email account. The corresponding email setup screen appears.
5. Enter all of the required information, and touch **Next** at the top of the screen. The Sync screen appears.
6. Select the types of content that you would like to sync from this account with your phone, such as Mail, Contacts, or Calendars. Touch **Save**. The email account is added to your phone.

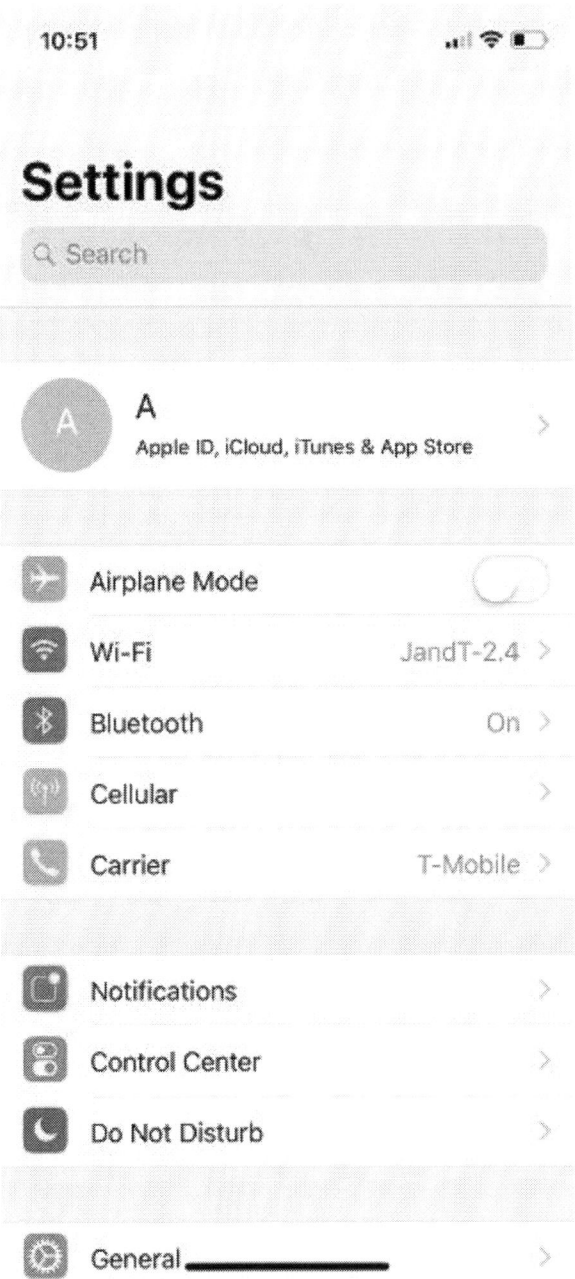
Figure 1: Settings Screen

Using the Mail Application

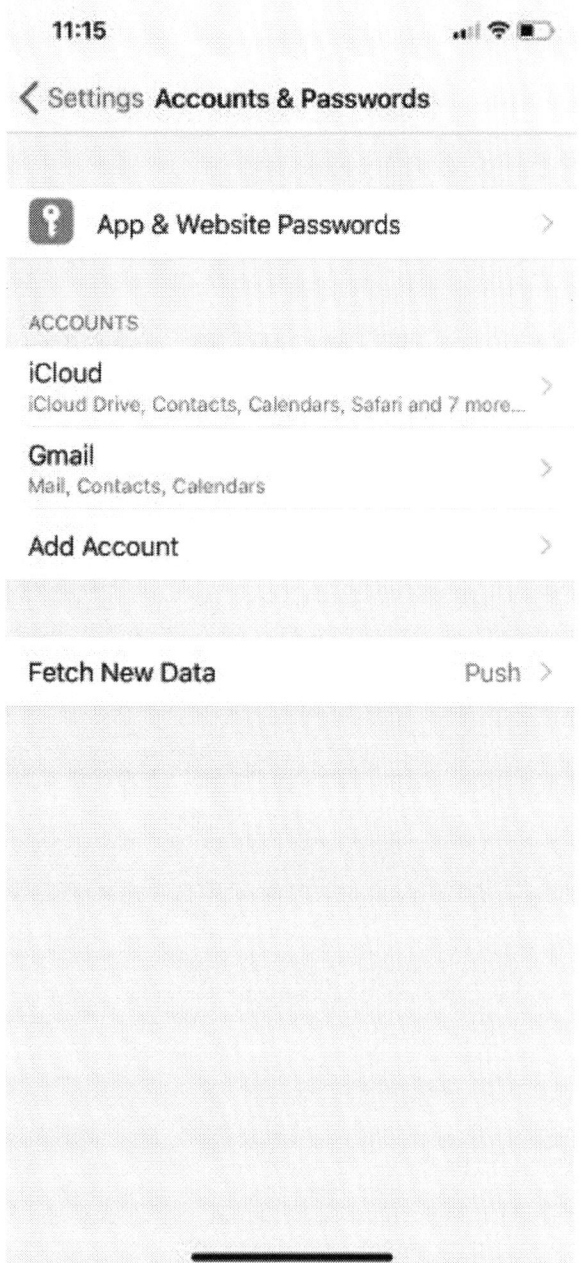

Figure 2: Accounts & Passwords Screen

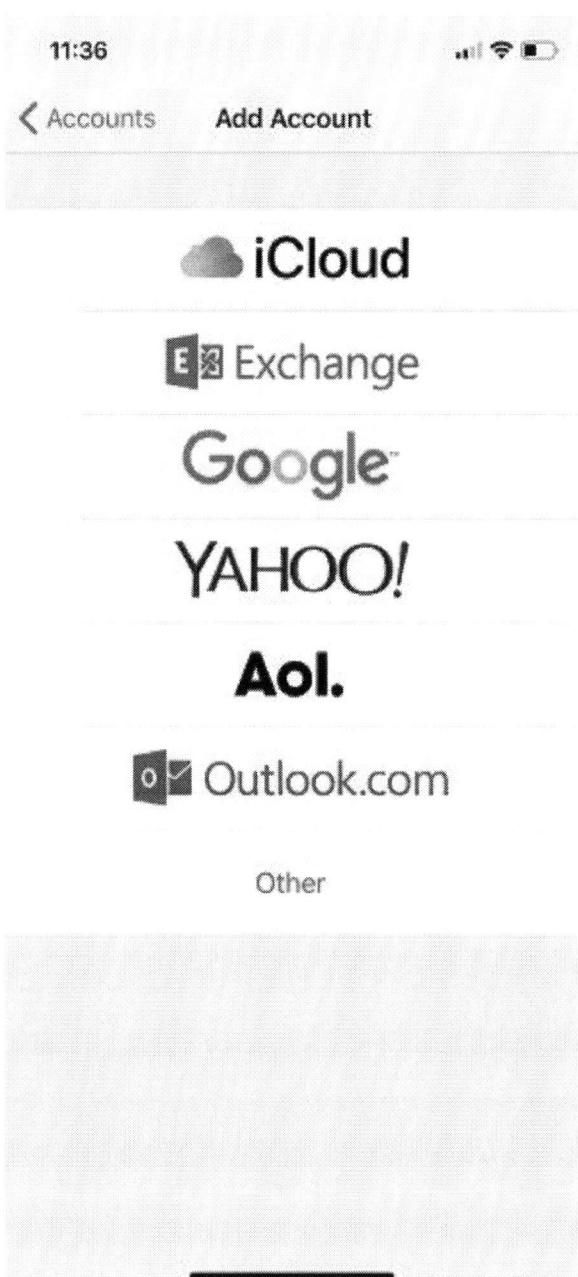

Figure 3: Account Type Screen

2. Reading Email

You can read your email on the phone via the Mail application. Before opening the Mail application, make sure you have set up your email account. Refer to *"Setting Up the Mail Application"* on page 186 to learn how. To read your email:

1. Touch the ✉ icon. The Mail application opens and the Inbox appears, as shown in **Figure 4**. If the emails are not shown, touch **Inbox** at the top of the screen.
2. Touch an email. The email opens.
3. Touch **Inbox** at the top of the screen in an email to return to the list of received emails.

Touch **Mailboxes** at the top of the Inbox to return to the list of mailboxes. The mailbox list varies depending on the email service.

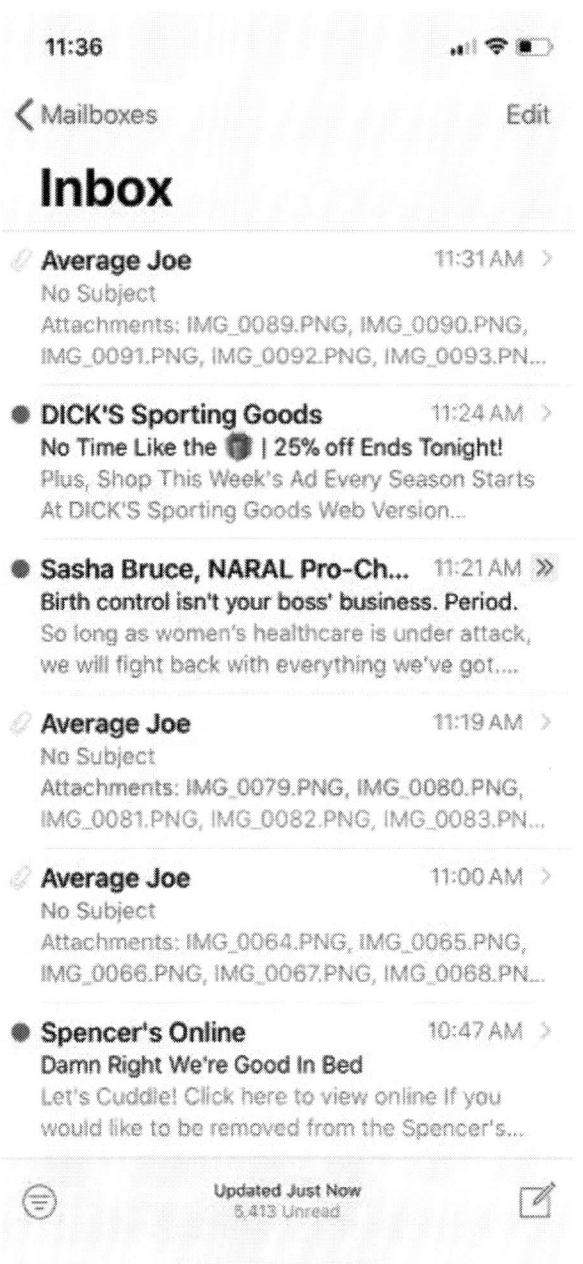

Figure 4: Email Inbox

3. Switching Accounts in the Mail application

If you have more than one active email account, you can switch between them, or view all of your email in one Inbox. To switch to another account:

1. Touch the ✉ icon. The Mail application opens and your emails appear.
2. Touch **Mailboxes** at the top of the screen while viewing a list of messages in a folder. A list of all active inboxes and accounts appears, as shown in **Figure 5**.
3. Touch an account. The Inbox associated with the selected account appears.

You can also touch **All Inboxes** to view all emails from the accounts attached to your phone in a single joint folder.

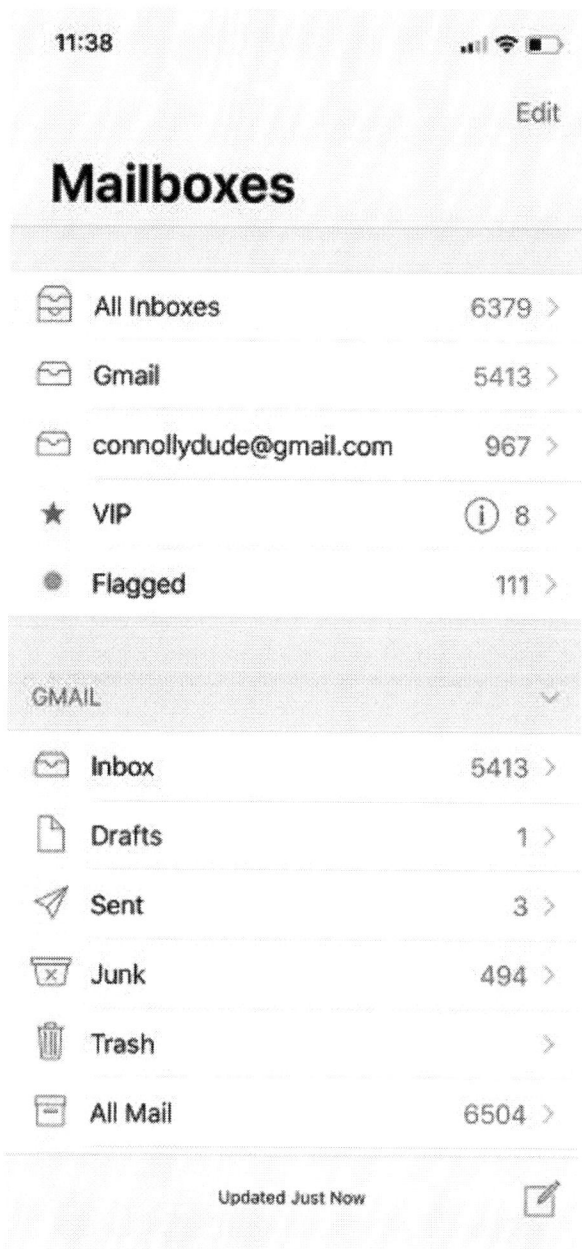

Figure 5: List of Active Inboxes and Accounts

4. Writing an Email

Compose email directly from the phone using the Mail application. To write an email while using the Mail application:

1. Touch the ◻ button. The New Message screen appears, as shown in **Figure 6**.
2. Start entering the name of a contact. A list of matching contacts appears as you type.
3. Touch the name of the contact that you wish to email. The contact's email address is added to the addressee list. Alternatively, enter an email address from scratch. Enter as many additional addressees as desired.
4. Touch the **return** key on the keyboard. The cursor jumps to the subject of the email. Enter a topic for the message.
5. Touch the **return** key on the keyboard. The cursor jumps to the body of the email. Enter the content of the email, and touch **Send** at the top of the screen. The email is sent.

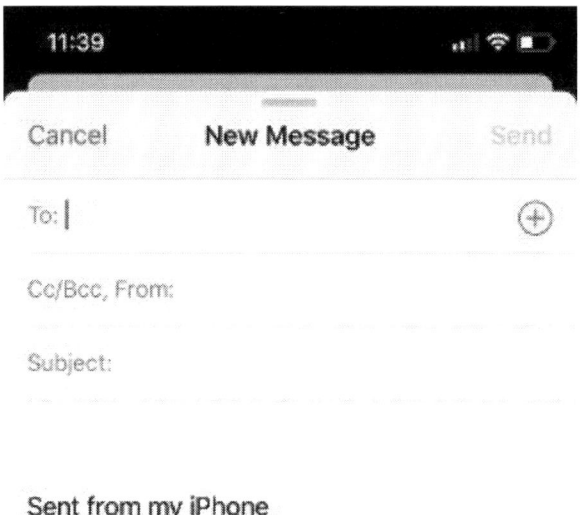

Figure 6: New Email Screen

5. Referring to Another Email when Composing a New Message

While composing an email, you may wish to refer to another message for reference. To do so, touch the top of the **New Message** window, and drag your finger to the bottom of the screen. The New Message window is hidden and you may use the Mail application normally. To continue writing your email where you left off, touch **New Message** at the bottom of the screen. If you have already entered a subject, 'New Message' is replaced by the subject.

6. Formatting Text

When writing an email on your phone, you can format the text to add bold, italics, underline, or increase the quote level.

To add bold, italics, or underline text while writing an email:
1. Touch and hold the text in the email that you wish to format. The Select menu appears above the text, as shown in **Figure 7**.
2. Touch **Select All**. All of the text is selected. To select a single word, touch **Select**. Blue dots appear around the word or phrase.
3. Touch and hold one of the blue dots and drag it in any direction. The text between the dots is highlighted and a Text menu appears, as shown in **Figure 8**.
4. Touch the button. 'Bold', 'Italics', and 'Underline' appear.
5. Touch one of the formatting options. The associated formatting is applied to the selected text.

You can also increase the left margin, or quote level, in an email. To increase the quote level:
1. Touch and hold any location in your email. The text cursor flashes in the selected location.
2. Touch the button in the Text menu. The Text Format menu appears.
3. Touch **Quote Level**. The Quote Level options appear.
4. Touch **Decrease** or **Increase** to adjust the Quote Level accordingly. The new Quote Level is set and applied to the paragraph where the text cursor is currently flashing.

Help Me! Guide to the iPhone X

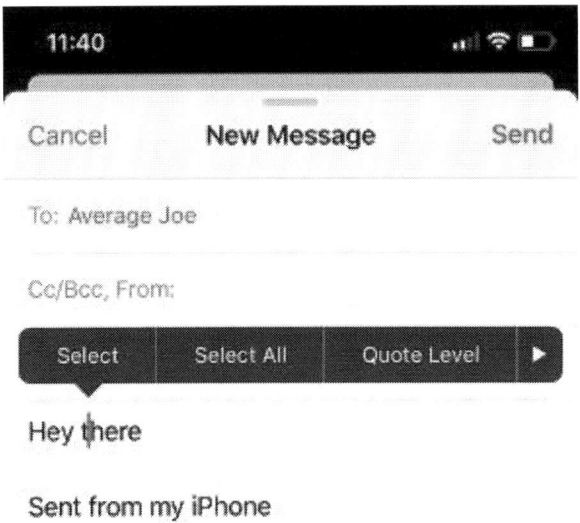

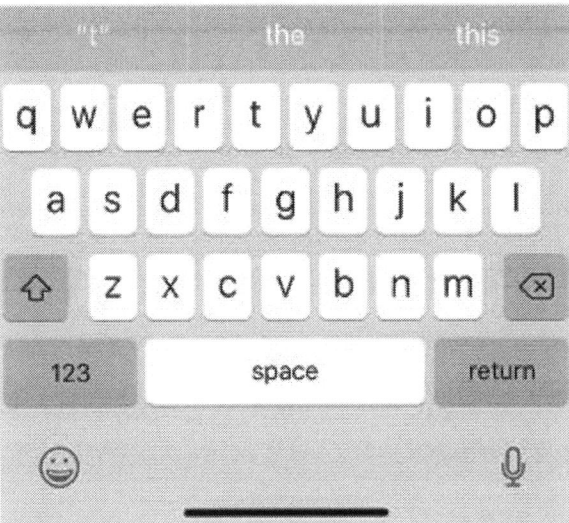

Figure 7: Select Menu

197

Using the Mail Application

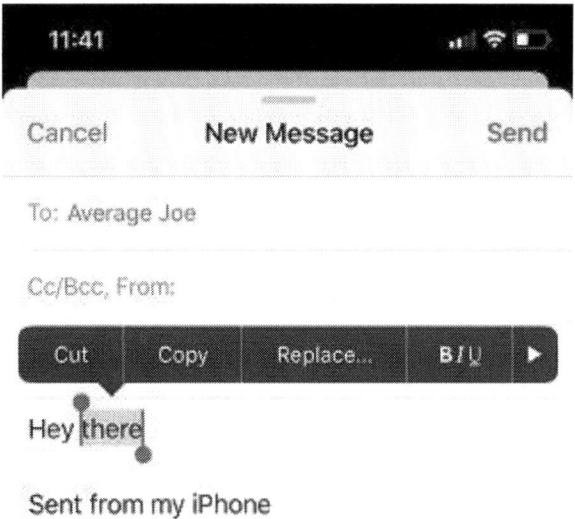

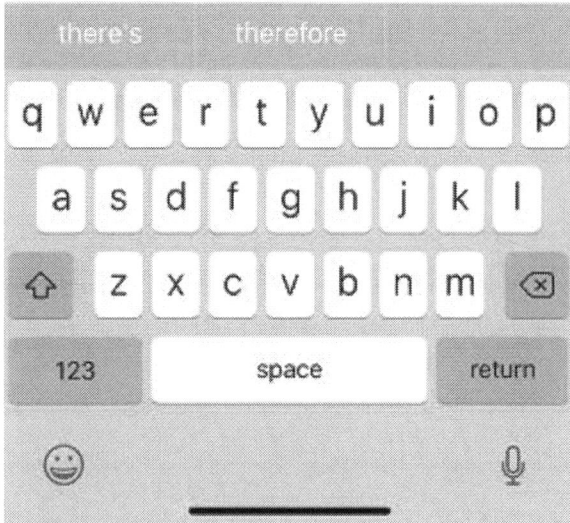

Figure 8: Text Menu

7. Replying to and Forwarding Email Messages

After receiving an email, you can reply to the sender or forward the email to a new recipient. To reply to, or forward an email:

1. Touch the ✉ icon. The Mail application opens.
2. Touch an email. The email appears.
3. Touch the ↩ button. The Reply menu appears, as shown in **Figure 9**.
4. Touch **Reply** to reply to the message, or touch **Forward** to forward the message. The New Message screen appears. The subject at the top is preceded by 'Re:' if replying, or 'Fwd:' if forwarding. The original email is copied in the body. If replying, the addressee field is filled in.
5. Touch the text field next to 'To:', and enter an addressee, if necessary. The addressee is entered. The address of the sender is automatically entered when replying to an email.
6. Touch the text field to the right of 'Subject' to enter a different subject for your message, if desired. The subject is entered.
7. Touch the text field below 'Subject' and enter a message, if desired. The message is entered.
8. Touch **Send** at the top of the screen. The email is sent.

*Note: When forwarding an email, the attachment menu will appear if the original message has an attachment. Touch **Include** if you wish to include the attachment when you forward the email. Otherwise, touch **Don't Include**.*

Using the Mail Application

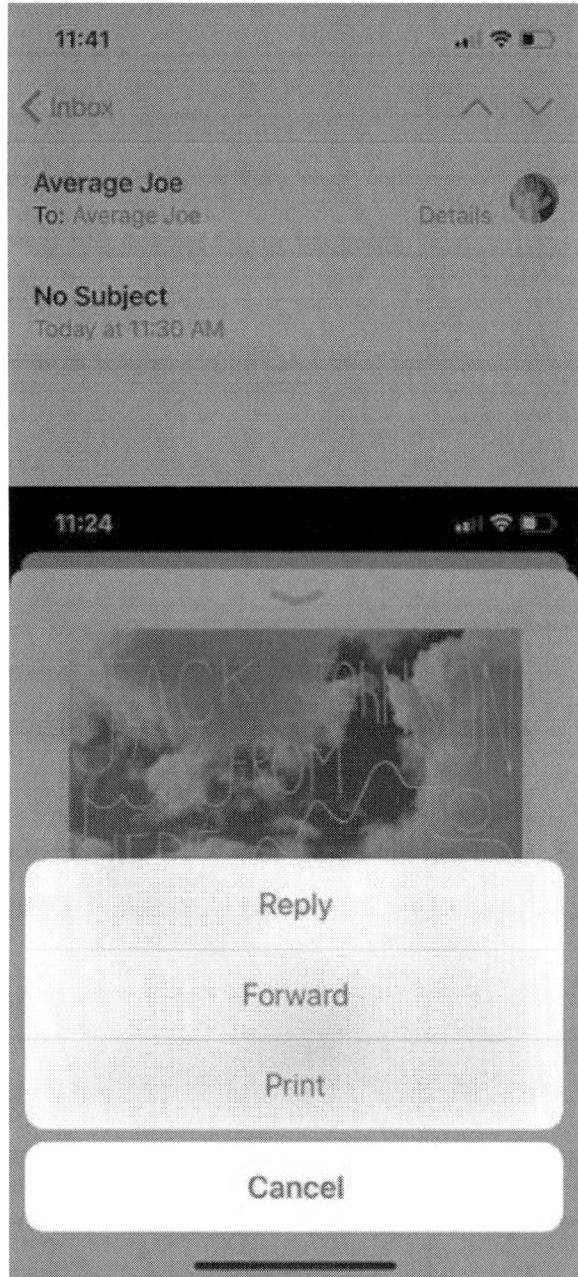

Figure 9: Reply Menu

200

8. Attaching a Picture or Video to an Email

While composing an email, you may wish to attach a picture or video to send to the recipient. To attach a picture or video to an email:
1. Touch and hold anywhere in the content of the email. The Select menu appears above the text.
2. Touch the ▶ button in the Select menu, and then touch **Insert Photo or Video**. A list of photo albums stored on your phone appears, as shown in **Figure 10**.
3. Touch the photo album that contains the photo that you wish to attach. The photo album opens and a list of photo thumbnails appears, as shown in **Figure 11**.
4. Touch the photo that you wish to attach. A preview of the photo appears.
5. Touch **Choose**. The selected photo is attached. Alternatively, touch **Cancel** to return to the list of photos.

You can also attach several photos or videos at a time by viewing a photo in the Photos application and touching the ⬆ icon. There is no limit to the number of photos that you can attach to an email when using an iPhone. However, the size of the email cannot exceed the limit set by your email provider. Refer to *"Managing Photos and Videos"* on page 137 to learn more.

Note: You may move or delete the photo in an email in the same way that you would move or delete text.

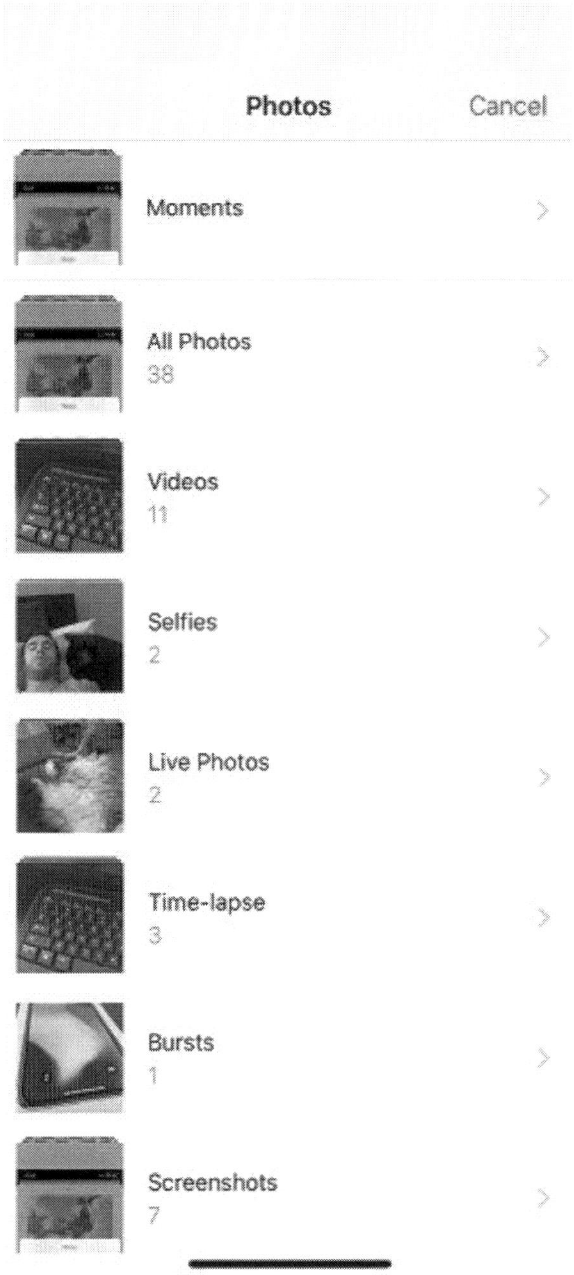

Using the Mail Application

Figure 10: List of Photo Albums

Figure 11: List of Photo Thumbnails

9. Moving an Email in the Inbox to Another Folder

You may wish to organize emails into folders so that you can find them more easily. To move an email in the Inbox to another folder:

1. Touch an email in the Inbox. The email opens.
2. Touch the 📁 button. A list of available folders appears, as shown in **Figure 12**.
3. Touch the name of a folder. The selected email is moved to the selected folder. To view a list of your folders, touch **Mailboxes** at the top of the screen while viewing the Inbox.

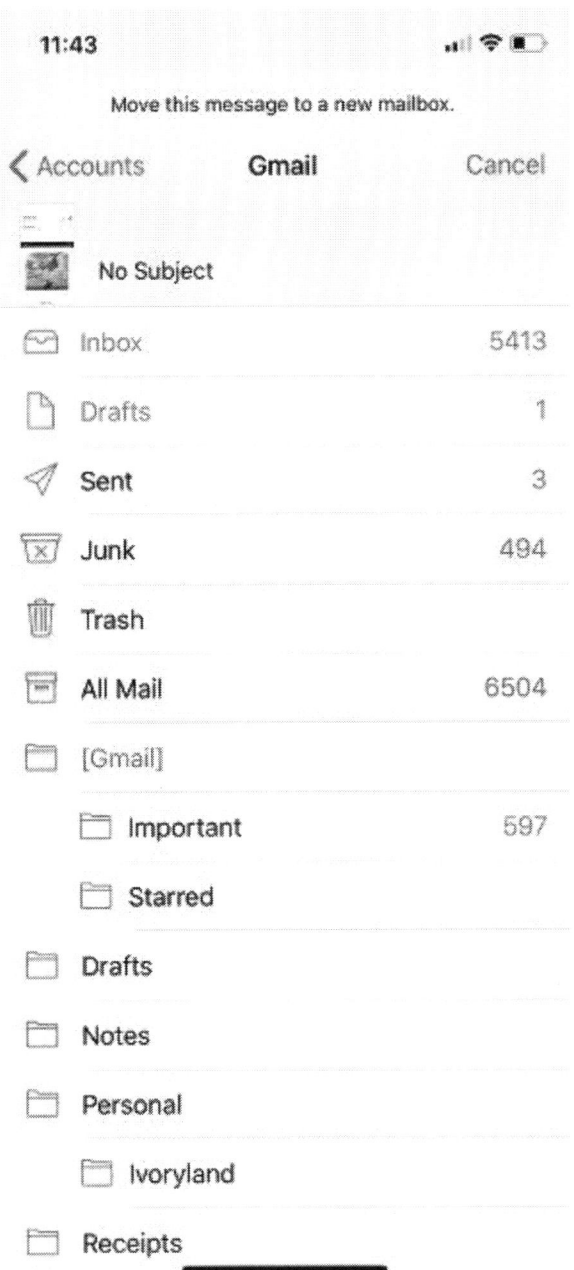

Figure 12: List of Available Folders

10. Flagging an Important Email

You may flag emails that are of the greatest importance in order to find them more quickly. This feature is especially useful if you do not have the time to read the email immediately, and wish to return to it in the near future. To flag an important email:
1. Touch an email in the Inbox. The email opens.
2. Touch the 🚩 button. The Flagging menu appears, as shown in **Figure 13**.
3. Touch **Flag**. The email is flagged as 'Important'. You may also touch **Mark as Unread** to flag the email so that you remember to read it later.

Help Me! Guide to the iPhone X

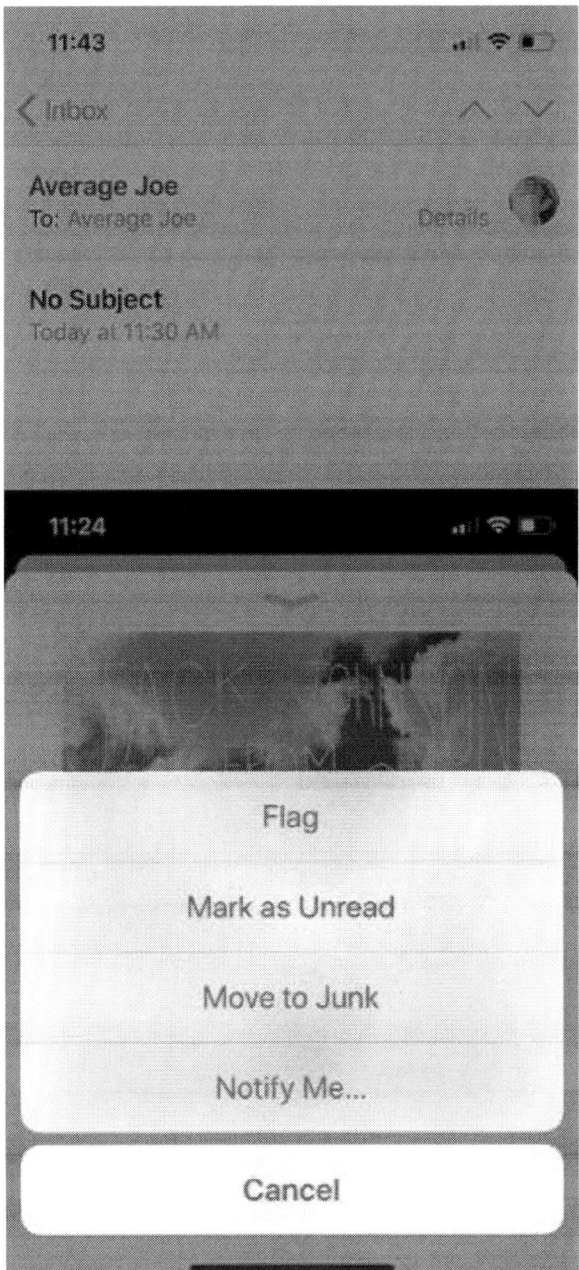

Figure 13: Flagging Menu

207

11. Archiving Emails

You may archive emails from your Inbox to free up space and improve organization. Archiving emails moves them to a folder that does not take up space on your phone. Therefore, you never need to delete an email, and can always recover it if you did not mean to delete it. You may archive as many emails as you like. To archive an email:

1. Touch the ![icon] icon. The Mail application opens.
2. Touch and hold an email in the list and drag your finger to the left until the email disappears. The email is sent to the 'All Mail' folder, and disappears from the Inbox. You can also archive an email by touching the ![icon] icon while viewing an open email.
3. Touch **Mailboxes** at the top of the screen, and then touch **All Mail** to view all emails, including those that have been archived.

12. Changing the Default Signature

The phone can set a default signature that will be attached to the end of each email that is sent from the phone. To set or change this signature:

1. Touch the ![icon] icon. The Settings screen appears.
2. Touch **Mail**. The Mail settings screen appears, as shown in **Figure 14**.
3. Scroll down and touch **Signature**. The Signature screen appears, as shown in **Figure 15**.
4. Enter a signature and then touch **Mail** at the top of the screen. The new signature is saved.

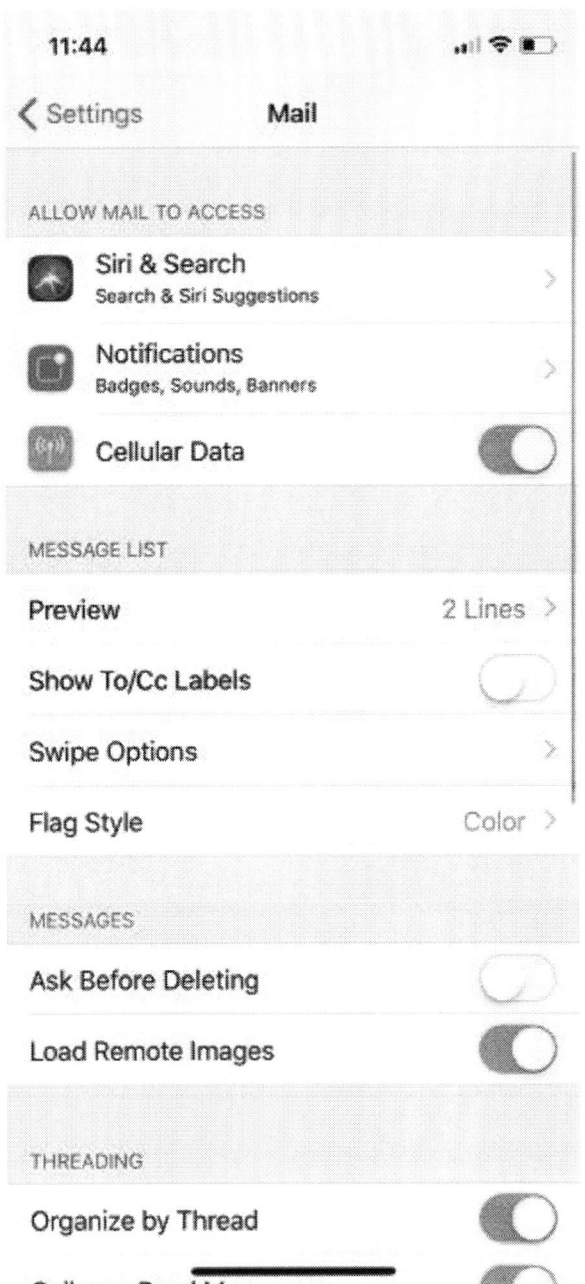
Figure 14: Mail Settings Screen

Using the Mail Application

Figure 15: Signature Screen

13. Changing Email Options

There are various options that change the way your Mail application works. Touch the ![icon] icon, and then touch **Mail** to change one of the following options:
- **Preview** - Choose the number of lines of an email message to preview in the Inbox.
- **Show To/Cc Label** - Choose whether to hide the 'To' and 'Cc' labels and show only addresses.
- **Swipe Options** - Changes the swipe action used to flag an email, or mark an email as 'Unread'.
- **Flag Style** - Choose the type of shape to use (color or shape) when flagging an email.
- **Ask Before Deleting** - Choose whether to display a confirmation before deleting an email.
- **Load Remote Images** - Choose whether to load images in an email automatically.
- **Organize by Thread** - Choose whether to group all emails with the same contact as a conversation.
- **Most Recent Message On Top** - Choose whether to always show the email that you received most recently at the top of a thread.
- **Complete Threads** - Choose whether to show an entire thread of emails with the same contact or group as a conversation even when you have moved some of the emails to other folders.
- **Always Bcc Myself** - Choose whether the Mail application sends a copy of each email to your own email address for your records.
- **Increase Quote Level** - Choose whether to increase the left margin when replying to or forwarding an email.
- **Default Account** - Choose the email address that will be used to send all emails when sending outside of the Mail application.

14. Unsubscribing from an Email List

You can now unsubscribe from mailing lists that crowd your inbox with unwanted emails. The Mail application automatically detects when an email is part of a mailing list. The following message appears at the top of the screen: "This message is from a mailing list."
Touch **Unsubscribe**. A confirmation dialog appears. Touch **Unsubscribe**. An email is sent on your behalf to remove you from the mailing list.

15. Viewing Emails in Conversation View

The Mail application lets you view email threads, or a list of emails that you have exchanged with a single contact or group, in the Inbox pane. If you have exchanged three or more emails with a contact or group, the ≫ icon appears on the conversation in the Inbox pane, as outlined in **Figure 16**. Touch the ≫ icon. The Conversation View appears, as shown in **Figure 17**. Touch the ⌄⌄ icon to return to the normal Inbox view.

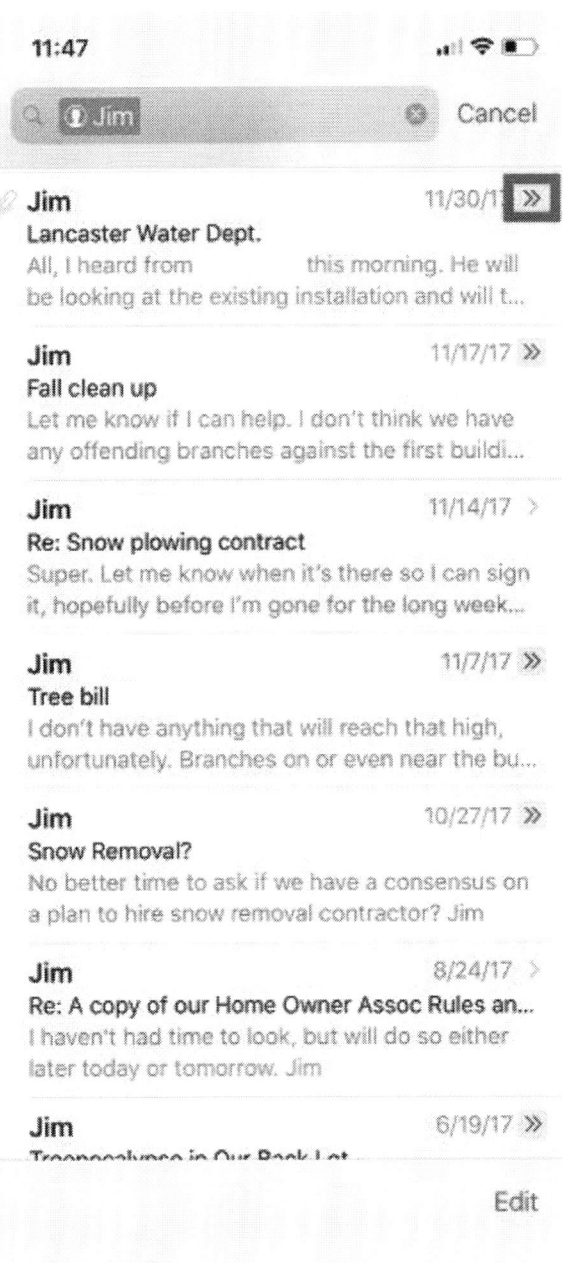

Figure 16: Conversation Icon Outlined

Using the Mail Application

Figure 17: Conversation View in the Inbox

16. Adding a Drawing in an Email

You can insert a hand-drawn picture into an email. To insert a hand-drawn picture:
1. Touch and hold anywhere in the content of the email. The Select menu appears above the text.
2. Touch the ▶ button twice and then touch **Insert Drawing**. The drawing screen appears, as shown in **Figure 18**.
3. Use the drawing tools at the bottom of the screen to draw your picture. You can also touch the + icon in the lower right-hand corner to add text, a signature, or to use the magnifier.
4. Touch **Done**. The Drawing menu appears, as shown in **Figure 19**.
5. Touch **Insert Drawing** to use it in the email or touch **Discard Changes** to discard the drawing. Once discarded, the drawing is gone forever.

Using the Mail Application

Figure 18: Drawing Screen

Figure 19: Drawing Menu

Managing Applications

Table of Contents

1. Signing In to an iTunes Account
2. Signing In to a Different iTunes Account
3. Editing iTunes Account Information
4. Searching for an Application to Purchase
5. Buying an Application
6. Using Wi-Fi to Download an Application
7. Switching Between Applications
8. Closing an Application Running in the Background
9. Organizing Applications into Folders
10. Reading User Reviews
11. Changing Application Settings
12. Deleting an Application
13. Sending an Application as a Gift
14. Redeeming a Gifted Application
15. Turning Automatic Application Updates On or Off

1. Signing In to an iTunes Account

In order to buy applications, you will need to have an iTunes account. To set up a new iTunes account:

1. Touch the ![icon] icon. The Settings screen appears, as shown in **Figure 1**.
2. Scroll down and touch **iTunes & App Store**. The iTunes & App Stores screen appears, as shown in **Figure 2**.
3. Touch **Sign In**. If you already have an Apple ID, enter your Apple ID and password, and touch **Sign In** again. To register for an Apple ID, navigate to **https://appleid.apple.com/account** using your computer's Web browser.

Managing Applications

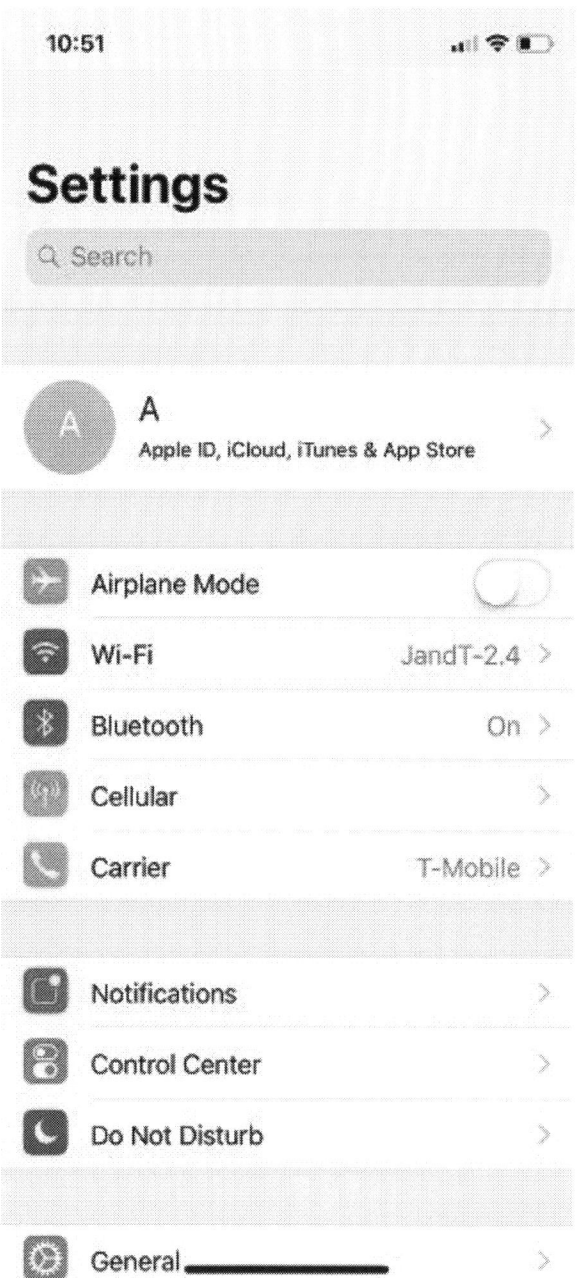

Figure 1: Settings Screen

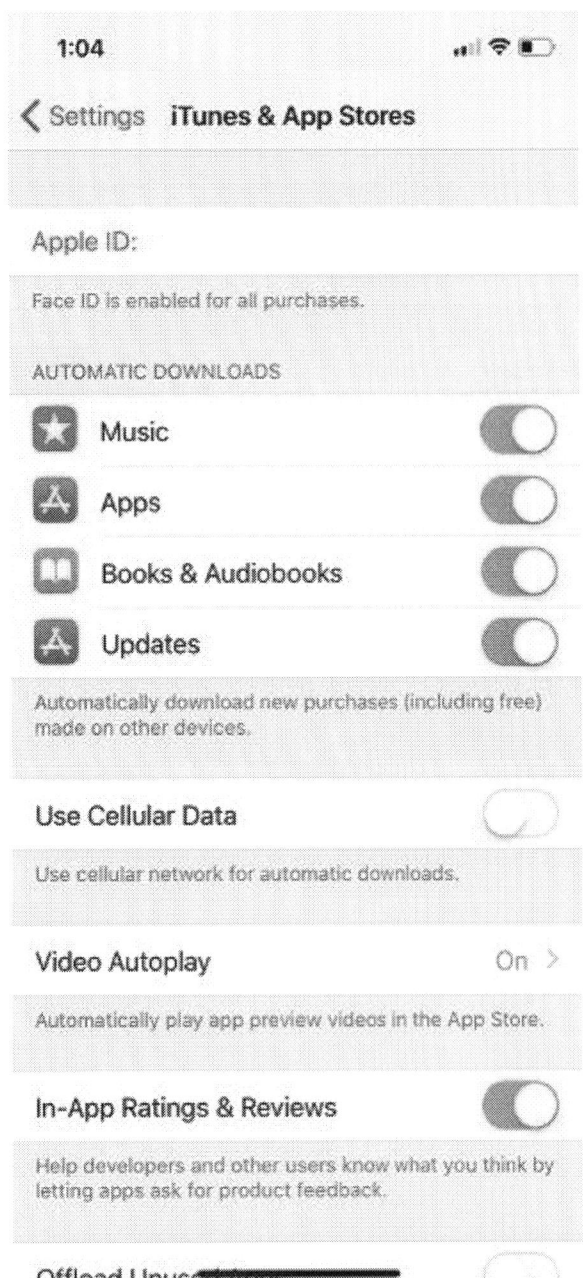

Figure 2: iTunes & App Stores Screen

2. Signing In to a Different iTunes Account

If more than one person uses your phone, you may wish to sign in with an alternate Apple ID. Only one Apple ID may be signed in at a time. To sign out and sign in to a different iTunes account:

1. Touch the icon. The Settings screen appears.
2. Scroll down and touch **iTunes & App Store**. The iTunes & App Stores screen appears. If someone is signed in to their iTunes account on the phone, their email appears at the top of the screen.
3. Touch the email address at the top of the screen. The Apple ID window appears, as shown in **Figure 3**.
4. Touch **Sign Out**. The account is signed out.
5. Touch **Sign In**. The virtual keyboard appears.
6. Enter your registered email address and password.
7. Touch **Sign In**. The account is signed in and the owner's email is shown at the top of the iTunes & App Stores screen.

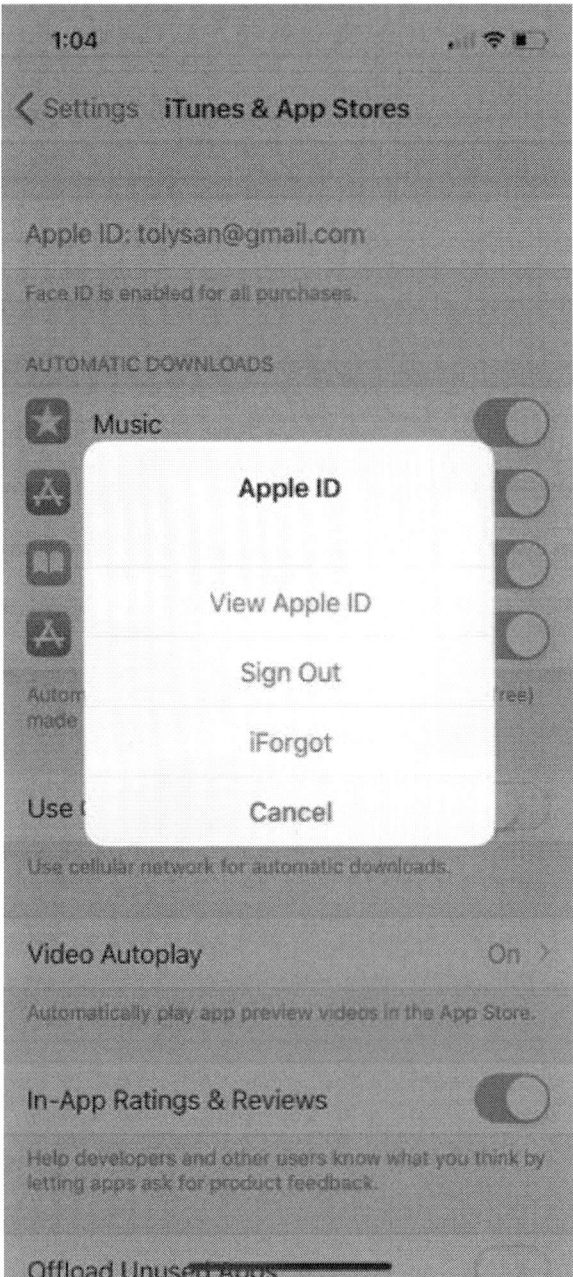
Figure 3: Apple ID Window

Managing Applications

3. Editing iTunes Account Information

You must keep your account information up to date in order to purchase applications from the iTunes Application Store. For instance, when your billing address changes or your credit card expires, you must change your information. To edit iTunes account information:

1. Touch the ![icon] icon. The Settings screen appears.
2. Scroll down and touch **iTunes & App Store**. The iTunes & App Stores screen appears. If someone is signed in to their iTunes account on the phone, their email appears at the top of the screen.
3. If you are not already signed in, enter your registered email and password, and touch **Done**. You are signed in.
4. Touch your email at the top of the screen. The Apple ID window appears.
5. Touch **View Apple ID**. The Account Settings screen appears with your personal account information.
6. Edit the fields as appropriate and then touch **Done**. The new information is saved.

4. Searching for an Application to Purchase

Use the Application Store to search for applications. There are three ways to search for applications:

Manual Search

To search for an application manually:

1. Touch the ![icon] icon. The Application Store opens, as shown in **Figure 4**.
2. Touch the ![icon] icon at the bottom of the screen. The Application Search screen appears, as shown in **Figure 5**.
3. Touch the search field and enter the name of an application.
4. Touch **Search**. A list of matching results appears.

223

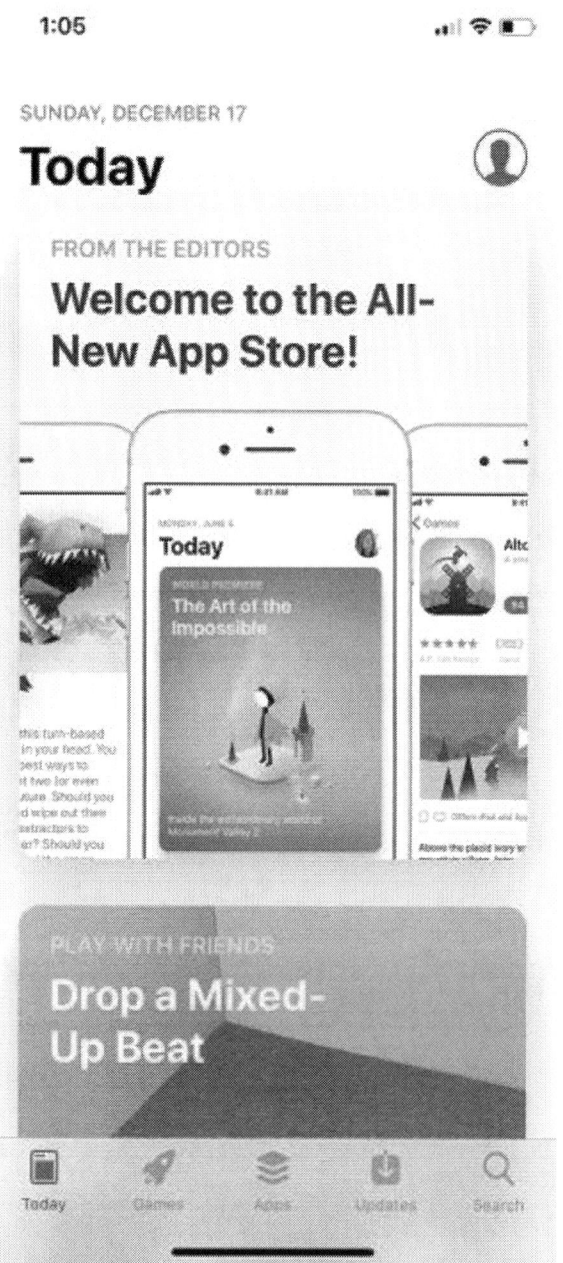

Figure 4: Application Store

Managing Applications

Figure 5: Application Search Screen

Browse by Category
To browse applications by category:

1. Touch the  icon. The Application Store opens.
2. Touch **Games** or **Apps** at the bottom of the screen. The corresponding screen appears.

Help Me! Guide to the iPhone X

3. Scroll down to the **Top Categories** section and touch **See All** on the right-hand side of the screen. The Categories screen appears, as shown in **Figure 6**.
4. Touch a category to browse it.

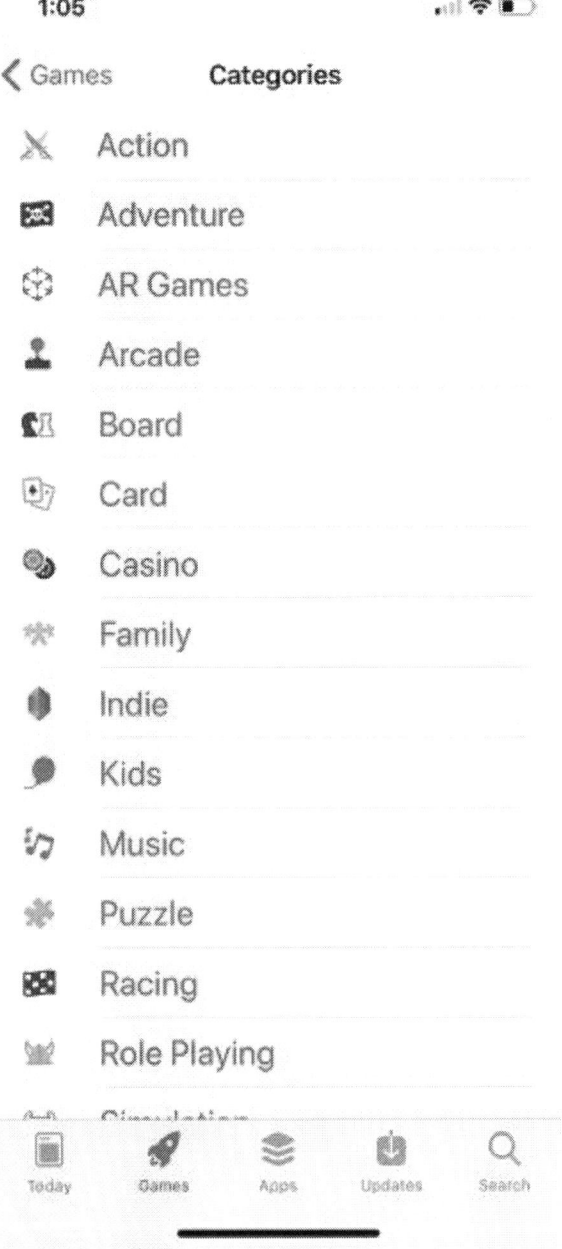

Figure 6: Categories Screen

226

Browse by Popularity
To browse applications by popularity:

1. Touch the ![app store icon] icon. The Application Store opens.
2. Touch **Games** or **Apps** at the bottom of the screen. The corresponding screen appears.
3. Scroll down to the **Top Paid** and **Top Free** sections, as shown in **Figure 7**.

Help Me! Guide to the iPhone X

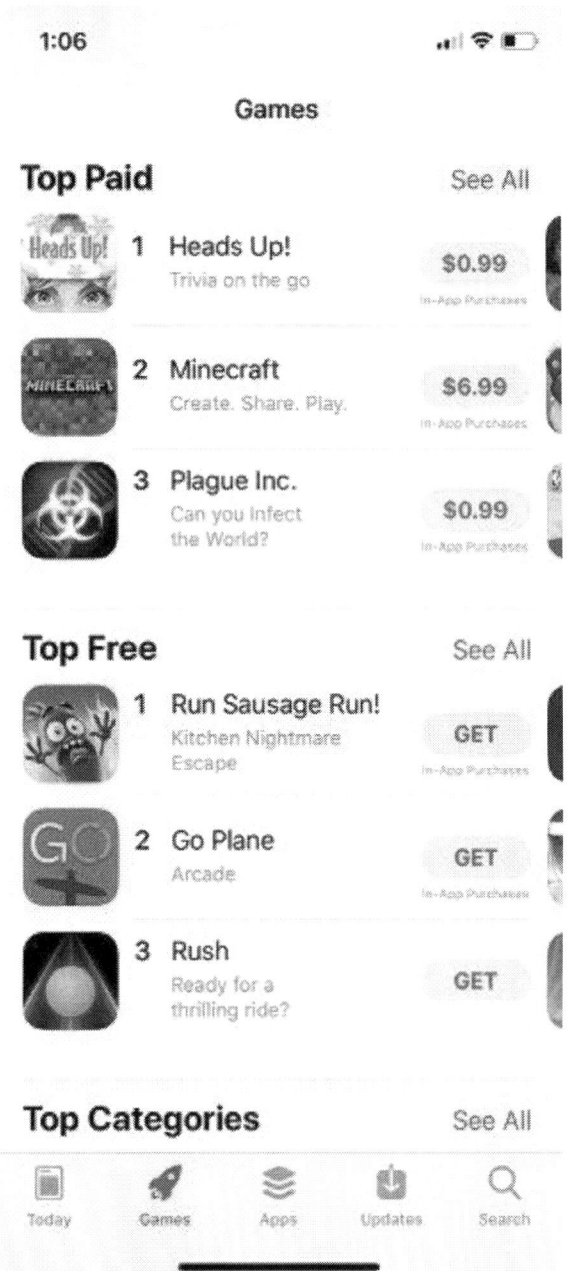

Figure 7: Top Paid and Top Free Sections

5. Buying an Application

You may purchase applications directly from your phone. To buy an application:

1. Touch the ![icon] icon. The Application Store opens.
2. Find an application. Refer to *"Searching for an Application to Purchase"* on page 223 to learn how.
3. Touch an application in the list. The Application description appears, as shown in **Figure 8**.
4. Touch the price of the application, or touch the word **FREE**, next to the name of the application. The Application Purchase window appears, as shown in **Figure 9**. If the application is already downloaded to your phone, 'INSTALLED' or 'UPDATE' appears, depending on whether you require an update. Touch **Purchase**, if paid, or touch **Install**, if the application is free. The password prompt appears.
5. Enter your iTunes password and touch **OK**. The phone returns to the Home screen, and the application is downloaded and installed.

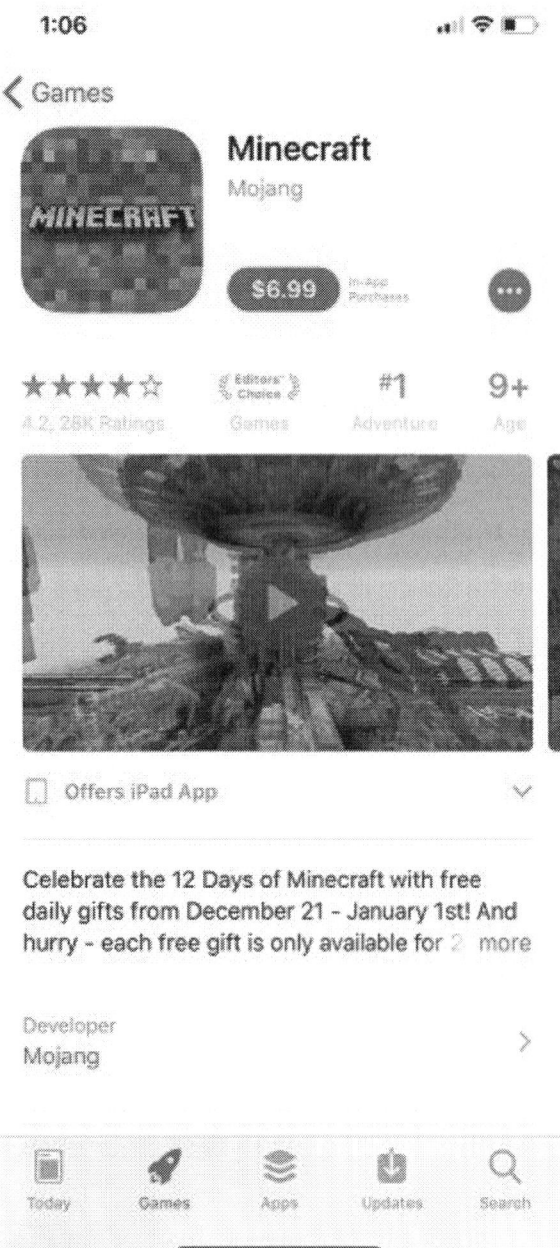

Figure 8: Application Description

Managing Applications

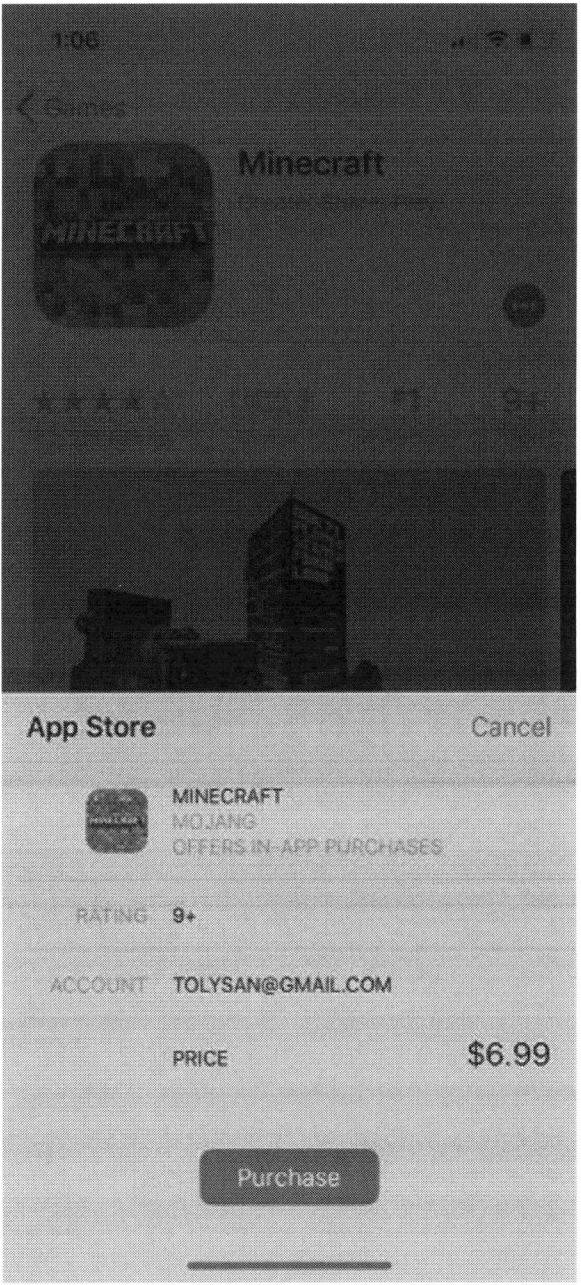

Figure 9: Application Purchase Window

231

6. Using Wi-Fi to Download an Application

Applications that are over 10MB in size require the phone to be connected to a Wi-Fi network to download. These applications will display the following message: "Application over 10MB. Connect to a Wi-Fi network or use iTunes on your computer to download >APP NAME<"", where APP NAME refers to the name of the application you are trying to download. Refer to *"Using Wi-Fi"* on page 26 to learn how to turn on Wi-Fi.

7. Switching Between Applications

The phone allows you to switch between running applications without having to exit any of them. For instance, you can listen to Pandora radio and read an eBook at the same time. To switch between applications:
1. Touch an application icon on one of your Home screens. The application opens.
2. Touch the bottom of the screen and slide your finger up to return to the Home screen.
3. Open another application.
4. Touch the bottom of the screen, slide your finger up, and hold it there for one second. The open applications appear, as shown in **Figure 10**.
5. Touch an application icon. The phone switches to the selected application.

When you open an application from inside another one, such as when you click a link in an email, a Back button appears in the upper left-hand corner of the screen. In the example of the email link, **Back to Mail** appears. Touch the Back button to return to the corresponding application.

Note: When switching to another application, the first application is never automatically closed. The application is simply running in the background. Refer to "Closing an Application Running in the Background" *on page 234 to learn how to close an application.*

Managing Applications

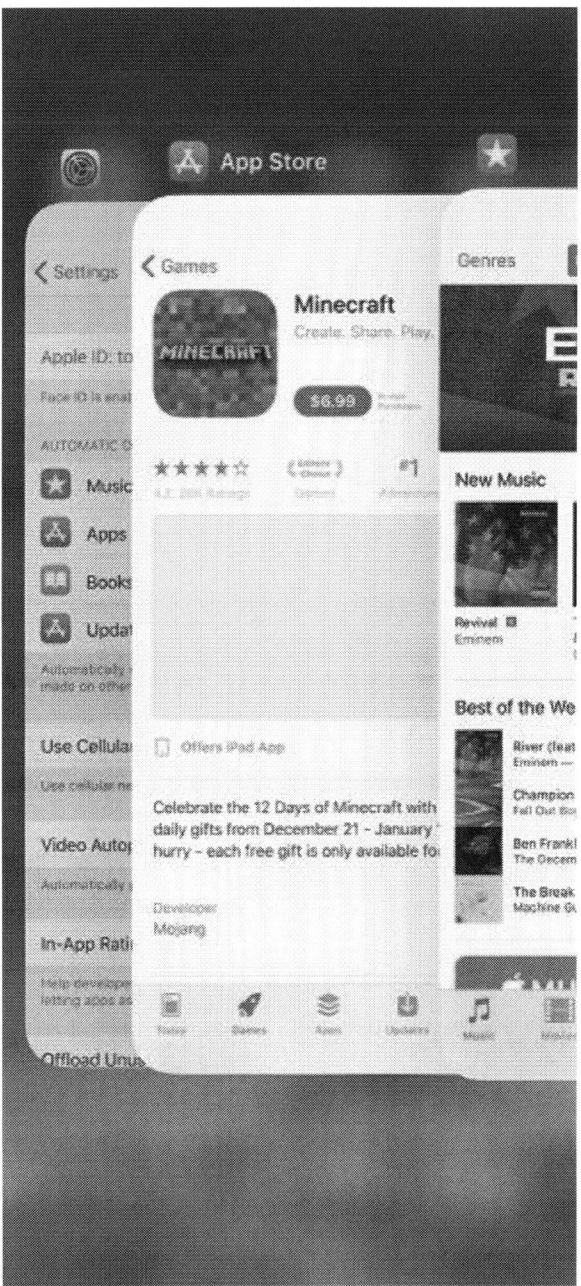

Figure 10: Open Applications

233

8. Closing an Application Running in the Background

After pressing the Home button to exit an application, it is not closed, but is left running in the background instead. It is good to have the application running because you can always switch to it quickly. However, if an application stops responding or if your battery is dying too quickly, you may wish to close it. To close an application running in the background:
1. Touch the bottom of the screen, slide your finger up, and hold it there for one second. The open applications appear.
2. Touch and hold an application icon for two seconds. The ● icon appears next to each application.
3. Touch the ● icon. The application is closed.

9. Organizing Applications into Folders

To learn how to organize applications into folders, refer to *"Creating an Icon Folder"* on page 24.

10. Reading User Reviews

In order to make a more informed decision when purchasing an application, you can read the reviews written by other users. However, be aware that people who have not used the application can also post reviews, which are uninformed. To read user reviews for an application:

1. Touch the ![App Store] icon. The Application Store opens.
2. Find an application. Refer to *"Searching for an Application to Purchase"* on page 223 to learn how.
3. Touch an application icon. The Application description appears.
4. Scroll down to the **Ratings & Reviews** section and touch **See All**. The reviews for the application appear.

11. Changing Application Settings

Some applications have settings that can be changed from the Settings screen. To change the application settings, touch the ![icon] icon. The Settings screen appears. Touch an application below 'Game Center' at the bottom of the screen. The Application Settings screen appears. The settings on this screen depend on the particular application.

12. Deleting an Application

You may delete most applications from your phone to free up space on your memory card or Home screen. To delete an unwanted application:
1. Touch and hold an application icon for three seconds. All of the applications on the Home screen begin to shake. Applications that can be erased have an ![x] button in their top left corner.
2. Touch the ![x] button next to an application icon. A confirmation dialog appears.
3. Touch **Delete**. The application is deleted.
4. Touch the bottom of the screen and slide your finger up. The application icons stop shaking and the ![x] buttons disappear.

Note: If you delete a paid application, you can download it again free of charge at any time. Refer to *"Buying an Application"* on page 229, and follow the instructions for buying the application to re-download it.

235

13. Sending an Application as a Gift

Applications can be sent as gifts. The recipient receives an email notification and can then download the gifted application from the Application Store. To send an application as a gift:

1. Touch the ![icon] icon. The Application Store opens.
2. Find the application that you want to give as a gift. Refer to *"Searching for an Application to Purchase"* on page 223 to learn how.
3. Touch the application icon. The application description appears.
4. Touch the ![icon] icon. The Application options appear, as shown in **Figure 11**.
5. Touch **Gift**. The Send Gift screen appears, as shown in **Figure 12**.
6. Touch **To:** and enter the email address of the recipient of the gift. Enter an optional message.
7. Touch **Today** to select when the gift should be shared, if the date is other than the current day.
8. Touch **Next** at the top of the screen. The Theme Selection screen appears.
9. Select a theme and touch **Next** at the top of the screen. The Gift Confirmation screen appears, as shown in **Figure 13**.
10. Touch **Buy** at the top of the screen. 'BUY NOW' appears as a confirmation.
11. Touch **BUY NOW**. The password prompt appears.
12. Enter your iTunes password and touch **OK**. The gift is purchased and sent.

Note: You are charged for the gifted application as soon as you purchase it.

Managing Applications

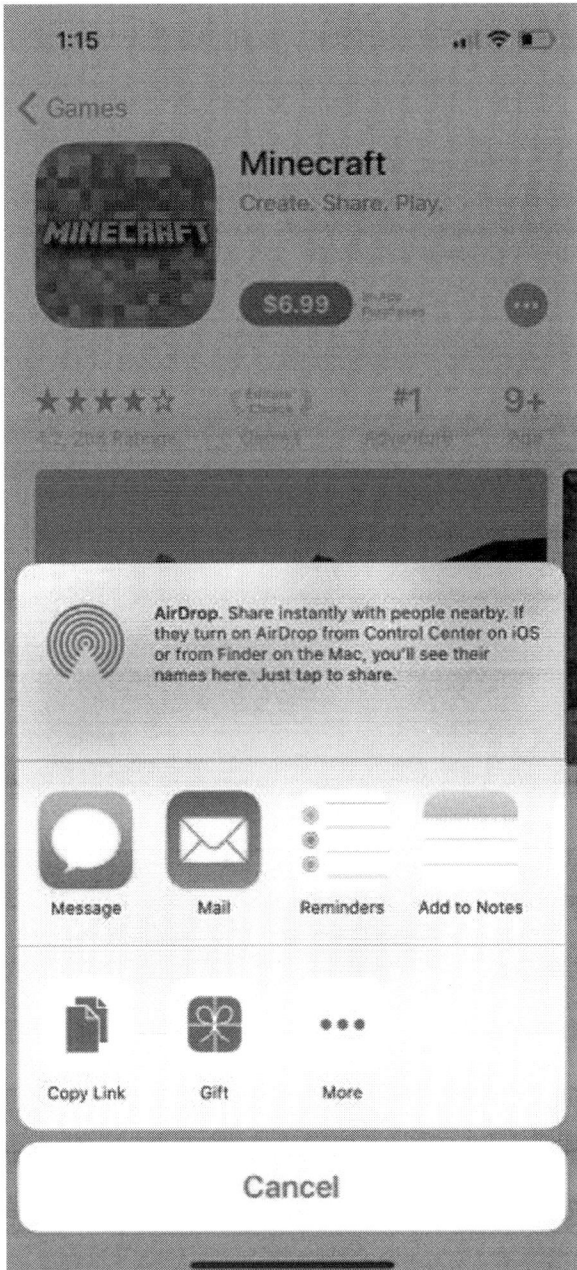

Figure 11: Application Options

237

Help Me! Guide to the iPhone X

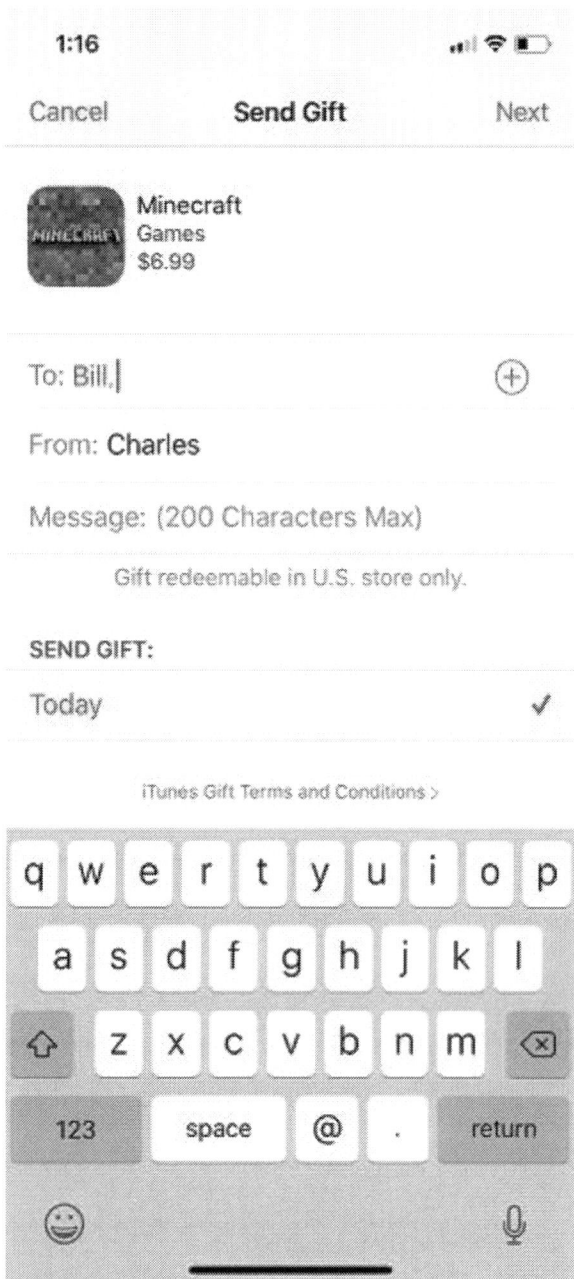

Figure 12: Send Gift Screen

238

Managing Applications

Figure 13: Gift Confirmation Screen

239

Help Me! Guide to the iPhone X

14. Redeeming a Gifted Application

When receiving an application as a gift, you must redeem it in order to download it. To redeem a gift and download the application using your phone:

1. Touch the icon. The email application opens.
2. Touch the email with the subject '**NAME sent you an iTunes Gift**', where NAME represents the name of the sender. The email opens. Refer to *"Reading Email"* on page 190 to learn how to find an email.
3. Touch the **Redeem Now** button in the email. The Application Store opens.
4. Touch **Redeem** at the top of the screen. The gifted application is downloaded and installed. If the application is over 10MB, you must first turn on Wi-Fi. Refer to *"Using Wi-Fi"* on page 26 to learn how to turn Wi-Fi on. If this is your first time downloading an application from the iTunes store, you will need to touch **Agree** several times to accept several pages of terms and conditions.

15. Turning Automatic Application Updates On or Off

The phone can automatically download updates for applications when new versions are released. To turn automatic application updates on or off:

1. Touch the icon. The Settings screen appears.
2. Scroll down and touch **iTunes & App Store**. The iTunes & App Stores screen appears.
3. Touch the switch next to 'Updates' under 'Automatic Downloads'. The switch appears and Automatic application updates are turned off.
4. Touch the switch next to 'Updates' under 'Automatic Downloads'. The switch appears and Automatic application updates are turned on.

240

Using Siri

Siri is a voice assistant that comes with the iPhone X. Follow the tips in this chapter to use Siri to its full potential.

Table of Contents

1. Making a Call
2. Sending and Receiving Text Messages
3. Managing the Address Book
4. Setting Up and Managing Meetings
5. Checking the Time and Setting Alarms
6. Sending and Receiving Email
7. Getting Directions and Finding Businesses
8. Playing Music
9. Searching the Web and Asking Questions
10. Looking Up Words in the Dictionary
11. Application-Specific Phrases.

Note: These phrases are only suggestions. Siri is flexible, and you can use many synonymous phrases.

1. Making a Call

To make a call using Siri, press and hold the **Sleep/Wake** button. Say one of the following phrases:
- **Call John** (use any name)
- **Call Suzy Mobile**
- **Call Dexter on his work phone**
- **Call 123 555 1345**
- **Call home**
- **FaceTime Jacob**

Using Siri

2. Sending and Receiving Text Messages

To send, read, or reply to a text message using Siri, press and hold the **Sleep/Wake** button. Say one of the following phrases:

- Tell Anne See you soon
- Send a message to Rob Burr
- Send a message to Larry saying What's your address?
- Send a message to Julie on her mobile saying I got an iPhone X!
- Send a message to 999 555 2222
- Text Jude and Prudence What are you guys up to today?
- Read my new messages
- Read it again
- Reply that's great news
- Tell him ETA is 20 minutes
- Call her

3. Managing the Address Book

To manage the address book using Siri, press and hold the Sleep/Wake button. Say one of the following phrases:

- What's Joe's address?
- What is Susan Park's phone number?
- When is my grandfather's birthday?
- Show Bobby's email address
- Show Pete Abred
- Find people named Apple
- My brother is Trudy Ages (assigns a relationship to the name)
- Who is Colin Card? (indicates Colin Card's relationship to you)
- Call my brother at home (calls the number assigned to the relationship)

4. Setting Up and Managing Meetings

To set up and manage meetings using Siri, press and hold the **Sleep/Wake** button. Say one of the following phrases:

- Set up a meeting at 10
- Set up a meeting with Zoe at 9
- Meet with Nikki at noon
- New appointment with Dan Delion Tuesday at 4
- Schedule a focus group meeting at 3:30 today in the boardroom
- Move my 2pm meeting to 3:30
- Add Wendy to my meeting with Waldo
- Cancel the focus group meeting
- What does the rest of my day look like?
- What's on my calendar for Monday?
- When is my next appointment?
- Where is my next meeting?

5. Checking the Time and Setting Alarms

To check the time and set alarms using Siri, press and hold the **Sleep/Wake** button. Say one of the following phrases:

- Wake me up tomorrow at 6am
- Set an alarm for 6:30am
- Wake me up in 8 hours
- Change my 5:30 alarm to 6:30
- Turn off my 4:30 alarm
- What time is it?
- What time is it in Moscow?
- What is today's date?
- What's the date this Friday?
- Set the timer for 30 minutes
- Show the timer
- Pause the timer
- Resume
- Reset the timer
- Stop it

Using Siri

6. Sending and Receiving Email

To send and receive email using Siri, press and hold the **Sleep/Wake** button. Say one of the following phrases:

- Email Dave about the trip
- Email New email to John Diss
- Mail Dad about dinner
- Email Dr. Spaulding and say Got your message
- Mail Jack and Jill about the party and say It was awesome
- Check email
- Any new email from Mom today?
- Show new mail about the apartment
- Show the email from Roger yesterday
- Reply Dear Mark I'm sorry for your loss

7. Getting Directions and Finding Businesses

To get directions and find businesses using Siri, press and hold the **Sleep/Wake** button. Say one of the following phrases:

- How do I get home?
- Show 10 Park Ave. Boston Massachusetts
- Directions to my parents' home
- Find coffee near me
- Where is the closest Starbucks?
- Find a Mexican restaurant in New Mexico
- Find a gas station within walking distance

8. Playing Music

To play music using Siri, press and hold the **Sleep/Wake** button. Say one of the following phrases:

- Play Hotel California
- Play Coldplay shuffled
- Play Dave Matthews Band
- Play some folk
- Play my roadtrip playlist

- Shuffle my party playlist
- Play
- Pause
- Skip

9. Searching the Web and Asking Questions

To search the web using Siri, press and hold the **Sleep/Wake** button. Say one of the following phrases:

- Search the web for Apple News
- Search for chili recipes
- Google the humane society
- Search Wikipedia for Duckbilled Platypus
- Bing Secondhand Serenade
- How many calories in a doughnut?
- What is an 18% tip on $180.45 for six people?
- How long do cats live?
- What's 25 squared?
- How many dollars is 60 euros?
- How many days until Christmas?
- When is the next solar eclipse?
- Show me the Ursula Major constellation
- What is the meaning of life?
- What's the price of gasoline in Boston?

10. Looking Up Words in the Dictionary

To look up words using Siri, press and hold the **Sleep/Wake** button. Say one of the following phrases:

- What is the meaning of meticulous?
- Define albeit
- Look up the word jargon

11. Application-Specific Phrases

To search or set up reminders that relate to specific applications, press and hold the **Sleep/Wake** button. Say one of the following phrases:

- Remind me about this when I get home (while viewing a web page)
- Show photos from Paris last June
- Remind me to reply to this (while viewing an email)
- Remind me to finish this note (while viewing a note in the Notes application)

Adjusting Wireless Settings

Table of Contents

1. Turning Airplane Mode On or Off
2. Turning Location Services On or Off
3. Customizing Cellular Data Usage
4. Turning Data Roaming On or Off
5. Setting Up a Virtual Private Network (VPN)
6. Turning Bluetooth On or Off
7. Using Wi-Fi to Sync Your Phone with Your Computer

1. Turning Airplane Mode On or Off

Most airplanes do not allow wireless communications while in flight. Continue using the phone by enabling Airplane mode before take-off. You may not place or receive calls, send or receive text messages or emails, or surf the Web while in Airplane mode. Airplane Mode is also useful when traveling outside of your area of service to avoid any roaming charges and to preserve battery life.

To turn Airplane Mode on or off, touch the icon. The Settings screen appears, as shown in **Figure 1**. Touch the switch next to 'Airplane Mode'. The switch appears and Airplane mode is turned on. To turn off Airplane Mode, touch the switch next to 'Airplane Mode'.

Adjusting Wireless Settings

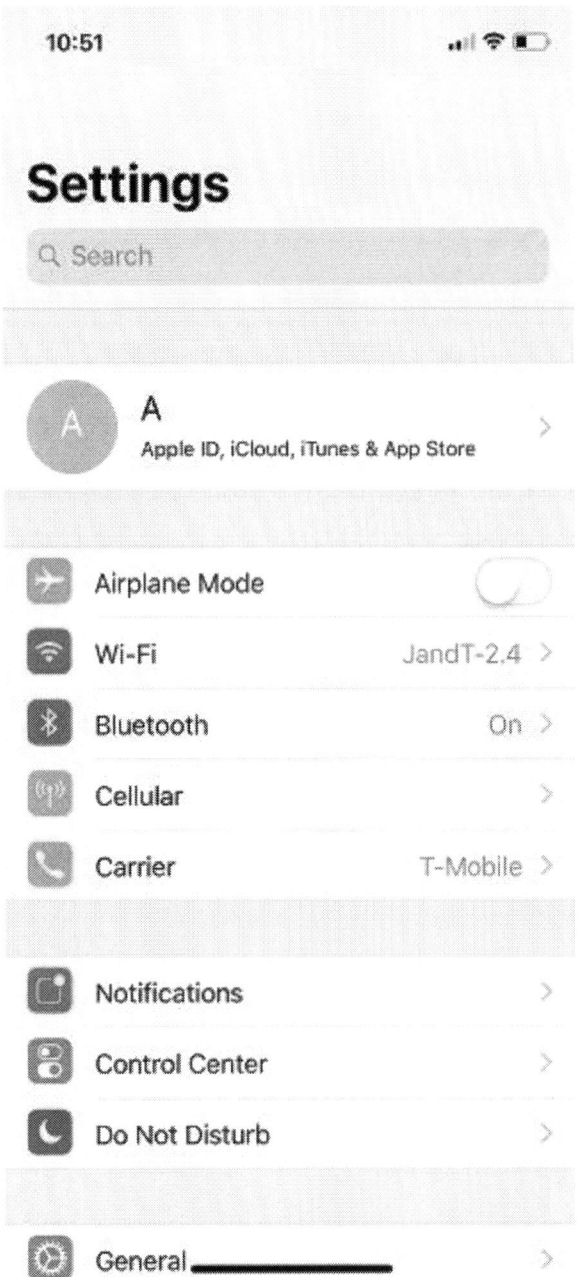

Figure 1: Settings Screen

2. Turning Location Services On or Off

Some applications, such as Maps, require the Location Services feature to be turned on, which determines your current location. To turn Location Services on or off:

1. Touch the icon. The Settings screen appears.
2. Scroll down and touch **Privacy**. The Privacy Settings screen appears, as shown in **Figure 2**.
3. Touch **Location Services**. The Location Services screen appears, as shown in **Figure 3**.
4. Touch the switch next to 'Location Services'. The switch appears and Location Services are turned on. To turn off Location Services, touch the switch next to 'Location Services'.

You can also customize the location preferences for each application listed on the Location Services screen. Touch the application, and then touch **Never** to turn off location services for that application permanently.

Scroll down and touch **System Services** to turn off Location Services for services, such as Find My iPhone and HomeKit.

Adjusting Wireless Settings

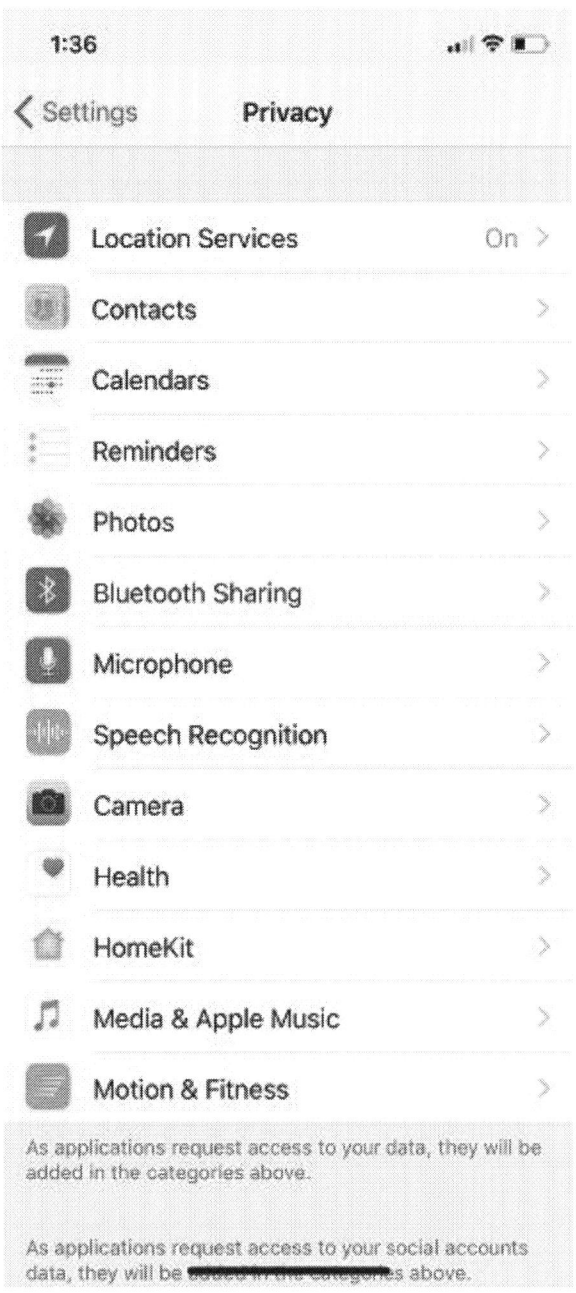

Figure 2: Privacy Settings Screen

Figure 3: Location Services Screen

Adjusting Wireless Settings

3. Customizing Cellular Data Usage

To surf the internet and download applications when not connected to Wi-Fi, you need to turn on cellular data. However, you can turn off cellular data if you wish to conserve battery life in an area with little or no 4G service. To turn cellular data on or off:

1. Touch the 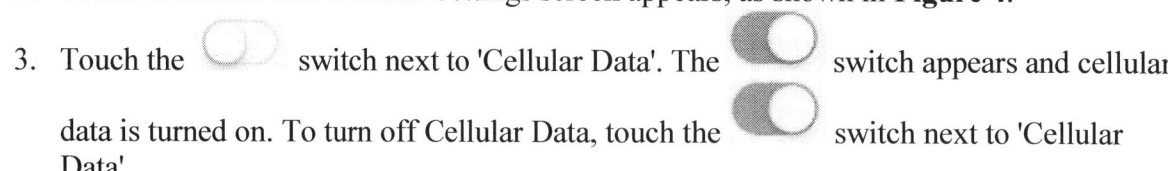 icon. The Settings screen appears.
2. Touch **Cellular**. The Cellular Settings screen appears, as shown in **Figure 4**.
3. Touch the switch next to 'Cellular Data'. The switch appears and cellular data is turned on. To turn off Cellular Data, touch the switch next to 'Cellular Data'.

You may also manage the cellular data usage from the Cellular Settings screen. To manage cellular data usage:

1. Touch the switch next to 'Mail', 'Passbook', or another application. Cellular data is turned off for the corresponding application.
2. Touch the switch next to the name of an application. Cellular data is turned on for the corresponding application.
3. Touch **System Services** to view the amount of data used by each service on your phone.

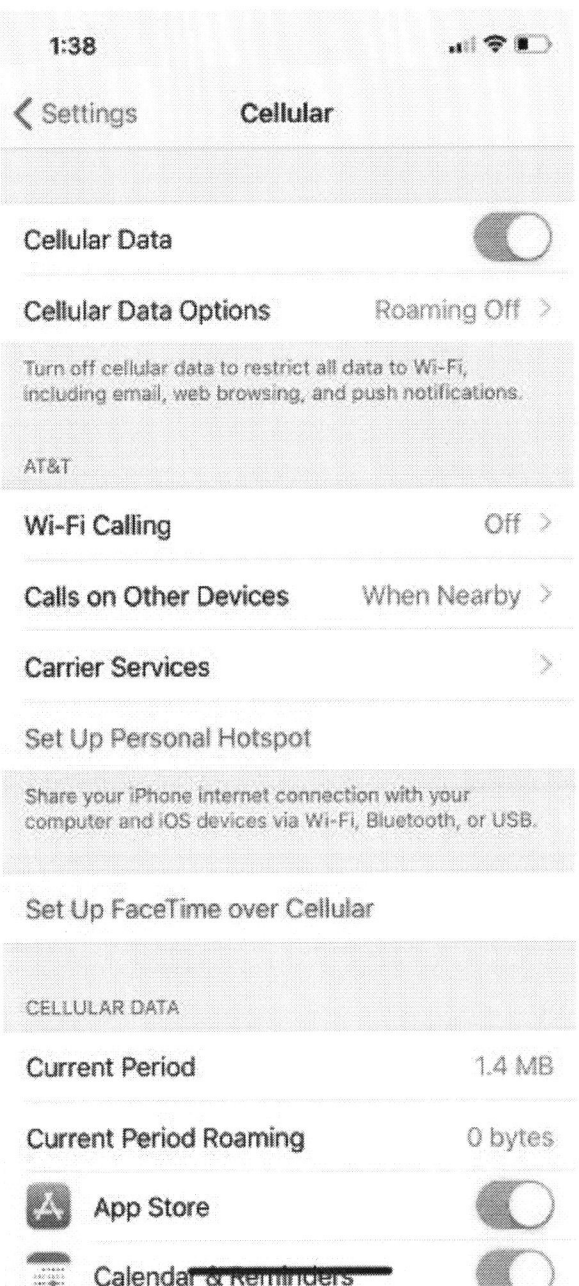
Figure 4: Cellular Settings Screen

Adjusting Wireless Settings

4. Turning Data Roaming On or Off

When you are in an area with no 4G coverage, the phone can use the Data Roaming feature to acquire signal from other networks. Be aware that Data Roaming can be extremely costly. Contact your network provider for details. To turn Data Roaming on or off:

1. Touch the icon. The Settings screen appears.
2. Touch **Cellular**. The Cellular Settings screen appears.
3. Touch **Cellular Data Options**. The Cellular Data Options screen appears.
4. Touch the switch next to 'Data Roaming'. The switch appears and Data Roaming is turned on. To turn off Data Roaming, touch the switch next to 'Data Roaming'.

5. Setting Up a Virtual Private Network (VPN)

You can use your phone to connect to an external network, such as a corporate one. To set up a VPN:

1. Touch the icon. The Settings screen appears.
2. Touch **General**. The General Settings screen appears, as shown in **Figure 5**.
3. Scroll down and touch **VPN**. The VPN screen appears, as shown in **Figure 6**.
4. Touch **Add VPN Configuration**. The Add VPN Configuration screen appears, as shown in **Figure 7**.
5. Touch each field and enter the required information.
6. Touch **Done**. The VPN is set up.

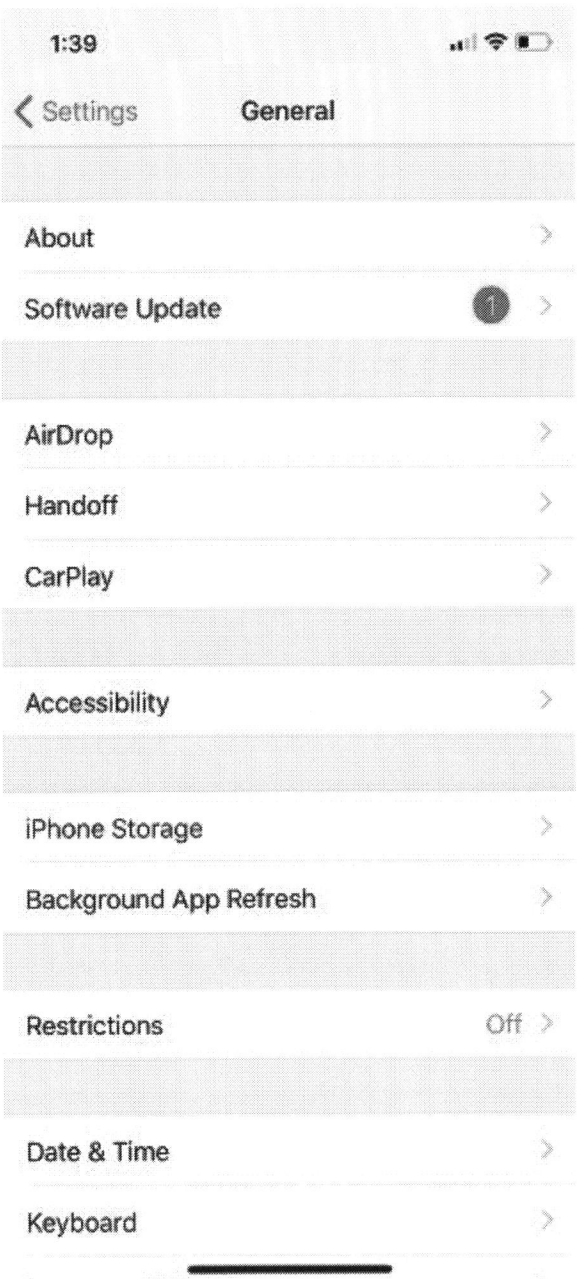

Figure 5: General Settings Screen

Adjusting Wireless Settings

Figure 6: VPN Screen

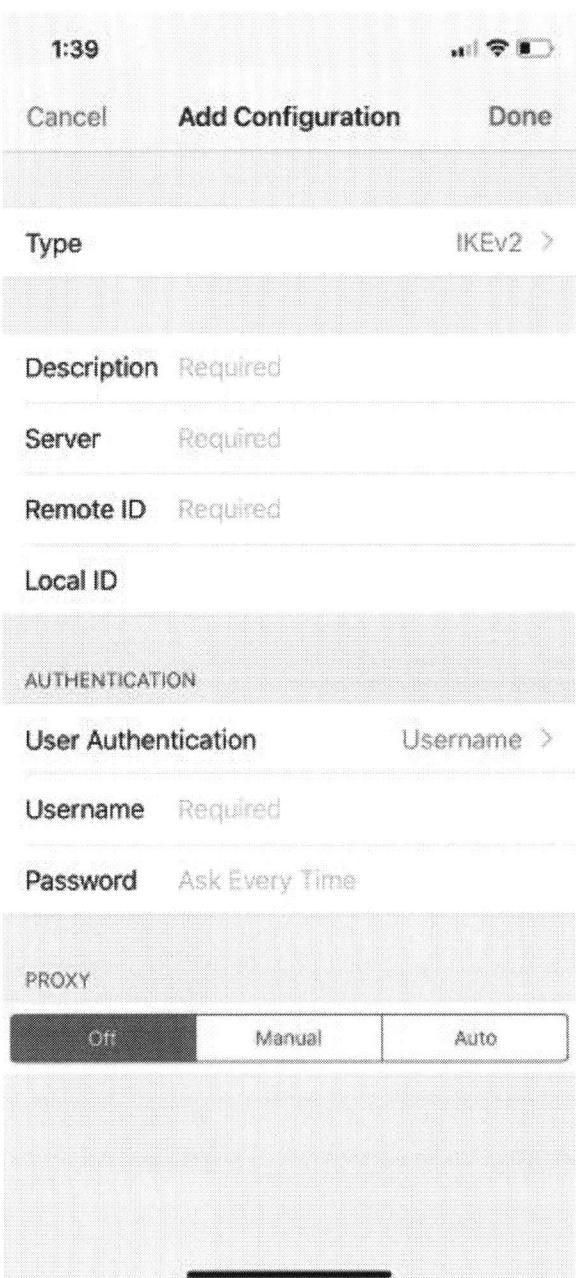

Figure 7: Add VPN Configuration Screen

6. Turning Bluetooth On or Off

A wireless Bluetooth headset or speaker can be used with the phone. Be aware that leaving Bluetooth turned on while the headset or speaker is not in use may deplete battery life quickly. To turn Bluetooth on or off:

1. Touch the ![icon] icon. The Settings screen appears.
2. Touch **Bluetooth**. The Bluetooth Settings screen appears, as shown in **Figure 8**.
3. Touch the ![switch] switch next to 'Bluetooth'. Bluetooth is turned on and a list of phones appears. If there are no Bluetooth phones near the phone, the list will be empty. To turn off Bluetooth, touch the ![switch] switch next to 'Bluetooth'. Bluetooth is turned off.

Figure 8: Bluetooth Settings Screen

Adjusting Wireless Settings

7. Using Wi-Fi to Sync Your Phone with Your Computer

Syncing your iPhone with your computer allows you to save your media library on your computer in case you have to erase your phone, or if you buy a new phone. Instead of connecting your iPhone to your computer to sync music, applications, and other media, you may sync wirelessly using Wi-Fi. Before you can use this feature, you must turn it on using iTunes on your computer.

Refer to **https://www.apple.com/support/itunes/** if you need help using iTunes. To use Wi-Fi to sync your phone with your computer:

Note: You may only use Wi-Fi syncing when your phone is plugged in to an outlet, and Wi-Fi is turned on.

1. Connect your phone to your computer using the cable that was provided when you purchased it. On some computers, iTunes opens automatically. If it does not, open iTunes.
2. Click the name of the phone at the top or left side of the screen, depending on the version of iTunes. The phone information screen appears. You may need to first click **Continue**, and then click **Get Started** before this screen appears.
3. Click **Sync with this DEVICENAME over Wi-Fi**, where DEVICENAME is the name of your phone. A check mark appears next to 'Sync with this DEVICENAME'.
4. Click **Apply**. The Wi-Fi Sync feature is turned on.
5. Disconnect your phone from your computer, and plug it into an outlet, as if you are charging it. Your phone should automatically Sync with your computer. If it does not sync, follow steps 6-9 below.
6. Touch the ⚙ icon. The Settings screen appears.
7. Touch **General**. The General Settings screen appears.
8. Scroll down and touch **iTunes Wi-Fi Sync**. The iTunes Wi-Fi Sync screen appears.
9. Touch **Sync Now**. Your phone syncs with your computer.

Help Me! Guide to the iPhone X

Adjusting Sound Settings

Table of Contents

1. Turning Vibration On or Off
2. Turning Volume Button Functionality On or Off
3. Setting the Default Ringtone
4. Customizing Notification and Alert Sounds
5. Turning Lock Sounds On or Off
6. Turning Keyboard Clicks On or Off
7. Controlling Siri's Voice
8. Adjusting Siri Settings

1. Turning Vibration On or Off

The iPhone can be set to vibrate every time it rings, or only while it is in Silent Mode.
To turn Ringer Vibration on or off:

1. Touch the icon. The Settings screen appears, as shown in **Figure 1**.
2. Scroll down and touch **Sounds & Haptics**. The Sounds & Haptics screen appears, as shown in **Figure 2**.
3. Touch the switch next to 'Vibrate on Ring' under the 'Vibrate' section. The switch appears and Ringer Vibration is turned on. The phone will vibrate whenever there is an incoming call.
4. Touch the switch. Ringer Vibration is turned off and the phone will not vibrate for incoming calls.

261

Adjusting Sound Settings

To turn Silent Mode vibration on or off:

1. Touch the icon. The Settings screen appears.
2. Touch **Sounds & Haptics**. The Sounds & Haptics screen appears.

3. Touch the switch next to 'Vibrate on Silent' under the 'Vibrate' section.

   The switch appears and Silent Mode vibration is turned on. The phone will vibrate whenever a call or message is received in Silent Mode.

4. Touch the switch. Silent Mode Vibration is turned off. The phone will not vibrate when it is in Silent Mode.

Note: To turn on Silent Mode on the phone, put the vibration switch in the down position so that a red dot appears beneath the switch. Silent mode is turned on and the icon appears on the screen. Refer to "Button Layout" *on page 17 to view the location of the Vibration switch.*

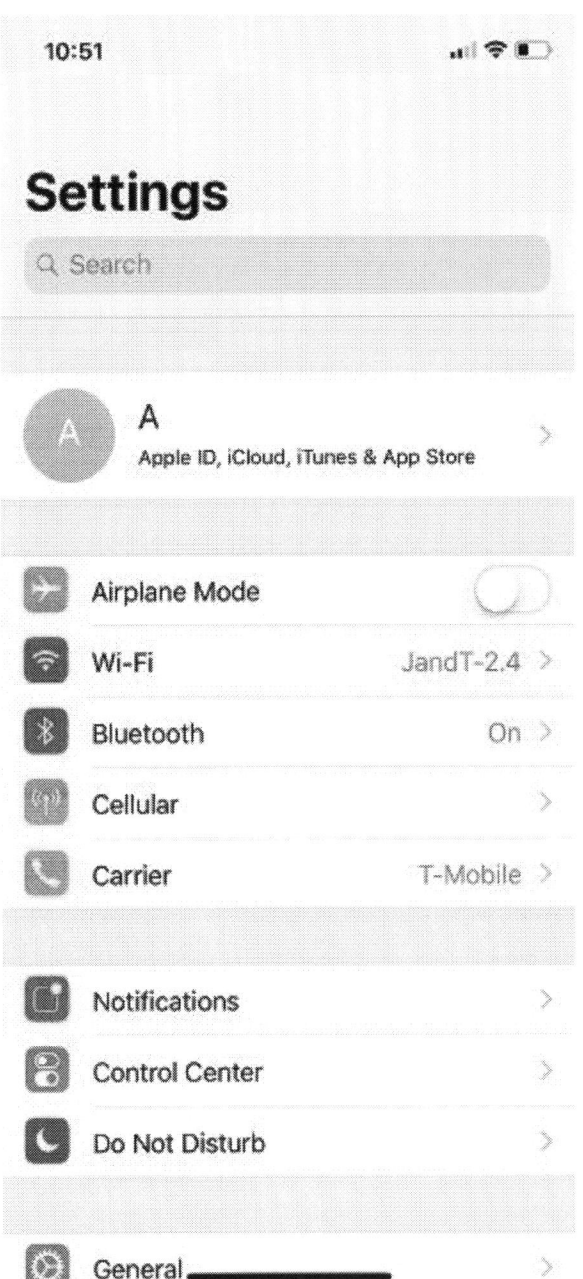
Figure 1: Settings Screen

Adjusting Sound Settings

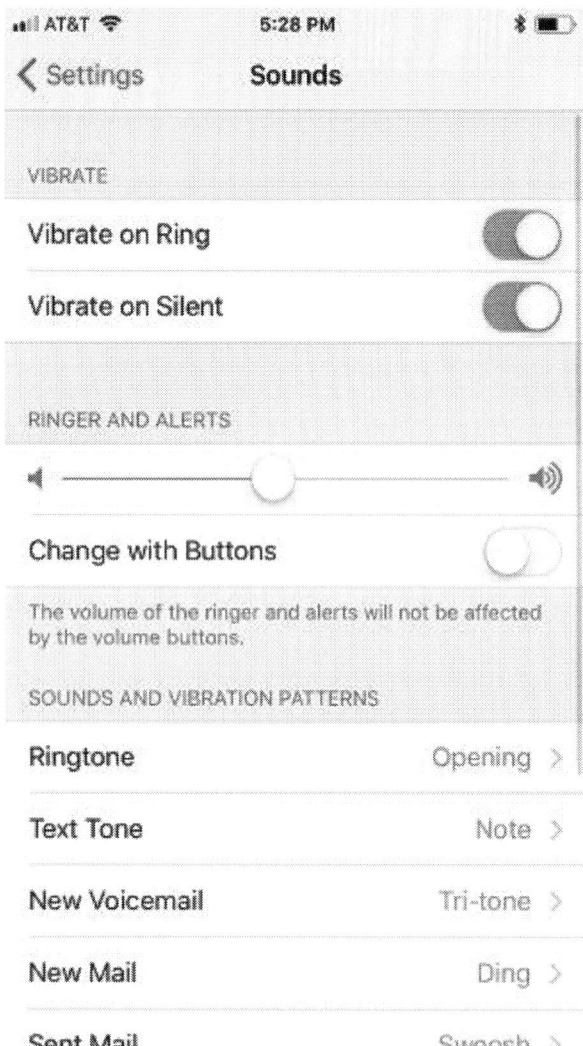

Figure 2: Sounds & Haptics Screen

2. Turning Volume Button Functionality On or Off

The volume buttons can be used to adjust the volume of the media, alerts, and the ringer. When the volume button functionality is disabled, they no longer work. To turn the volume button functionality on or off:

1. Touch the ![icon] icon. The Settings screen appears.
2. Scroll down and touch **Sounds**. The Sound Settings screen appears.
3. Touch the ![switch] switch next to 'Change with Buttons' under the 'Ringer and Alerts' section. The ![switch] switch appears and volume button functionality is turned off. To turn on Change with Buttons, touch the ![switch] switch next to 'Change with Buttons'.

3. Setting the Default Ringtone

You may change the ringtone that sounds every time somebody calls you. To set a default ringtone:

1. Touch the ![icon] icon. The Settings screen appears.
2. Touch **Sounds**. The Sound Settings screen appears.
3. Touch **Ringtone**. A list of ringtones appears, as shown in **Figure 3**.
4. Touch a ringtone. The new default ringtone is selected and a preview plays.
5. Touch **Sounds** at the top of the screen. The new ringtone is set as the default.

*Note: You can also touch **Store** at the top of the screen to purchase more ringtones.*

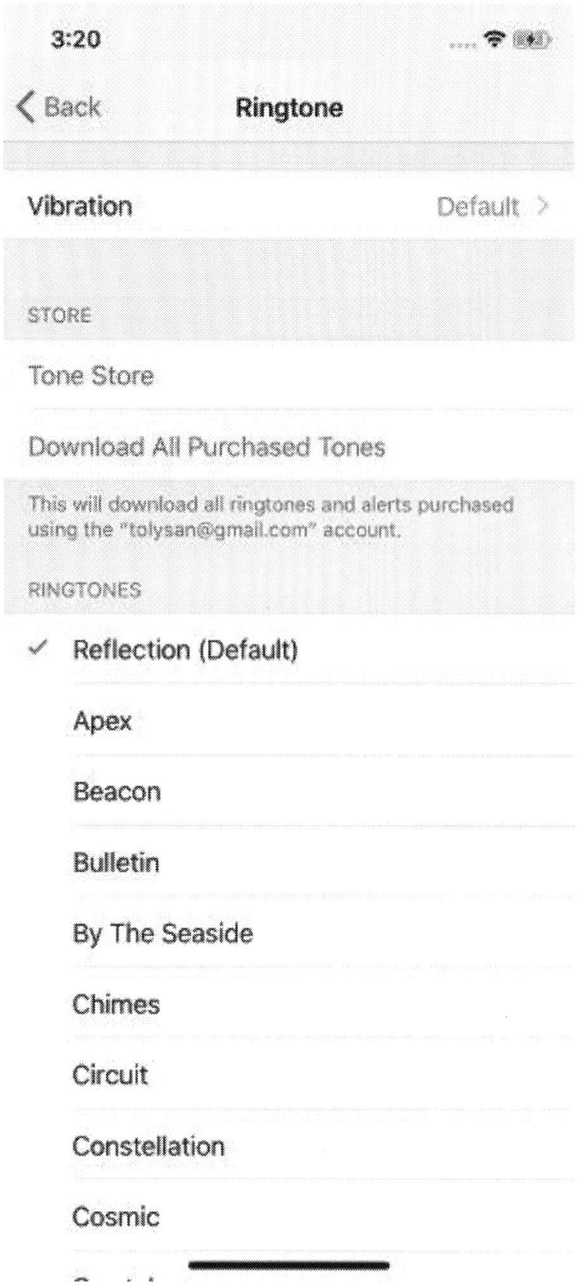

Adjusting Sound Settings

Figure 3: List of Ringtones

4. Customizing Notification and Alert Sounds

There are several notification and alert sounds that can be changed on the phone. To customize notification and alert sounds:

1. Touch the ![icon] icon. The Settings screen appears.
2. Touch **Sounds**. The Sound Settings screen appears.
3. Touch one of the following options to change the corresponding sound:
   - **Text Tone** - Plays when a new text message arrives.
   - **New Voicemail** - Plays when a new voicemail arrives.
   - **New Mail** - Plays when a new email arrives.
   - **Sent Mail** - Plays when an email is sent from the phone.
   - **Calendar Alerts** - Plays as a reminder for a calendar event.
   - **Reminder Alerts** - Plays as a notification of a previously set reminder.

5. Turning Lock Sounds On or Off

The phone can make a sound every time it is locked or unlocked. By default, this sound is turned on. To turn Lock Sounds on or off:

1. Touch the ![icon] icon. The Settings screen appears.
2. Touch **Sounds**. The Sound Settings screen appears.
3. Scroll down and touch the ![switch] switch next to 'Lock Sound'. The ![switch] switch appears and lock sounds are turned off. To turn on lock sounds, touch the ![switch] switch next to 'Lock Sound'.

6. Turning Keyboard Clicks On or Off

The phone can make a sound every time a key is touched on the virtual keyboard. By default, keyboard clicks are turned on. To turn Keyboard Clicks on or off:

1. Touch the ![icon] icon. The Settings screen appears.
2. Touch **Sounds**. The Sound Settings screen appears.
3. Touch the ![switch] switch next to 'Keyboard Clicks'. The ![switch] switch appears and Keyboard Clicks are turned off. To turn on Keyboard Clicks, touch the ![switch] switch next to 'Keyboard Clicks'.

7. Controlling Siri's Voice

By default, Siri's voice is never muted, even when you turn off your phone's volume. The iPhone lets you turn Siri's voice on or off using the vibration switch. To turn on Siri Volume Control:

1. Touch the icon. The Settings screen appears.
2. Touch **Siri & Search**. The Siri & Search Settings screen appears, as shown in **Figure 4**.
3. Touch **Voice Feedback**. The Voice Feedback screen appears, as shown in **Figure 5**.
4. Touch one of the following options to turn on the corresponding setting:
    - **Always On** - Leave Siri's voice feedback turned on permanently.
    - **Control with Ring Switch** - Mute Siri using the Vibration switch.
    - **Hands-Free Only** - Only use Siri's voice feedback when Hey Siri is turned on, or when you connect a Bluetooth headset or headphones.

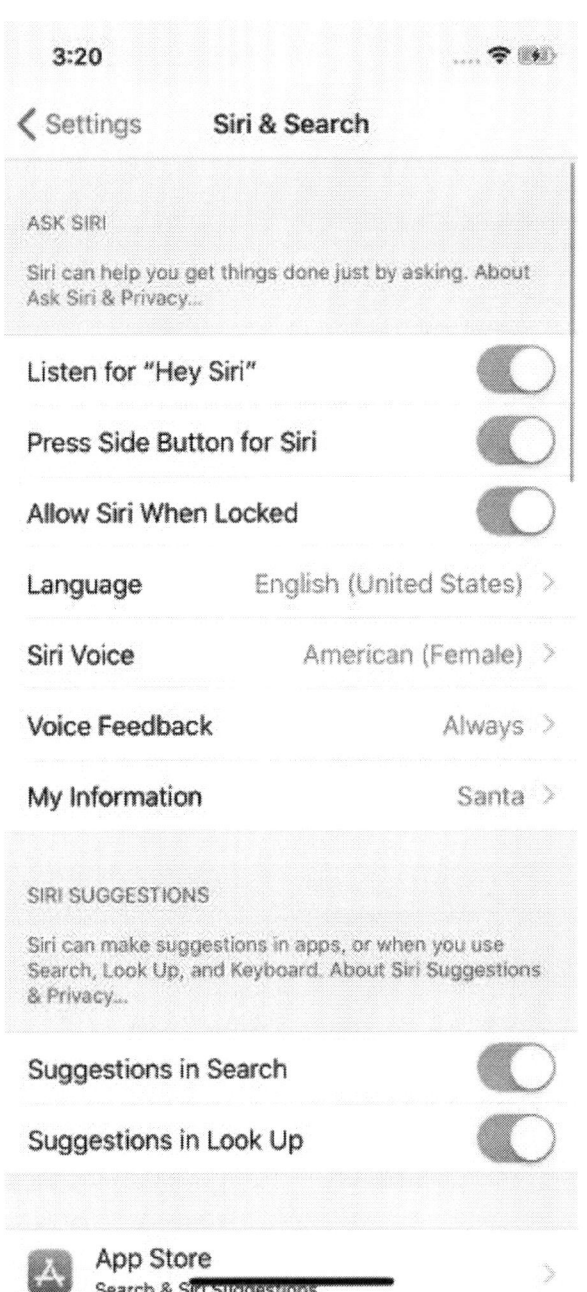
Figure 4: Siri & Search Settings Screen

Adjusting Sound Settings

Figure 5: Voice Feedback Screen

8. Adjusting Siri Settings

You can adjust certain settings for Apple's voice assistant, Siri. To adjust the Siri settings:

1. Touch the icon. The Settings screen appears.
2. Touch **Siri & Search**. The Siri & Search Settings screen appears.
3. Touch one of the following settings to change it:
    - **Listen for "Hey Siri"** - Allows you to turn on Siri by saying "Hey Siri" without pressing and holding the Home button. Requires a short setup process.
    - **Press Side Button for Siri** - Enables you to turn on Siri by pressing and holding the **Sleep/Wake** button.
    - **Allow Siri When Locked** - Lets you use Siri while your phone is locked.
    - **Language** - Select the language that Siri understands and uses to respond.
    - **Siri Voice** - Select the voice that Siri uses when responding.
    - **Voice Feedback** - Turn Siri's voice feedback on and off when the phone is muted or connected to a hands-free phone.

Adjusting Language and Keyboard Settings

Table of Contents

1. Customizing Spelling and Grammar Settings
2. Adding an International Keyboard
3. Adding a Keyboard Shortcut
4. Changing the Operating System Language
5. Changing the Keyboard Layout
6. Changing the Region Format

1. Customizing Spelling and Grammar Settings

Customize the Spelling and Grammar settings on your phone to improve typing accuracy when composing text messages or emails. To customize the Spelling and Grammar settings:

1. Touch the icon. The Settings screen appears.
2. Touch **General**. The General Settings screen appears, as shown in **Figure 1**.
3. Touch **Keyboard**. The Keyboard Settings screen appears, as shown in **Figure 2**.
4. Touch one of the switches on the right side of the screen to turn the corresponding setting on or off:
    - **Auto-Capitalization** - Capitalizes the first word of every sentence automatically.
    - **Auto-Correction** - Suggests and makes spelling corrections while you type.
    - **Check Spelling** - Underlines all misspelled words.
    - **Enable Caps Lock** - Allows you to turn Caps Lock on by quickly touching the key twice on the virtual keyboard. While Caps Lock is turned on, all capital letters are typed without the need to use the key.
    - **Predictive** - The Predictive Text feature offers suggestions for the next word in a sentence as you type, which is intelligently based on the words that you have already typed.
    - **Smart punctuation** - Changes the appearance of some punctuation as necessary, such as quotation marks.
    - **Enable Key Flicks** - Allows you to slide your finger down on a key to insert an alternate character.
    - **."" Shortcut** - Allows you to insert a period and an extra space when you quickly touch the space bar twice.

Adjusting Language and Keyboard Settings

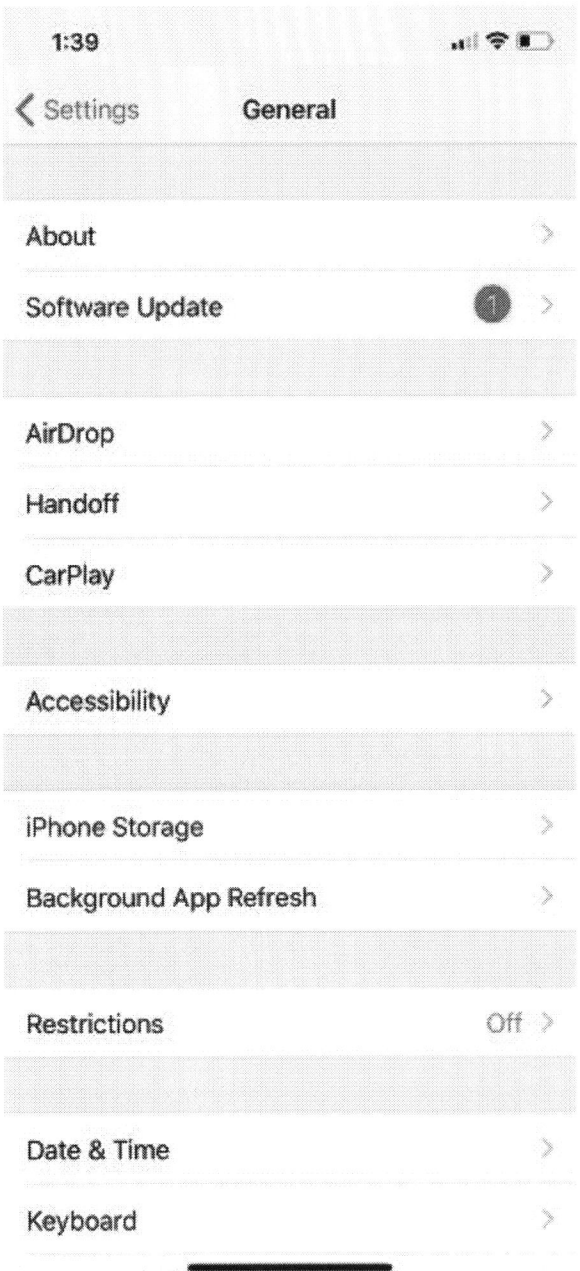

Figure 1: General Settings Screen

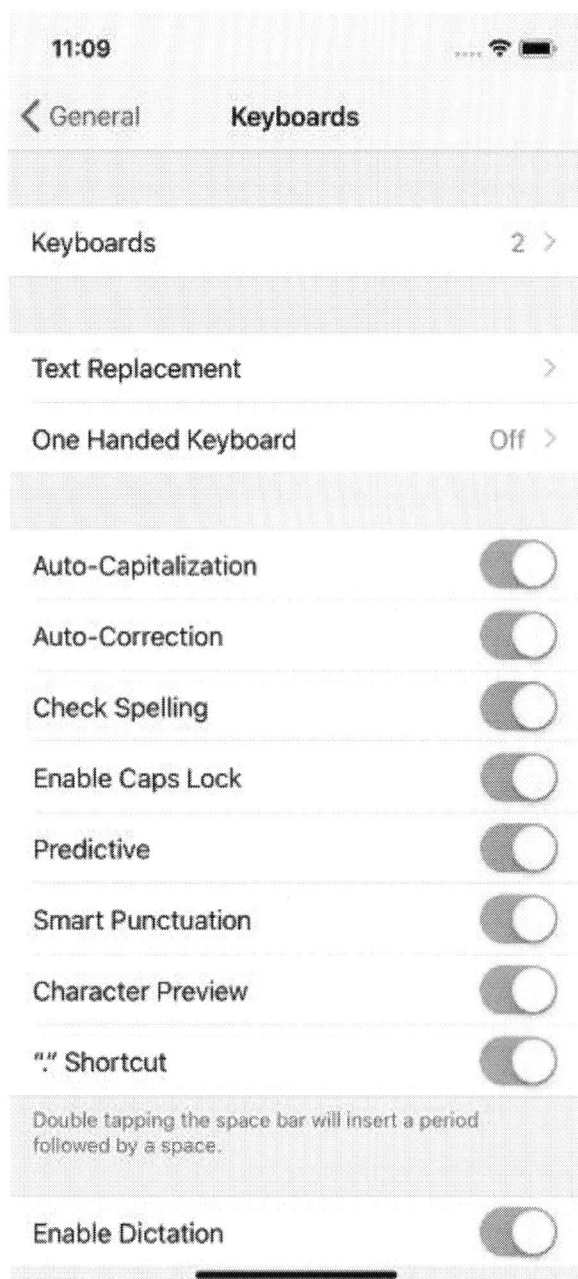
Figure 2: Keyboard Settings Screen

2. Adding an International Keyboard

The phone allows you to use international keyboards when entering text on the virtual keyboard. To add an international keyboard:

1. Touch the icon. The Settings screen appears.
2. Touch **General**. The General Settings screen appears.
3. Touch **Keyboard**. The Keyboard Settings screen appears.
4. Touch **Keyboards**. The Keyboards screen appears, as shown in **Figure 3**.
5. Touch **Add New Keyboard**. A list of international keyboards appears, as shown in **Figure 4**.
6. Touch a keyboard. The keyboard is added. While typing, touch the key at the bottom of the virtual keyboard to switch to an international one.
7. You may remove a keyboard from the list by touching and holding it, and then sliding your finger to the left until 'Delete' appears. Touch **Delete** to remove the keyboard.

Note: If you only add the Emoji keyboard (emoticons) in addition to the English keyboard, the key appears instead of the key.

Figure 3: Keyboards Screen

Figure 4: List of International Keyboards

3. Adding a Keyboard Shortcut

The phone allows you to add custom Keyboard shortcuts. For example, "ur" for "your" or "ttyl" for "talk to you later" are substituted when the corresponding abbreviation is typed. To add a Keyboard shortcut:

1. Touch the icon. The Settings screen appears.
2. Touch **General**. The General Settings screen appears.
3. Scroll down and touch **Keyboard**. The Keyboard Settings screen appears.
4. Touch **Text Replacement**. A list of existing shortcuts appears, as shown in **Figure 5**.
5. Touch the icon. The Add Text Replacement screen appears, as shown in **Figure 6**.
6. Enter the desired phrase to be substituted for the shortcut. Touch **return**.
7. Enter the desired shortcut and touch **Save** at the top of the screen. The keyboard shortcut is added. To use the shortcut, type it and touch the space bar.

Adjusting Language and Keyboard Settings

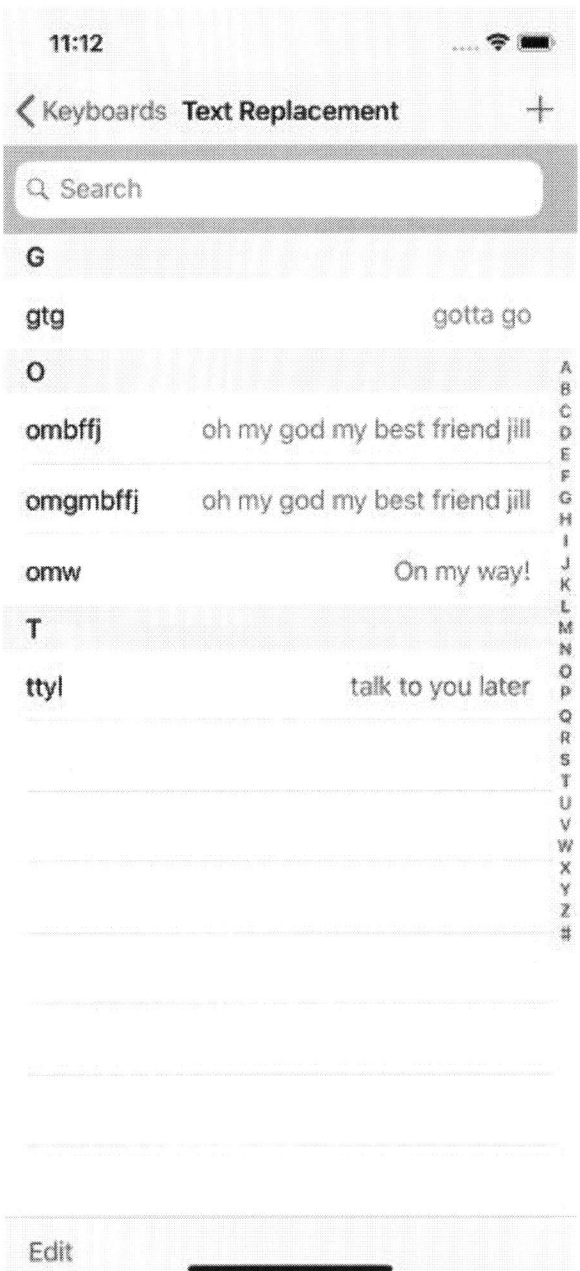

Figure 5: List of Existing Shortcuts

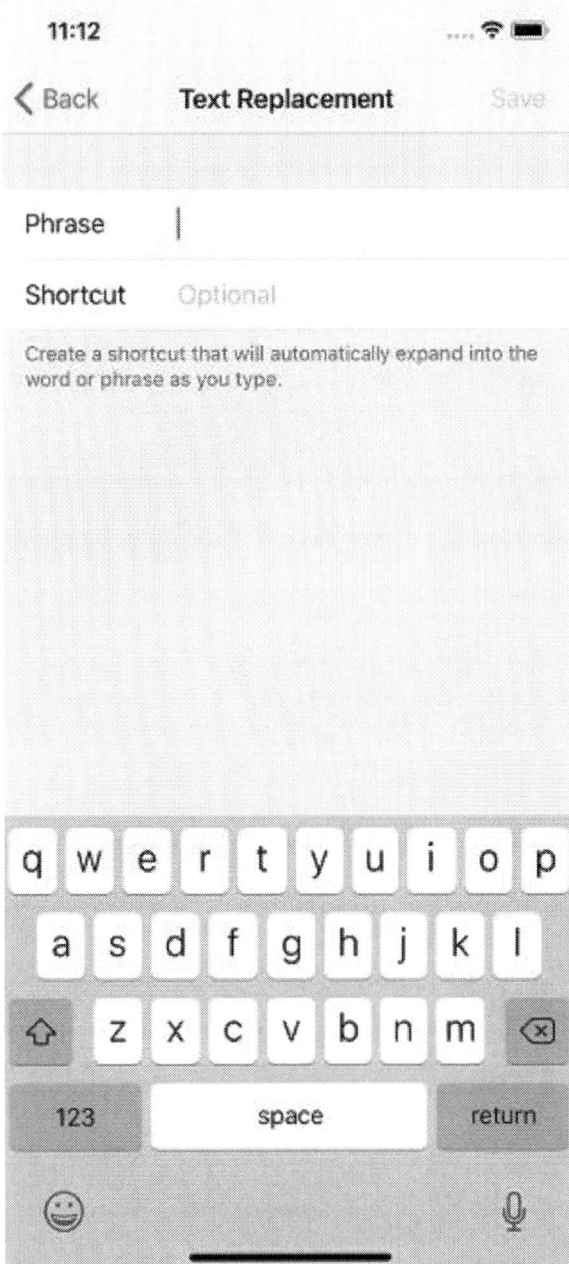

Figure 6: Text Replacement Screen

4. Changing the Operating System Language

The iOS on the phone can be changed to display all menus and options in a language other than English. To change the Operating System Language:

1. Touch the ![icon] icon. The Settings screen appears.
2. Touch **General**. The General Settings screen appears.
3. Scroll down and touch **Language & Region**. The Language & Region screen appears, as shown in **Figure 7**.
4. Touch **iPhone Language**. A list of available languages appears, as shown in **Figure 8**.
5. Touch a language, then touch **Done** at the top of the screen. A confirmation dialog appears.
6. Touch **Continue**. The selected language is applied and all menus and options reflect the change.

Note: It may take some time to install the language. This delay is normal.

Help Me! Guide to the iPhone X

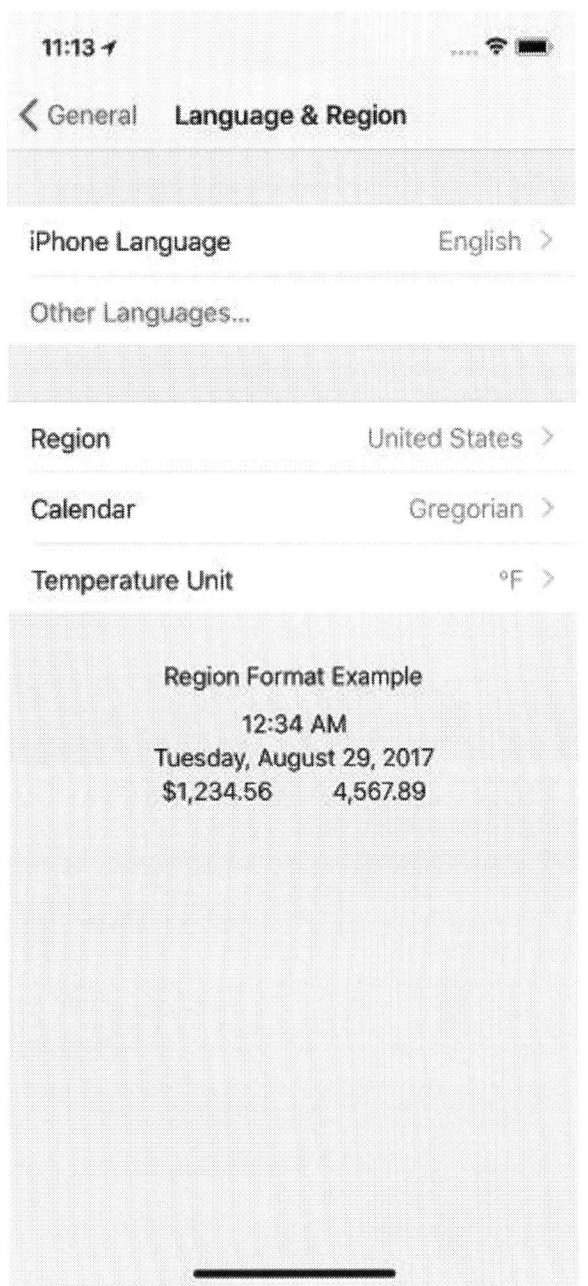

Figure 7: Language & Region Screen

Adjusting Language and Keyboard Settings

Figure 8: List of Available Languages

283

Help Me! Guide to the iPhone X

5. Changing the Keyboard Layout

The layout of the keyboard in most languages can be changed, according to personal preference. For instance, the English keyboard can be set display in default QWERTY, as shown in **Figure 9**, AZERTY, as shown in **Figure 10**, or QWERTZ as shown in **Figure 11**. To change the Keyboard Layout:

1. Touch the icon. The Settings screen appears.
2. Touch **General**. The General Settings screen appears.
3. Scroll down and touch **Keyboard**. The Keyboard Settings screen appears.
4. Touch **Keyboards**. The Keyboards screen appears.
5. Touch the language of the keyboard that you wish to change. The Keyboard Layout screen appears.
6. Touch the desired layout. The new Keyboard Layout is set.

Note: The English keyboard layouts are shown below only as an example. The keyboard layouts vary based on the language that you select. Some languages do not offer various layouts.

Figure 9: QWERTY Keyboard

Figure 10: AZERTY Keyboard

284

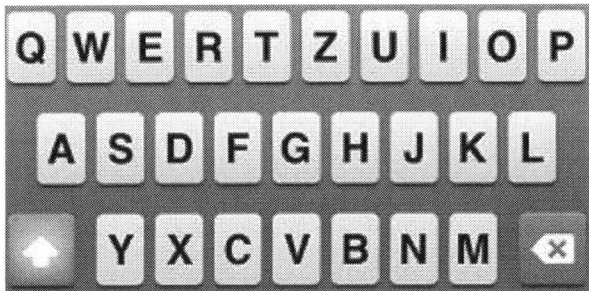

Figure 11: QWERTZ Keyboard

6. Changing the Region Format

The region format on the phone determines how dates, times, and phone numbers are universally displayed. For instance, a European country may display the 30th day of the first month in the year 2011 as 30/01/2011, whereas the U.S. would display the same date as 01/30/2011. To change the region format:

1. Touch the icon. The Settings screen appears.
2. Touch **General**. The General Settings screen appears.
3. Touch **Language & Region**. The Language & Region screen appears.
4. Touch **Region**. A list of regions appears, as shown in **Figure 12**.
5. Touch the desired region. The new region format is set.

Help Me! Guide to the iPhone X

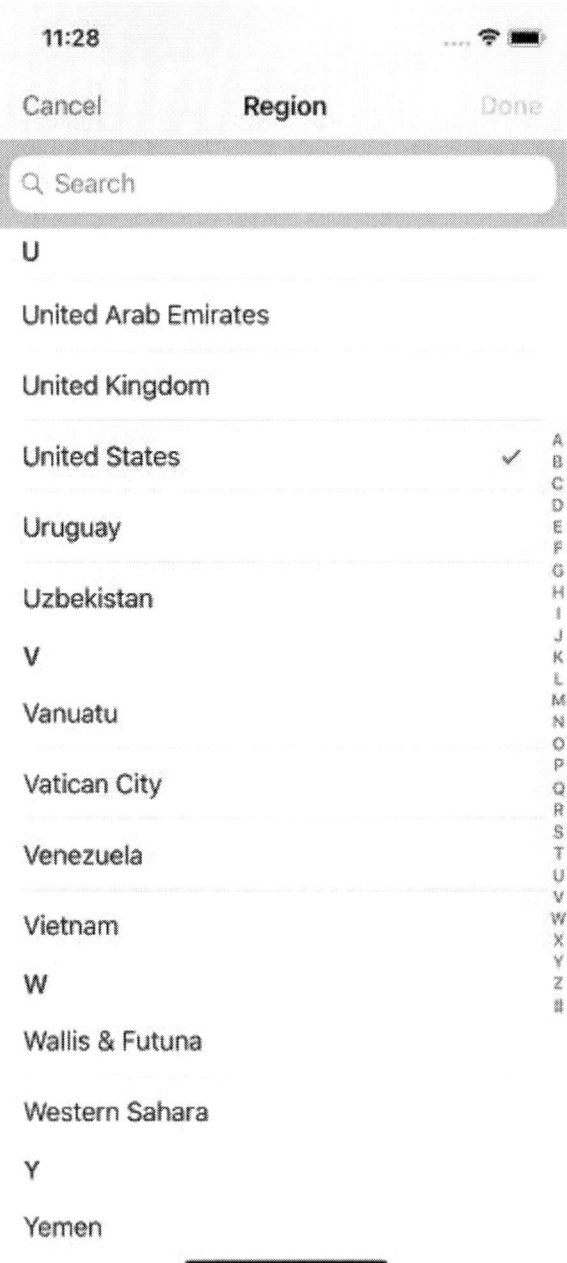

Figure 12: List of Regions

Adjusting General Settings

Table of Contents

1. Changing Auto-Lock Settings
2. Adjusting the Brightness
3. Turning Night Shift On or Off
4. Assigning a Passcode Lock
5. Setting Up a Face ID Lock
6. Turning 24-Hour Mode On or Off
7. Resetting the Home Screen Layout
8. Resetting All Settings
9. Erasing and Restoring the Phone
10. Managing Notification Settings
11. Changing the Wallpaper
12. Restricting Access to Private Information
13. Turning Raise to Wake On or Off

1. Changing Auto-Lock Settings

The phone can lock itself when it is idle in order to save battery life, and to avoid unintentionally pressing buttons. When it is locked, the phone can still receive calls and text messages. By default, the phone is set to automatically lock after one minute. To change the length of time that will pass before the phone locks itself:

1. Touch the ![] icon. The Settings screen appears.
2. Touch **Display & Brightness**. The Display & Brightness screen appears, as shown in **Figure 1**.
3. Touch **Auto-Lock**. The Auto-Lock screen appears, as shown in **Figure 2**.
4. Touch an amount of time, or touch **Never** if you do not want the phone to automatically lock itself. The change is applied and the phone will wait the selected amount of time before automatically locking itself.

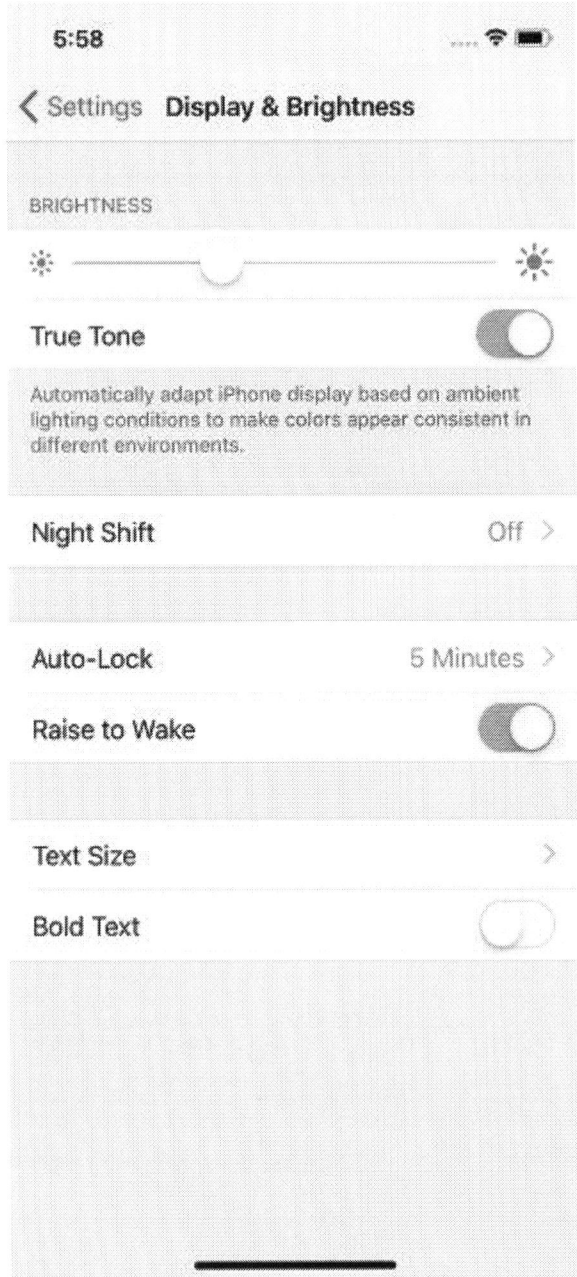

Figure 1: Display & Brightness Screen

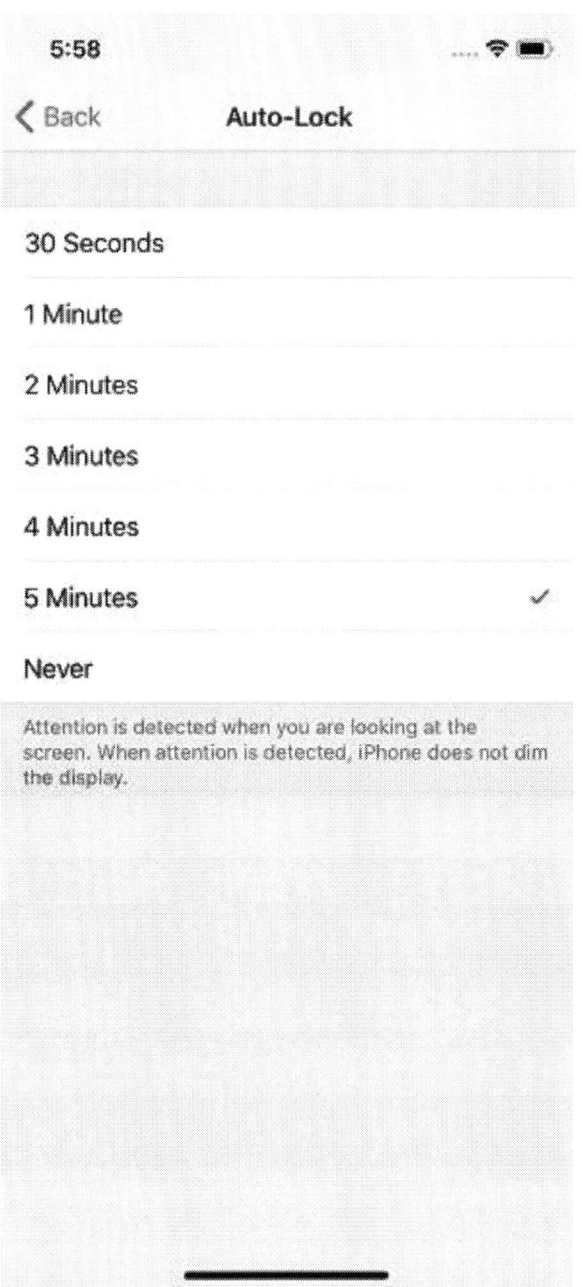

Figure 2: Auto-Lock Screen

Adjusting General Settings

2. Adjusting the Brightness

You may wish to increase the brightness of the screen on your phone when you are in a sunny area. On the other hand, you may wish to decrease the brightness in a dark area to conserve battery life. To adjust the brightness:

1. Touch the ![icon] icon. The Settings screen appears.
2. Touch **Display & Brightness**. The Display & Brightness Settings screen appears.
3. Touch the ![icon] on the ━━━━━━━━ bar and drag it towards the small ![icon] icon to decrease the brightness or towards the large ![icon] icon to increase it.

3. Turning Night Shift On or Off

The Night Shift feature allows you to set the display to use warm colors, which are easier on the eyes. This is a feature that is especially useful in the evening hours when you do not want to strain your eyes. In addition to turning Night Shift on or off, you can schedule it to automatically turn on during a certain time period. To configure Night Shift:

1. Touch the ![icon] icon. The Settings screen appears.
2. Touch **Display & Brightness**. The Display & Brightness Settings screen appears.
3. Touch **Night Shift**. The Night Shift screen appears, as shown in **Figure 3**.
4. Touch **Manually Enable Until Tomorrow**. Night Shift is turned on until 12:00am on the following day. To schedule Night Shift, touch **From To** and select a time range.

You can also manually turn on Night Shift in the Control Center by force touching the ![icon] icon and then touching **Night Shift**. Refer to *"Accessing Quick Settings through the Control Center"* on page 31 to learn more.

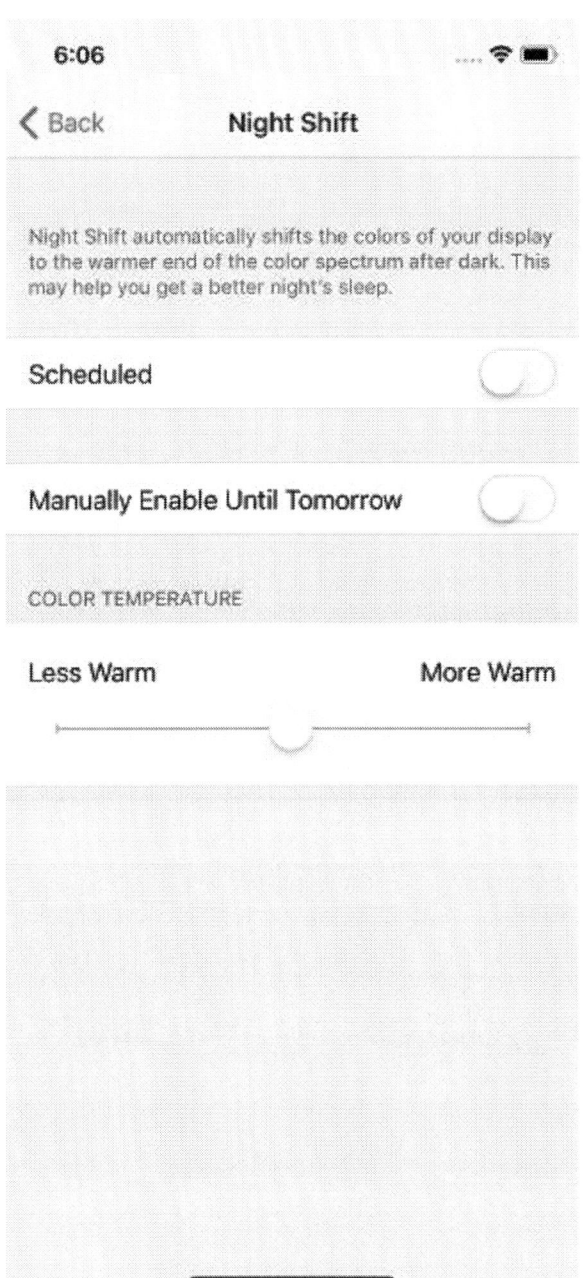

Figure 3: Night Shift Screen

Adjusting General Settings

4. Assigning a Passcode Lock

The phone can prompt for a four-digit or alphanumeric password. To set up a password lock:

1. Touch the ⚙ icon. The Settings screen appears.
2. Touch **Face ID & Passcode**. The Face ID & Passcode screen appears, as shown in **Figure 4**.
3. Touch **Turn Passcode On**. The Set Passcode screen appears, as shown in **Figure 5**. To set a 4-Digit numeric, an alphanumeric, or a custom numeric passcode, touch **Passcode Options**, and select an option from the Passcode Options list, as shown in **Figure 6**.
4. Enter a passcode. A confirmation screen appears.
5. Enter the passcode again. The new passcode is set.
6. Touch one of the following options on the Passcode Lock screen to change the corresponding setting:
    - **Require Passcode** - Set the time the phone waits before asking the user for the passcode. It is recommended to choose the default, **Immediately**, since an unauthorized user will not have access to your phone for any period of time if this option is chosen. Choosing one of the other options causes the phone to wait a set amount of time after being locked before requiring a passcode.
    - **Erase Data** - Erases all data after a user enters the passcode incorrectly ten times in a row.

Warning: You will not be able to recover your data if this feature is on when an incorrect passcode is entered ten times consecutively.

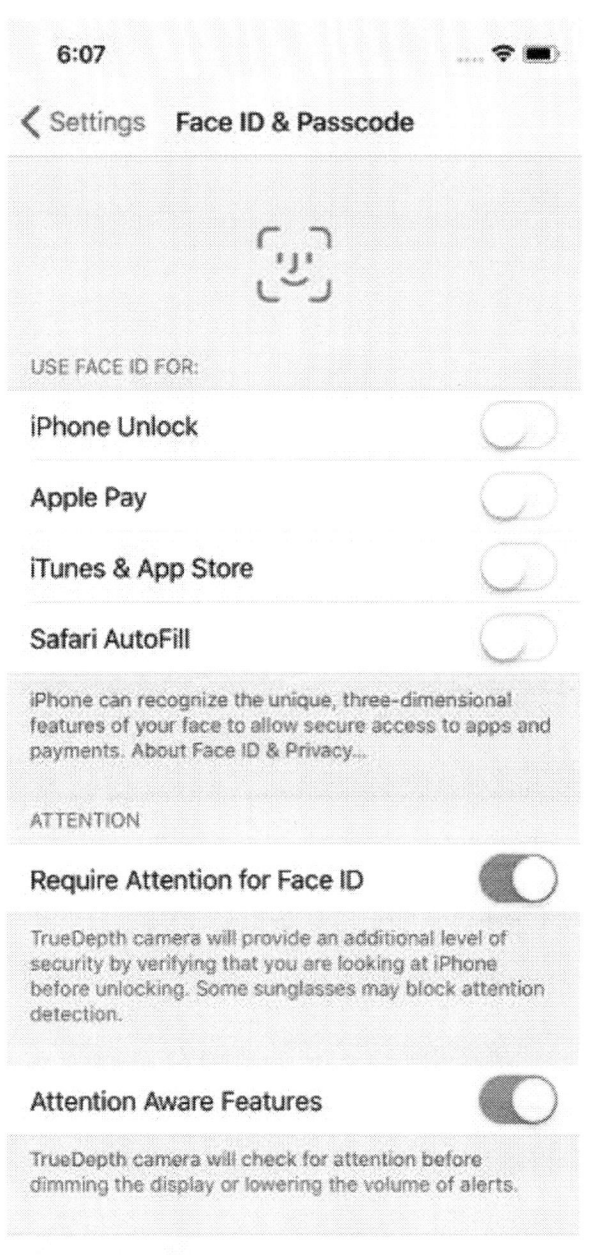

Figure 4: Touch ID & Passcode Screen

Adjusting General Settings

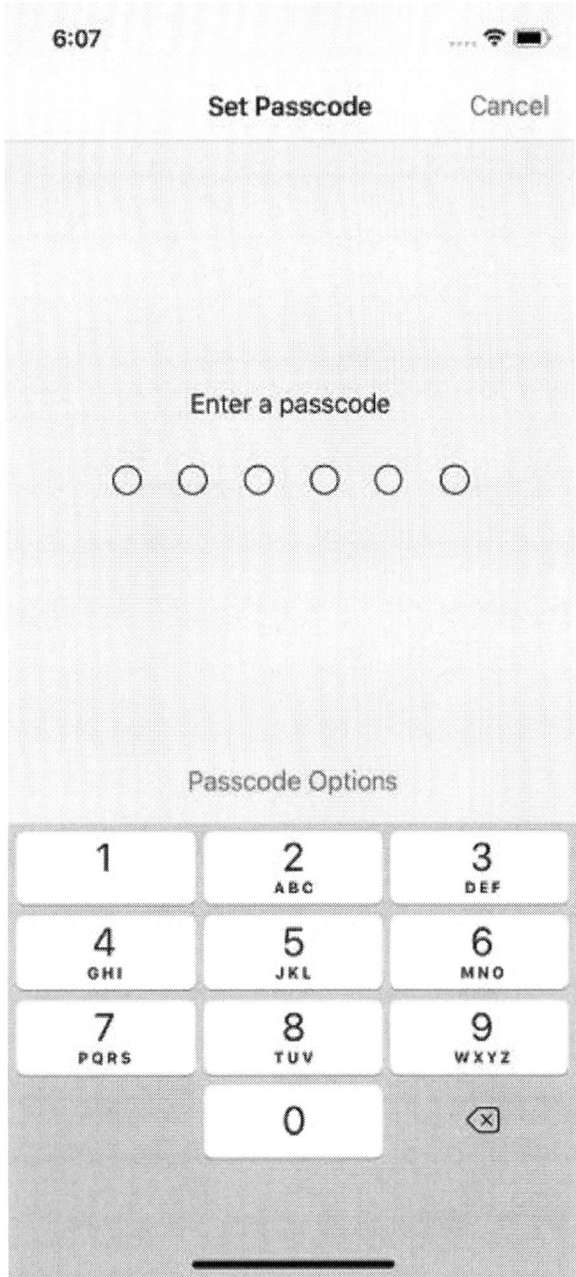

Figure 5: Set Passcode Screen

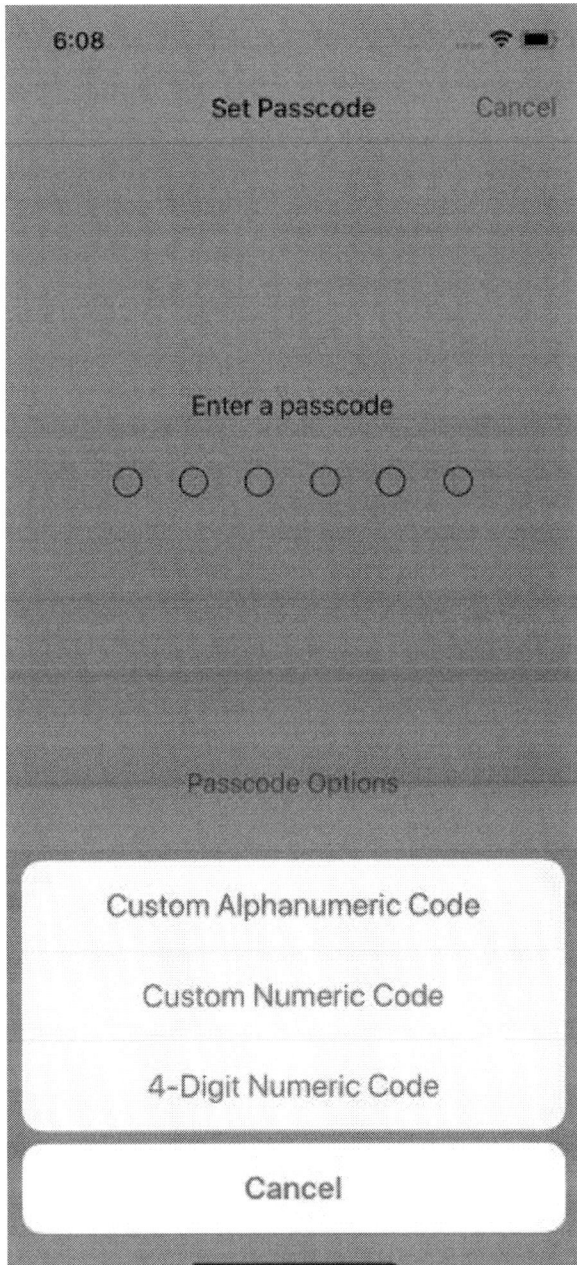

Figure 6: Passcode Options

5. Setting Up a Face ID Lock

The iPhone X allows you to unlock the screen using your face. To set up Face ID:

1. Touch the icon. The Settings screen appears.
2. Touch **Face ID & Passcode**. The Face ID & Passcode screen appears.
3. Scroll down and touch **Set Up Face ID**. The Face ID Setup screen appears, as shown in **Figure 7**.
4. Touch **Get Started**. Move your face around to complete the circle, as instructed.
5. Repeat the same process again. Face ID is set up. If you have not already done so, enter a passcode that you can use when Face ID is not available.

Figure 7: Face ID Setup Screen

Adjusting General Settings

6. Turning 24-Hour Mode On or Off

The phone can display the time in regular 12-hour mode or in 24-hour mode, commonly referred to as military time. To turn 24-hour mode on or off:

1. Touch the icon. The Settings screen appears.
2. Touch **General**. The General Settings screen appears.
3. Scroll down and touch **Date & Time**. The Date & Time screen appears, as shown in **Figure 8**.
4. Touch the switch next to '24-Hour Time'. The switch appears 24-Hour mode is turned on. To turn off 24-Hour mode, touch the switch next to '24-Hour Time'.

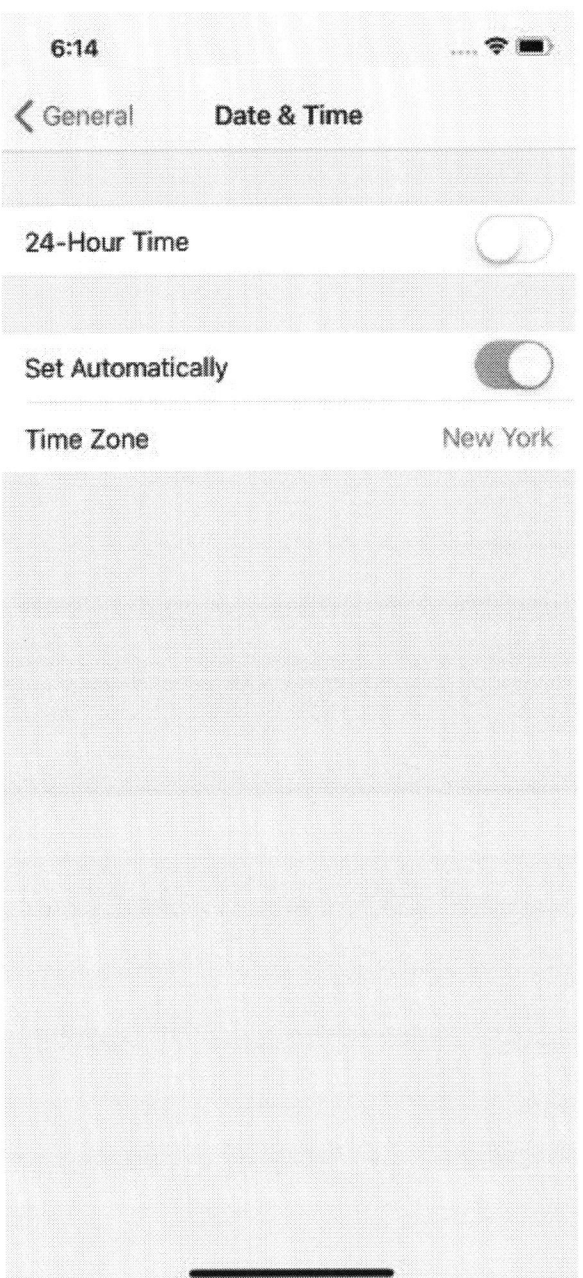

Figure 8: Date & Time Screen

Adjusting General Settings

7. Resetting the Home Screen Layout

You can reset the Home screen on your phone to look like it did when you first purchased it. To reset the Home Screen Layout:

Note: Resetting the Home screen layout does not delete any applications, but simply rearranges them on the Home screen.

1. Touch the icon. The Settings screen appears.
2. Touch **General**. The General Settings screen appears.
3. Scroll down and touch **Reset**. The Reset screen appears, as shown in **Figure 9**.
4. Touch **Reset Home Screen Layout**. A confirmation dialog appears at the bottom of the screen.
5. Touch **Reset Home Screen**. The Home Screen Layout is reset.

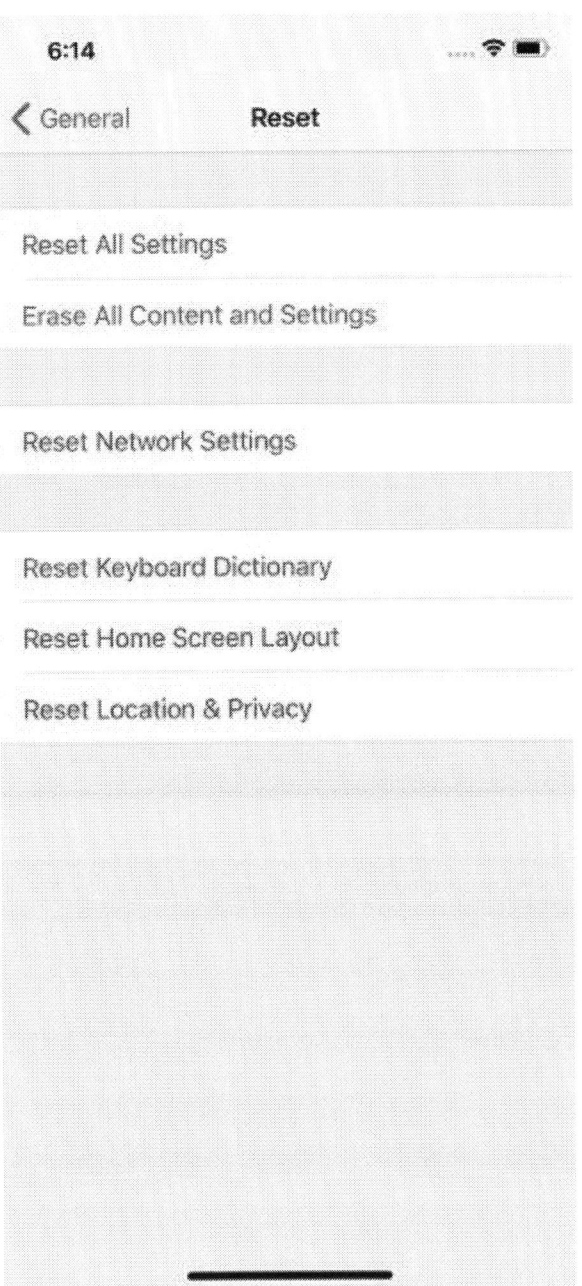

Figure 9: Reset Screen

8. Resetting All Settings

You can reset all of the settings on your phone to the state they were in when you first purchased it. To reset all settings:

Note: Resetting the settings will NOT delete any data from your phone.

1. Touch the icon. The Settings screen appears.
2. Touch **General**. The General Settings screen appears
3. Scroll down and touch **Reset**. The Reset screen appears.
4. Touch **Reset All Settings**. A confirmation dialog appears at the bottom of the screen. You will also need to enter your passcode, if you have one.
5. Touch **Reset All Settings**. All settings are reset to defaults.

9. Erasing and Restoring the Phone

You can delete all of the data and reset all settings to completely restore the phone to its original condition. To erase and restore the phone to its original condition:

Warning: Any erased data is not recoverable. Make sure that you back up all of the data that you wish to keep.

1. Touch the icon. The Settings screen appears.
2. Touch **General**. The General Settings screen appears.
3. Touch **Reset**. The Reset screen appears.
4. Touch **Erase All Content and Settings**. Enter the phone's passcode if you have set one. A confirmation dialog appears.
5. Touch **Erase Now**. The phone is erased and restored to its original condition.

10. Managing Notification Settings

You may customize the types of notifications that appear in the Notifications Center. To manage notification settings:

1. Touch the ![icon] icon. The Settings screen appears.
2. Touch **Notifications**. The Notifications Settings appear, as shown in **Figure 10**.
3. Touch one of the notification types, such as phone or Messages, to turn the notifications on or off, or to customize the number of notifications that appear. The Notification Customization screen appears, as shown in **Figure 11** (Messages Notification Customization).
4. Touch the ![switch] switch next to 'Allow Notifications'. The ![switch] switch appears and notifications will no longer appear for the selected type.
5. Touch one of the following options to customize the notifications:

Note: The following options vary based on the notification type. You may also need to first touch your account, as in the case of adjusting Mail notifications.

- **Sounds** - Select the sound that plays when a new notification of the selected type arrives.
- **Badge App Icon** - Turn the notification type icon that appears next to a notification on or off.
- **Show on Lock Screen** - Enable notifications of the selected type to appear on the Lock screen.
- **Show in History** - Enable notifications from the selected application to appear in the notification history on the cover sheet.
- **Show as Banners** - Enable notifications to appear as temporary or persistent banners when the phone is unlocked. Persistent banners remain on the screen until you interact with them.
- **Show Previews** - Enable notifications to show additional information in the text. Touch **Show Previews** and select **Never** to always have the phone show only the name of the application. Touch **When Unlocked** to have the phone show only the name of the application when the phone is unlocked. Touching **Always (Default)** enables the phone to always show additional information in the notification.
- **Repeat Alerts** - Enables the phone to send you the same notification up to 10 times every two minutes.

Adjusting General Settings

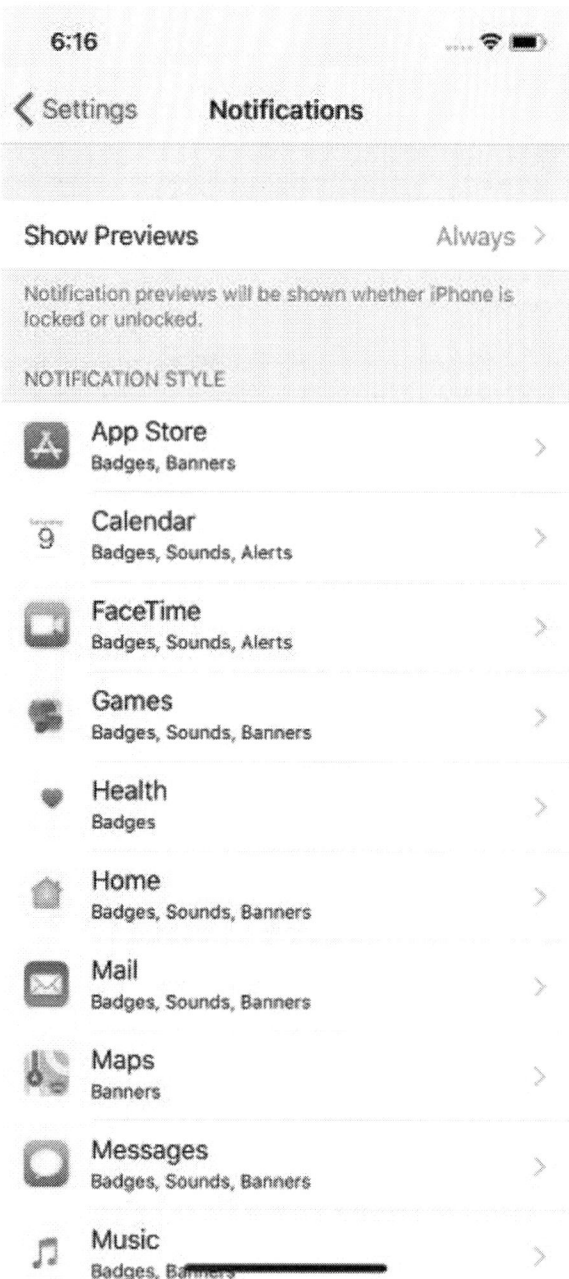

Figure 10: Notifications Settings

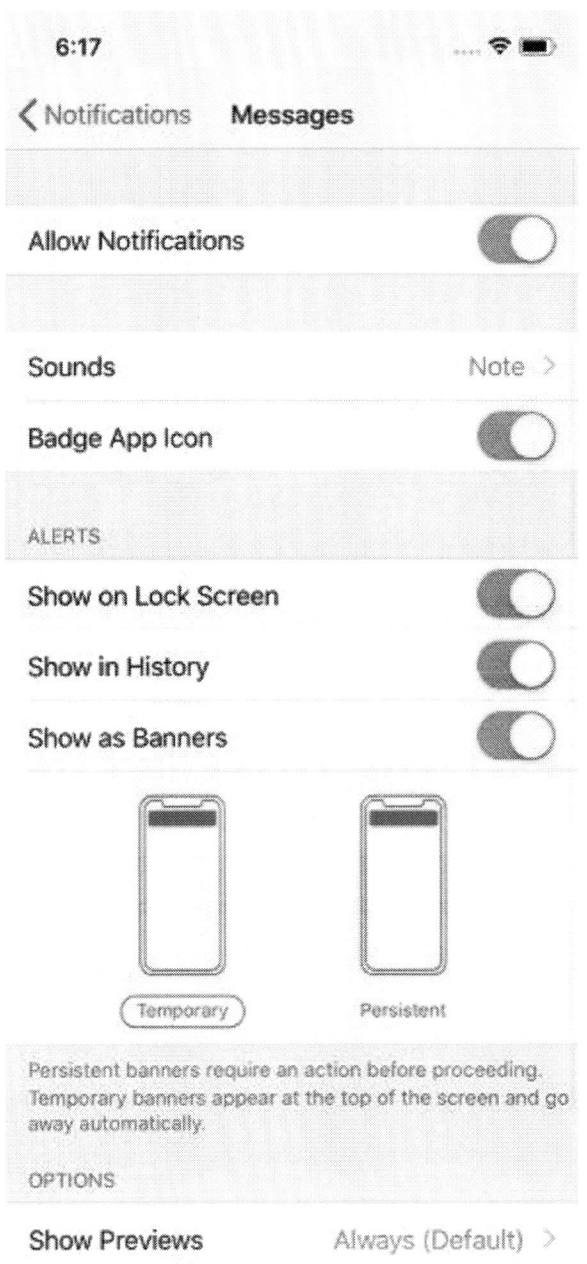

Figure 11: Notification Customization Screen

11. Changing the Wallpaper

The wallpaper is the image that appears on the Lock screen, and on the Home screen behind the application icons. To change the wallpaper:

1. Touch the ![] icon. The Settings screen appears.
2. Touch **Wallpaper**. The Wallpaper Settings appear, as shown in **Figure 12**.
3. Touch **Choose a New Wallpaper**. The Wallpaper Selection screen appears, as shown in **Figure 13**.
4. Touch the image above 'Dynamic' or 'Stills', or touch one of the photo albums under 'Photos'. The corresponding image thumbnails appear.
5. Touch an image thumbnail. The image appears in full-screen, as shown in **Figure 14**.
6. Touch **Set Lock Screen**, **Set Home Screen**, or **Set Both** to set the corresponding wallpaper. The new wallpaper is set.

Figure 12: Wallpaper Settings

Adjusting General Settings

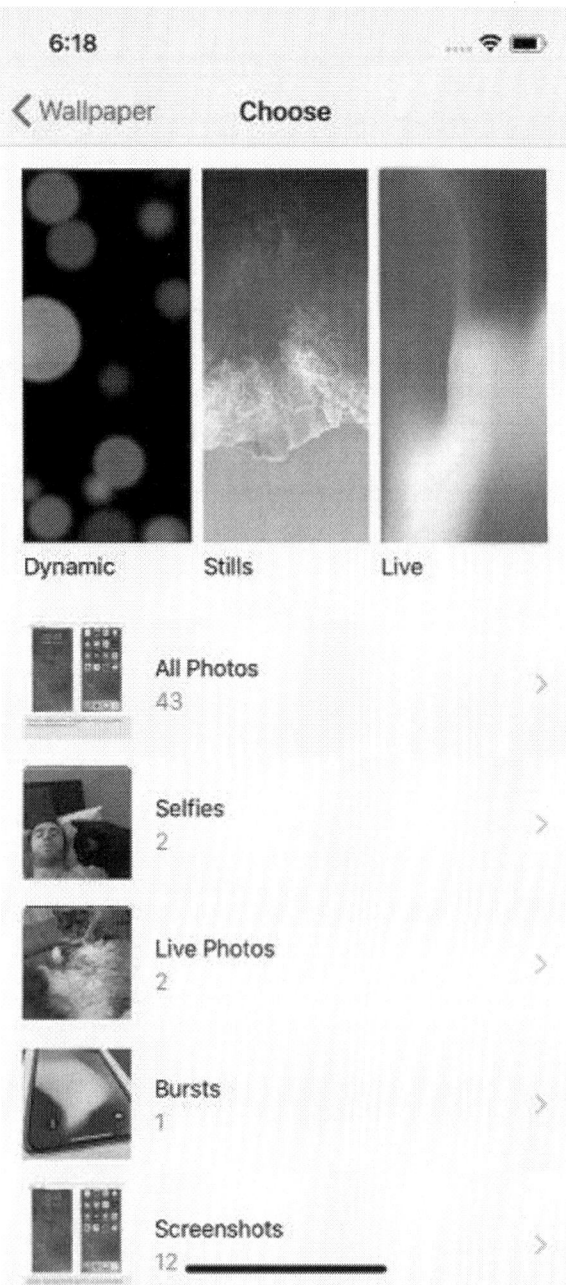

Figure 13: Wallpaper Selection

Help Me! Guide to the iPhone X

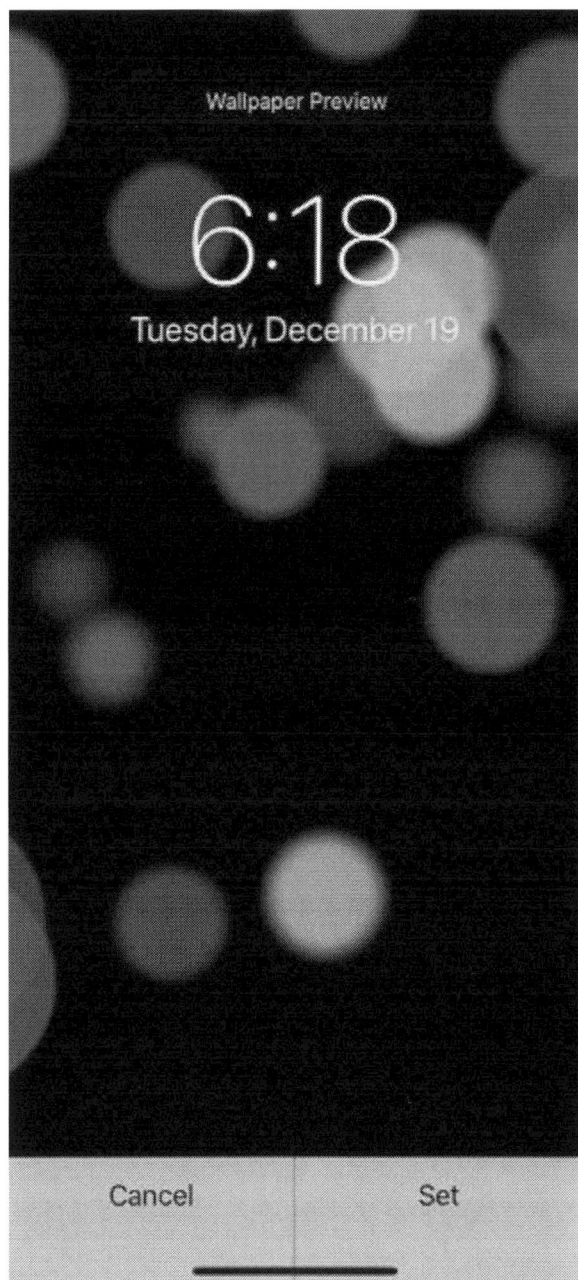

Figure 14: Wallpaper Image in Full-Screen

12. Restricting Access to Private Information

Some applications may request to use your some of the information stored on your phone, or even to access your camera. If you touch **Allow**, the application will have access to the requested information until you take away the access. To restrict access to private information:

1. Touch the ⚙ icon. The Settings screen appears.
2. Touch **Privacy**. The Privacy Settings screen appears, as shown in **Figure 15**.
3. Touch one of the information types, such as 'Contacts' or 'Calendars'. The list of applications appear that have requested access to the selected type of information.
4. Touch the ⬤◯ switch next to the name of the requesting application. The ◯⬤ switch appears, and the selected application will no longer have access to the type of information selected in step 3.

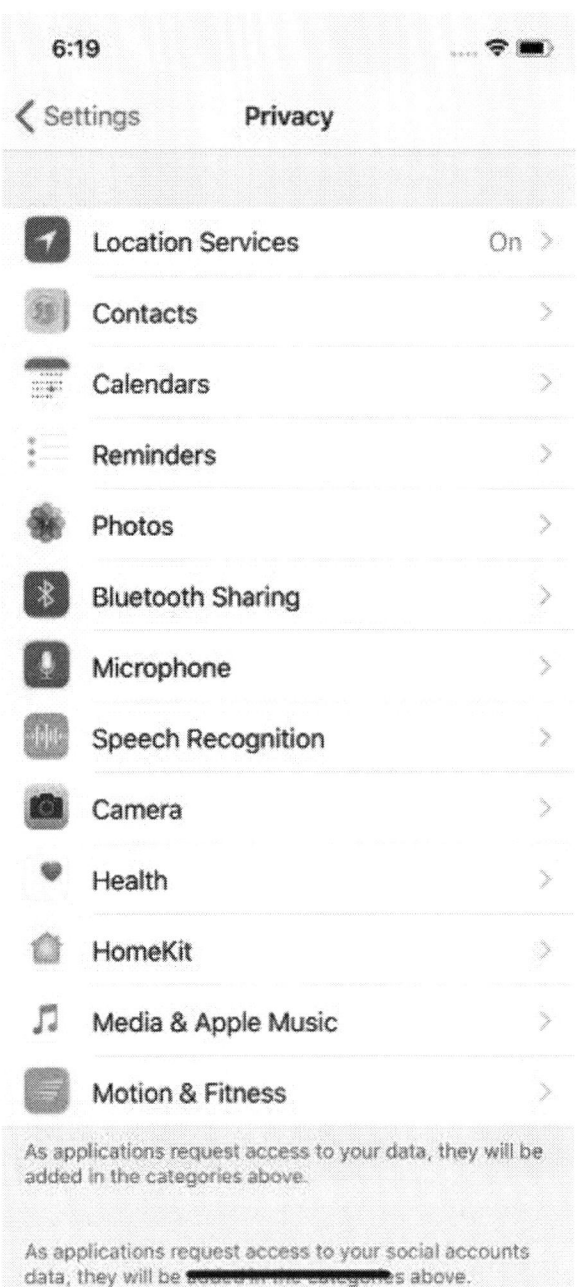

Figure 15: Privacy Settings Screen

13. Turning Raise to Wake On or Off

The Raise to Wake feature allows you to turn on your iPhone's screen when you pick it up or take it out of your pocket. Then, all you have to do is unlock it. To turn Raise to Wake on or off:

1. Touch the ⚙ icon. The Settings screen appears.
2. Touch **Display & Brightness**. The Display & Brightness Settings screen appears.
3. Touch the ⚪ switch next to 'Raise to Wake'. The Raise to Wake feature is turned on. To turn off Raise to Wake, touch the 🔘 switch next to 'Raise to Wake'.

Adjusting Accessibility Settings

Table of Contents

1. Managing Vision Accessibility Features
2. Managing Hearing Accessibility Features
3. Turning Guided Access On or Off
4. Managing Physical & Motor Accessibility Features
5. Answering Phone Calls Automatically

1. Managing Vision Accessibility Features

Vision accessibility features allow people with visual disabilities to use the phone with greater ease. To manage vision accessibility features:

1. Touch the ![icon] icon. The Settings screen appears.
2. Touch **General**. The General Settings screen appears, as shown in **Figure 1**.
3. Touch **Accessibility**. The Accessibility Settings screen appears, as shown in **Figure 2**.
4. Touch one of the following options to turn vision accessibility features on or off:
    - **VoiceOver** - This feature speaks an item on the screen when you touch it once, activates it when you touch it twice, and scrolls through a list or page of text when you touch the screen with three fingers. You can use a variety of voices for Voiceover, including Siri's male or female voice.
    - **Zoom** - This features zooms in on an item when you touch the screen twice using three fingers, moves around when you drag three fingers on the screen, and changes the level of zoom when you touch the screen with three fingers twice and drag.
    - **Magnifier** - This feature lets you use the phone's camera as a magnifying glass. When enabled, press the Sleep/Wake button three times quickly to turn it on.
    - **Invert Colors** (Under **Display Accommodations**) - This feature inverts all of the colors on the screen. For instance, black text on a white screen becomes white text on a black screen.
    - **Color Filters** (Under **Display Accommodations**) - This feature changes all color on the phone's screen to black and white, red/green, green/red ,or blue/yellow, depending on the type of color blindness.
    - **Auto-Brightness** (Under **Display Accommodations**) - Enables the phone to automatically control the brightness depending on the surrounding lighting.
    - **Reduce White Point** (Under **Display Accommodations**) - Decreases the intensity of bright colors like white.

- **Larger Text** - This feature increases the default size of the font. Use the font slider to adjust the default font size.
- **Bold Text** - This feature makes all text on the phone bold in order to make it easier to read. Enabling or disabling this feature requires you to restart the phone.
- **Button Shapes** - This feature allows all buttons, such as the back button in the upper left-hand corner of each menu screen, to have outlines.
- **Increase Contrast** - This feature improves the contrast on certain backgrounds in order to make it easier to read certain text.
- **Reduce Motion** - This feature turns off all screen animations, such as when you close an application to return to the Home screen.
- **On/Off Labels** - This feature turns and switches into and switches, respectively.

Adjusting Accessibility Settings

Figure 1: General Settings Screen

Help Me! Guide to the iPhone X

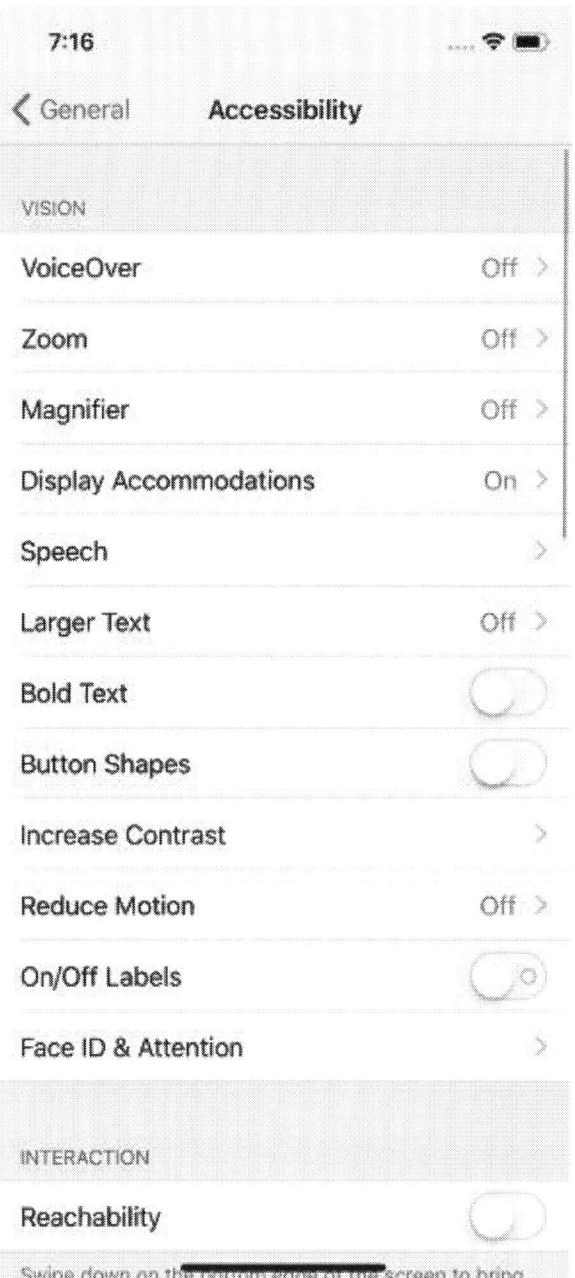

Figure 2: Accessibility Settings Screen

Adjusting Accessibility Settings

2. Managing Hearing Accessibility Features

Hearing accessibility features allow people with hearing disabilities to use the phone with greater ease. To manage hearing accessibility features:
1. Touch the ![icon] icon. The Settings screen appears.
2. Touch **General**. The General Settings screen appears.
3. Touch **Accessibility**. The Accessibility Settings screen appears.
4. Touch one of the following options to turn hearing accessibility features on or off:
    - **Subtitles & Captioning** - This feature allows subtitles and closed captioning to be enabled for videos, where available.
    - **Audio Descriptions** - This feature allows automatically plays audio descriptions for certain media, where available.
    - **LED Flash for Alerts** - This feature allows the camera flash to be used to provide notification alerts, such as incoming calls or text messages.
    - **Mono Audio** - This feature turns off stereo audio, leaving only one speaker working.
    - **Siri** - Turn on **Type to Siri** to type your Siri search instead of using your voice. When **Type to Siri** is turned on, you cannot use your voice with Siri.

3. Turning Guided Access On or Off

Guided Access is a feature that is made for people with learning disabilities, allowing the user to stay in a single application and control the features that are available. To turn Guided Access on or off:
1. Touch the ![icon] icon. The Settings screen appears.
2. Touch **General**. The General Settings screen appears.
3. Touch **Accessibility**. The Accessibility Settings screen appears.
4. Scroll down and touch **Guided Access**. The Guided Access Settings screen appears, as shown in **Figure 3**.
5. Touch the ![switch] switch next to 'Guided Access'. Guided Access is turned on.
6. Touch **Passcode Settings**, then touch **Set Guided Access Passcode** to set up a passcode that will allow you to exit the application when you are done using it.

Figure 3: Guided Access Settings Screen

Adjusting Accessibility Settings

4. Managing Physical & Motor Accessibility Features

Physical and Motor accessibility features allow people with motor disabilities to use the phone with greater ease. To manage physical & motor accessibility features:
1. Touch the icon. The Settings screen appears.
2. Touch **General**. The General Settings screen appears.
3. Touch **Accessibility**. The Accessibility Settings screen appears.
4. Touch one of the following options to turn physical and motor accessibility features on or off:
    - **Switch Control** - This feature allows an adaptive accessory to be used to highlight items on the screen to control the functions of the phone. The Switch Control screen allows various settings, such as timing, switch stabilization, point scanning, audio, and visual settings, to be adjusted.
    - **Assistive Touch** - This feature allows you to create custom gestures in order to access various services on the phone.
    - **Side Button** - This feature allows you to slow down the speed at which you need to press the Sleep/Wake button to access certain features.
    - **Call Audio Routing** - This feature allows you to answer calls directly on your headset or speakerphone by default.
    - **Shake to Undo** - This feature allows you to turn the Shake to Undo feature on or off. By default, shaking the phone causes it ask you whether you would like to undo typing. Refer to *"Quickly Deleting Recently Typed Text"* on page 351 to learn more.
    - **Accessibility Shortcut** - This feature allows you to select an accessibility feature that will be turned on when you press the Sleep/Wake button three times quickly at any time. If you choose more than one feature, a menu will appear allowing you to select the Accessibility feature that you wish to enable.

Touch Accommodations
This feature allows you to customize certain touch gestures when interacting with the phone's screen. The following settings are turned on or off when this setting is enabled or disabled.
- **Hold Duration** - Adjust the amount of time that you must touch and hold the screen before a touch is recognized.
- **Ignore Repeat** - Adjust the amount of time that passes before a touch is recognized as a separate touch from the first. For instance, if you set the time to 2 seconds and touch the screen twice within one second, only the first touch is recognized.

- **Tap Assistance** - Allows you to touch the screen and drag your finger to make a selection. Your touch is not recognized until you lift your finger. Touch **Use Initial Touch Location** to have the phone register your touch where you first touched the screen. Touch **Use Final Touch Location** to have the phone register your touch where you last touched the screen.

5. Answering Phone Calls Automatically

The iPhone can automatically answer an incoming phone call after a set period of time. To enable the phone to answer calls automatically:

1. Touch the icon. The Settings screen appears.
2. Touch **General**. The General Settings screen appears.
3. Touch **Accessibility**. The Accessibility Settings screen appears.
4. Touch **Call Audio Routing**. The Call Audio Routing screen appears, as shown in **Figure 4**. To select how you will hear the audio on the phone call, touch **Bluetooth Headset** or **Speaker** (speakerphone). If you touch **Automatic**, the iPhone will automatically determine the best choice based on whether you have connected a Bluetooth headset.
5. Touch **Auto-Answer Calls**. The Auto-Answer Calls screen appears, as shown in **Figure 5**.
6. Touch the next to **Auto-Answer Calls**. The feature is turned on and the phone will now answer calls automatically. To set the period of time to wait, touch the + and - buttons next to **Seconds**.

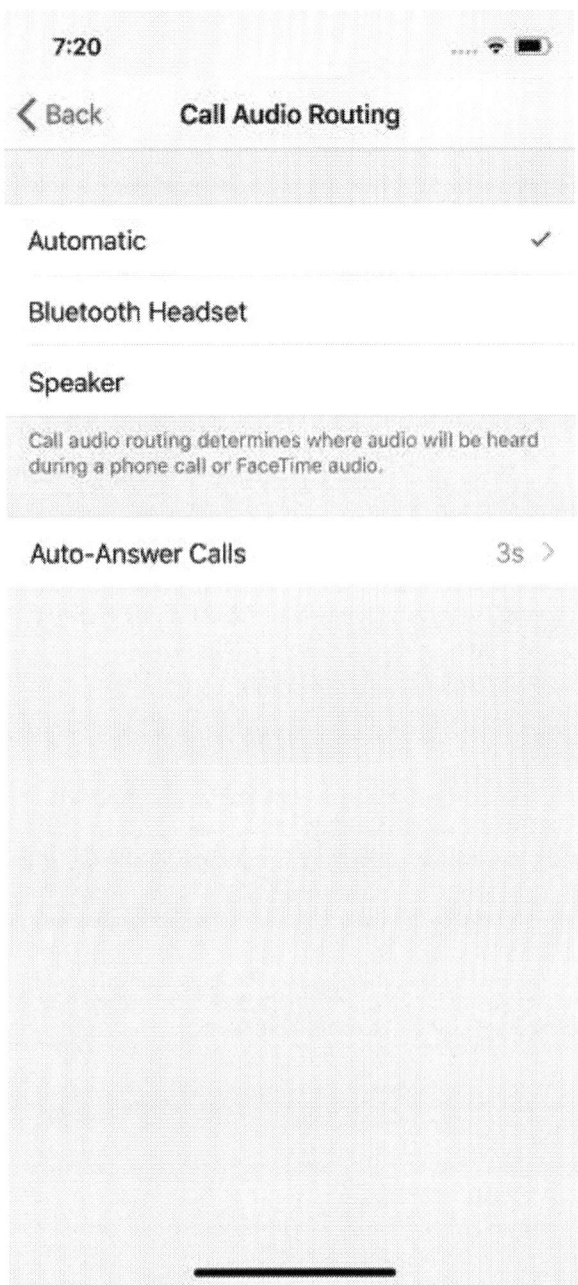

Figure 4: Call Audio Routing Screen

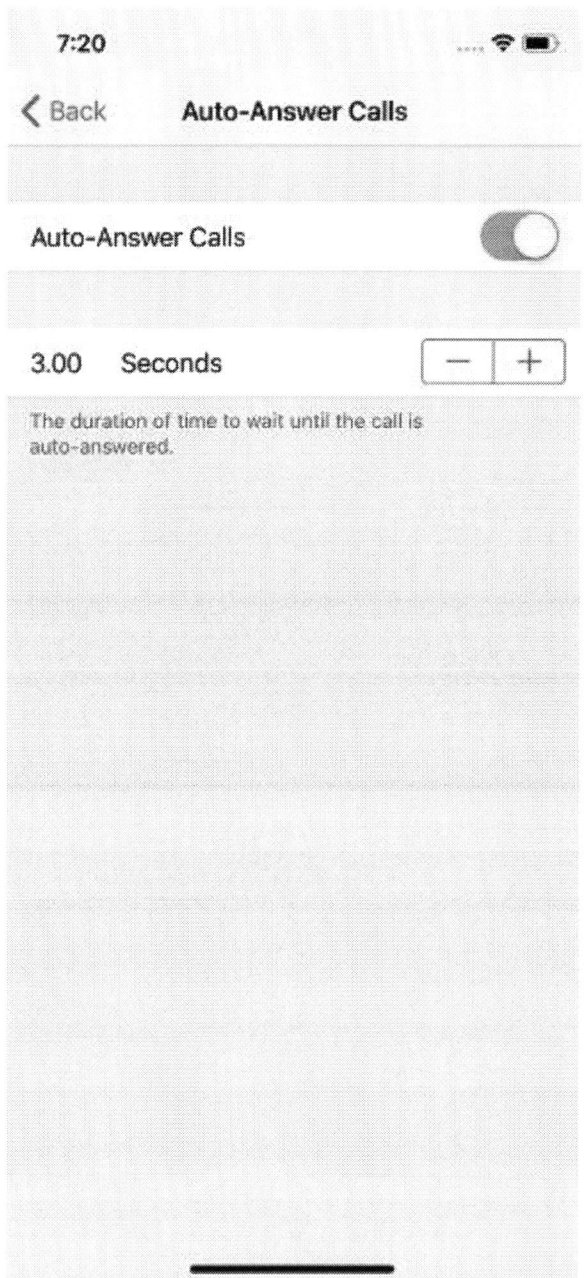

Figure 5: Auto-Answer Calls Screen

Adjusting Phone Settings

Table of Contents

1. Turning Call Forwarding On or Off
2. Turning Call Waiting On or Off
3. Turning Caller ID On or Off
4. Turning the International Assist On or Off
5. Blocking Specific Numbers
6. Editing Preset Text Message Responses
7. Turning Wi-Fi Calling On or Off

1. Turning Call Forwarding On or Off

The phone can be set to forward all calls to a specified number. To turn Call Forwarding on or off:

1. Touch the ![icon] icon. The Settings screen appears, as shown in **Figure 1**.
2. Scroll down and touch **Phone**. The Phone Settings screen appears, as shown in **Figure 2**.
3. Touch **Call Forwarding**. The Call Forwarding screen appears.
4. Touch the ![switch] switch next to 'Call Forwarding'. The 'Forward to' field appears, as shown in **Figure 3**.
5. Use the keypad to enter the phone number to which the phone should forward. When finished, touch **Call Forwarding** at the top of the screen. Call Forwarding is set up, and the Call Forwarding screen appears.

Adjusting Phone Settings

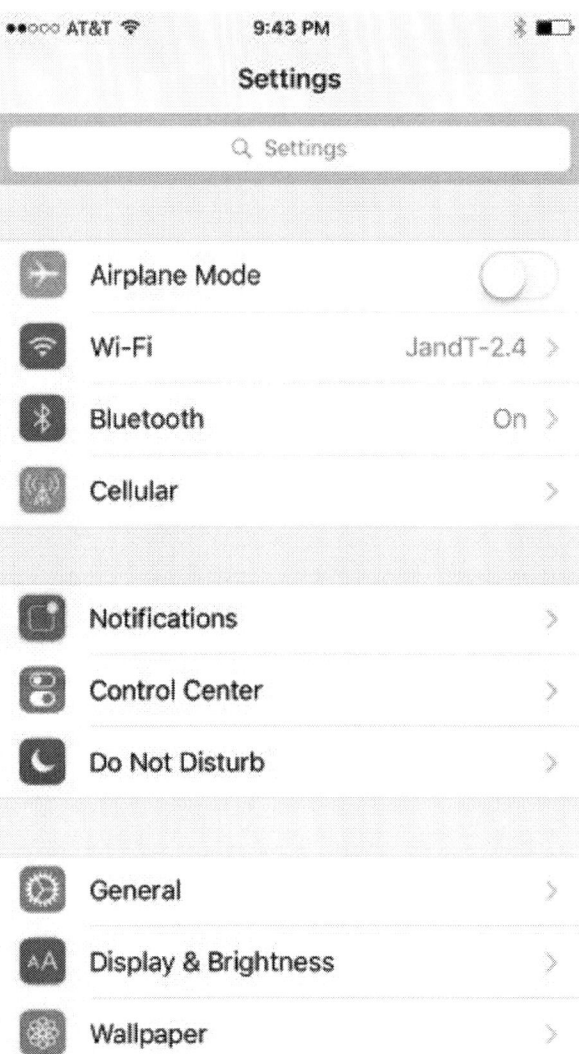

Figure 1: Settings Screen

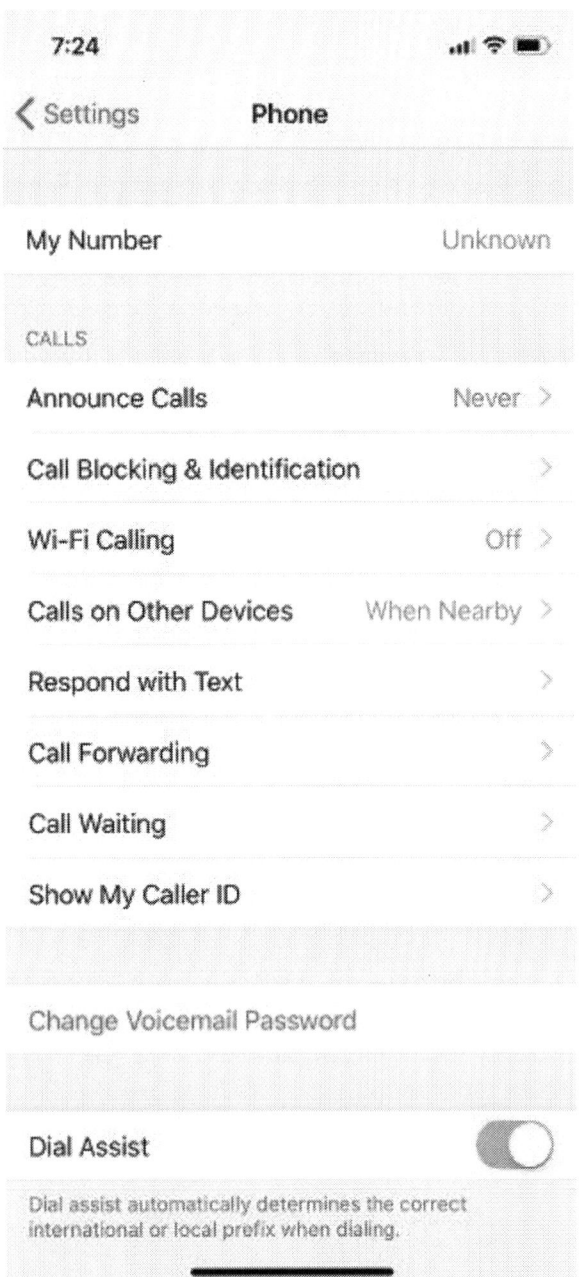

Figure 2: Phone Settings Screen

Adjusting Phone Settings

Figure 3: Forward To Screen

2. Turning Call Waiting On or Off

While you are on the line with someone, the Call Waiting feature allows the iPhone to alert you when there is a second incoming call. To turn Call Waiting on or off:

1. Touch the icon. The Settings screen appears.
2. Scroll down and touch **Phone**. The Phone Settings screen appears.
3. Touch **Call Waiting**. The Call Waiting screen appears, as shown in **Figure 4**.
4. Touch the switch next to 'Call Waiting'. The switch appears and Call Waiting is turned off. To turn off Call Waiting, touch the switch next to 'Call Waiting'.

Adjusting Phone Settings

Figure 4: Call Waiting Screen

3. Turning Caller ID On or Off

The Caller ID feature shows your phone number or name (if your number is stored in the recipient's Phonebook) on the called party's phone. In order to preserve privacy and make your phone number appear as "Private Number", turn the Caller ID feature off. To turn Caller ID on or off:

1. Touch the ![icon] icon. The Settings screen appears.
2. Scroll down and touch **Phone**. The Phone Settings screen appears.
3. Touch **Show My Caller ID**. The Show My Caller ID screen appears, as shown in **Figure 5**.
4. Touch the ![switch] switch next to 'Show My Caller ID'. The ![switch] switch appears and Caller ID is turned off. To turn off Caller ID, touch the ![switch] switch next to 'Show My Caller ID'.

Note: When Caller ID is turned off, even those who have your phone number stored in their Phonebook will not be able to view your number when receiving a call from you.

Adjusting Phone Settings

Figure 5: Show My Caller ID Screen

4. Turning the International Assist On or Off

The International Assist feature is useful while traveling abroad. This feature will automatically add the correct international prefix to every phone number that you dial when calling a U.S. phone number. To turn International Assist on or off:

1. Touch the icon. The Settings screen appears.
2. Scroll down and touch **Phone**. The Phone Settings screen appears.
3. Touch the switch next to 'Dial Assist'. The switch appears and International Assist is turned on. To turn off Dial Assist, touch the switch next to 'Dial Assist'.

Note: The International Assist feature does not work in all areas.

5. Blocking Specific Numbers

The phone can block contacts with specified numbers from calling or texting you. In order to block a number, you must first add it to your Phonebook. To specify numbers to block:

1. Touch the icon. The Settings screen appears.
2. Scroll down and touch **Phone**. The Phone Settings screen appears.
3. Touch **Call Blocking & Identification**. The Call Blocking & Identification screen appears, as shown in **Figure 6**.
4. Touch **Block Contact**. Your Phonebook appears.
5. Touch a contact. The contact's number is added to the Blocked list.

Adjusting Phone Settings

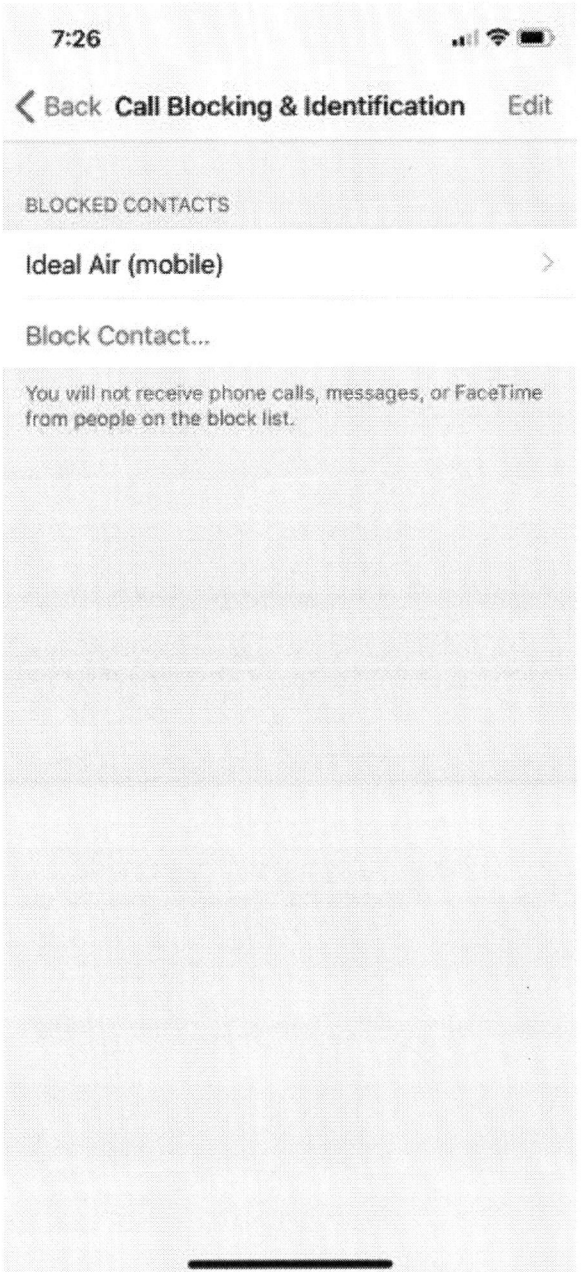

Figure 6: Call Blocking & Identification Screen

6. Editing Preset Text Message Responses

The phone allows you to respond with a preset text if you are unable to answer a call. To edit the preset text message responses:

1. Touch the ⚙ icon. The Settings screen appears.
2. Scroll down and touch **Phone**. The Phone Settings screen appears.
3. Touch **Respond with Text**. The Respond with Text screen appears, as shown in **Figure 7**.
4. Touch one of the messages under 'Respond With' to edit it.
5. Touch **Phone** at the top of the screen. The new preset text messages are saved.

Adjusting Phone Settings

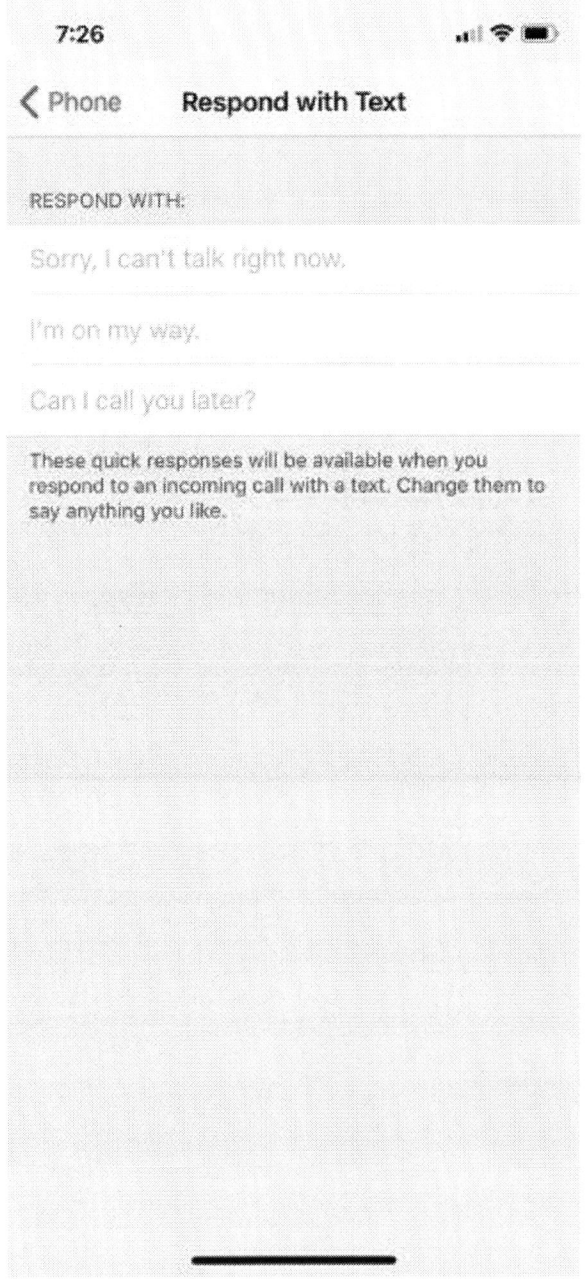

Figure 7: Respond with Text Screen

7. Turning Wi-Fi Calling On or Off

To save your minutes and to improve call quality, you can use your Wi-Fi network or a Wi-Fi hotspot to make phone calls. To turn Wi-Fi calling on or off:

1. Touch the icon. The Settings screen appears.
2. Scroll down and touch **Phone**. The Phone Settings screen appears.
3. Touch **Wi-Fi Calling**. The Wi-Fi Calling screen appears.
4. Touch the switch next to **Wi-Fi Calling on This iPhone**. A confirmation dialog appears.
5. Touch **Enable**. An emergency call notice appears.
6. Touch **Continue** and verify your emergency address. You only need to do this the first time you turn on Wi-Fi calling.
7. Touch **Verify address**. Wi-Fi calling is turned on. To turn off Wi-Fi calling, touch the switch next to **Wi-Fi Calling on This iPhone**.

Adjusting Text Message Settings

Table of Contents

1. Turning iMessage On or Off
2. Turning Read Receipts On or Off in iMessage
3. Turning 'Send as SMS' On or Off
4. Turning MMS Messaging On or Off
5. Turning the Subject Field On or Off
6. Turning the Character Count On or Off
7. Turning Group Messaging On or Off
8. Setting the Amount of Time to Keep Messages
9. Setting the Expiration Time for Audio Messages
10. Turning Raise to Listen On or Off
11. Blocking Unknown Senders

1. Turning iMessage On or Off

The iMessage feature allows you to send free text messages to iPhone, iPad, or iPod Touch. Turn on iMessage to send a message to another phone, or to an iPad or iPod touch, using the email address assigned to the recipient's iMessage account. By default, iMessage is turned on. You cannot send a text message using the iPad or iPod Touch without turning on iMessage. When iMessage is turned off on the iPhone and you send a text message to another phone, standard text messaging rates apply as set forth by your network provider. To turn iMessage on or off:

1. Touch the ![icon] icon. The Settings screen appears, as shown in **Figure 1**.
2. Scroll down and touch **Messages**. The Message Settings screen appears, as shown in **Figure 2**.
3. Touch the ![switch] switch next to 'iMessage'. The ![switch] switch appears and iMessage is turned on. To turn off iMessage, touch the ![switch] switch next to 'iMessage'.

Adjusting Text Message Settings

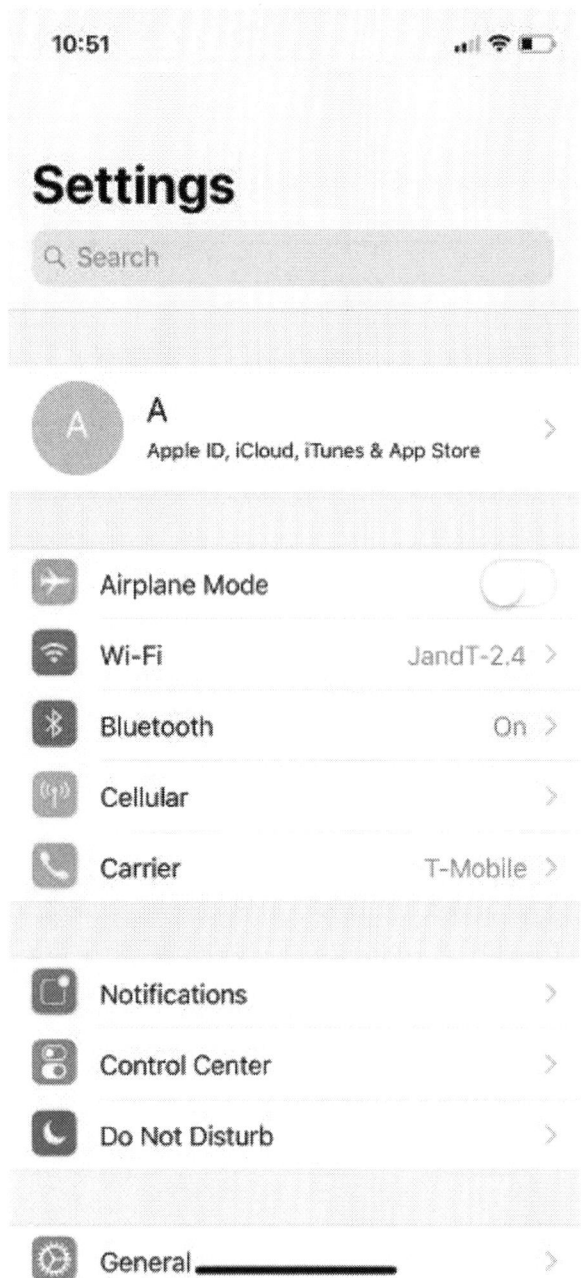

Figure 1: Settings Screen

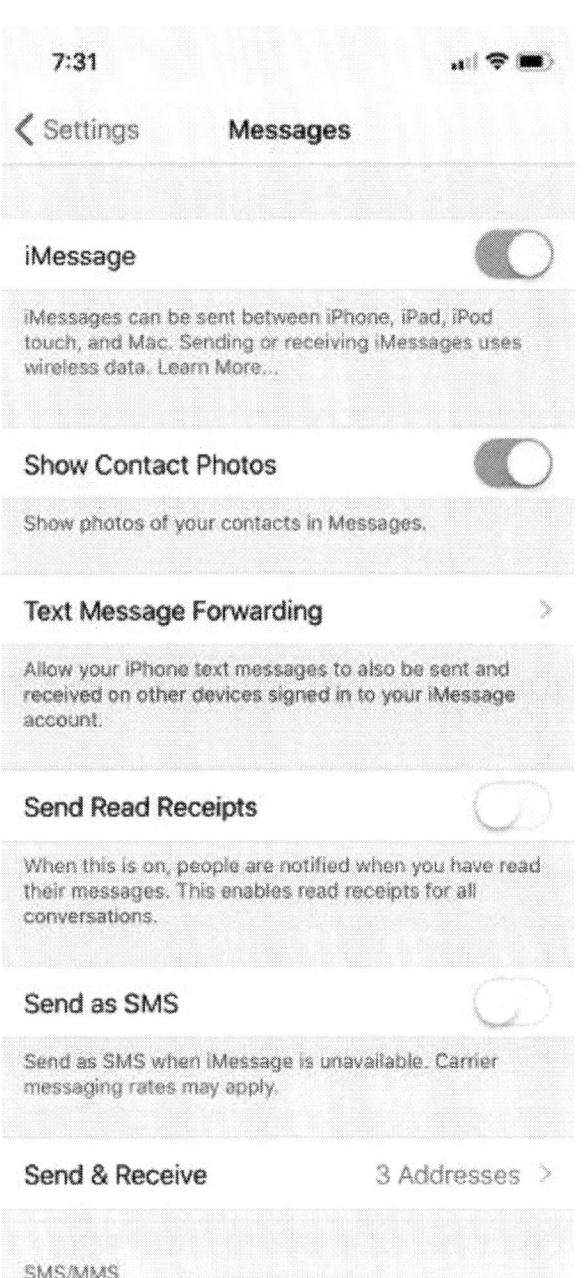

Figure 2: Message Settings Screen

2. Turning Read Receipts On or Off in iMessage

After receiving and opening a message from an iPhone, iPad, or iPod Touch, your phone can notify the sender that you have opened and read the message. These notifications are called Read Receipts, and appear under the original message on the sender's screen as "Read", followed by a time. Read Receipts are only compatible with the three Apple phones listed above. To turn Read Receipts on or off:

1. Touch the 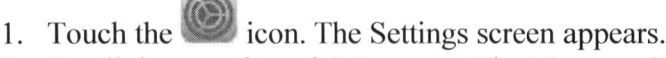 icon. The Settings screen appears.
2. Scroll down and touch **Messages**. The Message Settings screen appears.
3. Touch the ⚪ switch next to 'Send Read Receipts'. The 🟢 switch appears and Read Receipts are turned on. To turn off Read Receipts, touch the 🟢 switch next to 'Send Read Receipts'.

3. Turning 'Send as SMS' On or Off

When a message cannot be sent via iMessage, your iPhone can attempt to send it as a regular text message, also known as an SMS. To turn Send as SMS on or off:

1. Touch the 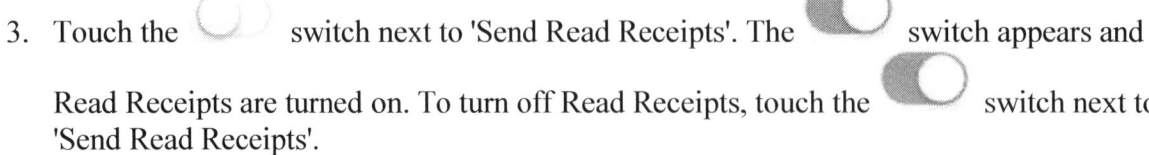 icon. The Settings screen appears.
2. Scroll down and touch **Messages**. The Message Settings screen appears.
3. Touch the ⚪ switch next to 'Send as SMS'. The 🟢 switch appears and 'Send as SMS' is turned on. To turn off Send as SMS, touch the 🟢 switch next to 'Send as SMS'.

Note: When 'Send as SMS' is turned off, you will only be able to send a message to an iPhone, iPad, or iPod, which has iMessage enabled.

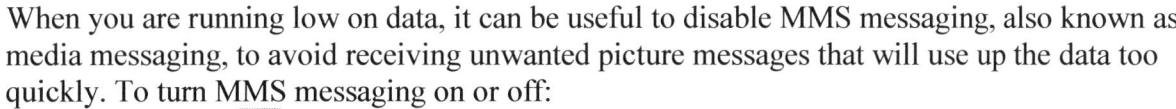

4. Turning MMS Messaging On or Off

When you are running low on data, it can be useful to disable MMS messaging, also known as media messaging, to avoid receiving unwanted picture messages that will use up the data too quickly. To turn MMS messaging on or off:

1. Touch the icon. The Settings screen appears.
2. Scroll down and touch **Messages**. The Message Settings screen appears.
3. Touch the switch next to 'MMS Messaging'. The switch appears and MMS Messaging is turned off. To turn off MMS Messaging, touch the switch next to 'MMS Messaging'.

5. Turning the Subject Field On or Off

The iPhone can attach a subject to each text message it sends when the subject field is enabled. On most phones, the subject will appear in parentheses preceding the message content. To turn the subject field on or off:

1. Touch the icon. The Settings screen appears.
2. Scroll down and touch **Messages**. The Message Settings screen appears.
3. Touch the switch next to 'Show Subject Field'. The switch appears and the Subject field is turned on. To turn off Show Subject Field, touch the switch next to 'Show Subject Field'.

6. Turning the Character Count On or Off

The Messaging application can show you the number of characters that you have typed when entering a message. To turn the character count on or off:

1. Touch the icon. The Settings screen appears.
2. Scroll down and touch **Messages**. The Message Settings screen appears.
3. Touch the switch next to 'Character Count'. The switch appears and the Character Count is turned on. To turn off Character Count, touch the switch next to 'Character Count'.

Adjusting Text Message Settings

7. Turning Group Messaging On or Off

When sending a text message, responses from any of the recipients are sent to everyone that you originally messaged. This feature is known as Group Messaging. To turn Group Messaging on or off:

1. Touch the  icon. The Settings screen appears.
2. Scroll down and touch **Messages**. The Message Settings screen appears.
3. Touch the  switch next to 'Group Messaging'. The switch appears and the Group Messaging is turned on. To turn off Group Messaging, touch the switch next to 'Group Messaging'.

8. Setting the Amount of Time to Keep Messages

When using iMessage, text messages can be automatically deleted after a certain period of time. To set the amount of time to keep messages:

1. Touch the icon. The Settings screen appears.
2. Scroll down and touch **Messages**. The Message Settings screen appears.
3. Touch **Keep Messages**. The Keep Messages screen appears, as shown in **Figure 3**.
4. Touch **30 Days** or **1 Year** to select the amount of time, or touch **Forever** to prevent the phone from erasing any messages.

Figure 3: Keep Messages Screen

9. Setting the Expiration Time for Audio Messages

When an audio message is sent using iMessage, it can be set to expire after two minutes, at which point it is removed from your phone. Refer to *"Adding a Voice Message to a Conversation (iMessage Only)"* on page 104 to learn how to attach audio messages in iMessage. To set the expiration time for audio messages:

1. Touch the ![icon] icon. The Settings screen appears.
2. Scroll down and touch **Messages**. The Message Settings screen appears.
3. Touch **Expire** under 'Audio Messages'. The Audio Message Expiration screen appears, as shown in **Figure 4**.
4. Touch **After 2 Minutes**, or touch **Never** to keep audio messages.

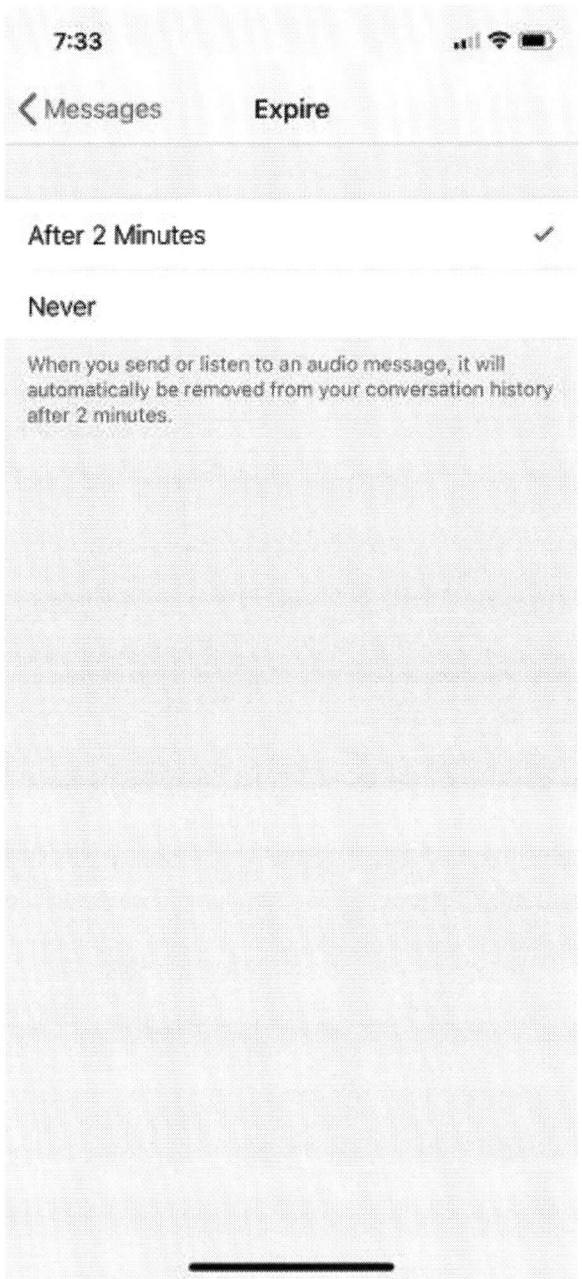

Figure 4: Audio Message Expiration Screen

10. Turning Raise to Listen On or Off

The Raise to Listen feature allows you to raise the iPhone to your ear to listen to audio messages. To turn Raise to Listen on or off:

1. Touch the icon. The Settings screen appears.
2. Scroll down and touch **Messages**. The Message Settings screen appears.
3. Touch the switch next to 'Raise to Listen'. The switch appears and the Raise to Listen is turned on. To turn off Raise to Listen, touch the switch next to 'Raise to Listen'.

11. Blocking Unknown Senders

You can prevent numbers that you do not know from messaging you. In order to block a number, you must first add it to your Phonebook. To specify numbers to block:

1. Touch the icon. The Settings screen appears.
2. Scroll down and touch **Messages**. The Message Settings screen appears.
3. Touch **Blocked**. The Blocked screen appears, as shown in **Figure 5**.
4. Touch **Add New**. Your Phonebook appears.
5. Touch a contact. The contact's number is added to the Blocked list.

Figure 5: Blocked Screen

Tips and Tricks

Table of Contents

1. Maximizing Battery Life
2. Taking and Editing a Screenshot
3. Scrolling to the Top of a Screen
4. Saving an Image While Browsing the Internet
5. Inserting a Period
6. Adding an Extension to a Contact's Number
7. Navigating the Home Screens
8. Typing Alternate Characters
9. Quickly Deleting Recently Typed Text
10. Resetting the Phone
11. Calling a Phone Number on a Website
12. Taking Notes
13. Recovering Signal After Being in an Area with No Service
14. Changing the Number of Rings Before the Phone Goes to Voicemail
15. Deleting a Song in the Music Application
16. Taking a Picture from the Lock Screen
17. Assigning a Custom Ringtone to a Contact
18. Opening the Photos Application without Closing the Camera
19. Inserting Emoticons
20. Hiding the Keyboard in the Messages Application
21. Controlling Web Surfing Using Gestures
22. Navigating the Menus Using Gestures
23. Pausing or Cancelling an Application Download
24. Making a Quick Note for a Contact
25. Using a Search Engine that Does Not Track Your Searches
26. Preventing Applications from Refreshing in the Background
27. Leaving Your Home Screen Free of Icons
28. Call Waiting in FaceTime
29. Viewing Battery Usage
30. Attaching Any File Type to an Email
31. Viewing Favorite Contacts Using 3D Touch
32. Moving the Text Cursor Like a Computer Mouse
33. Saving Data by Sending Smaller Pictures
34. Filtering Email to Customize Your Inbox
35. Using 3D Touch in the Control Center
36. Deleting Unused Applications Automatically

37. Disabling In-App Ratings and Reviews
38. Scanning a Document in the Notes Application
39. Sharing Your Wi-Fi Password Over the Air
40. Shutting Down Your Phone without Using the Sleep/Wake Button
41. Viewing and Deleting All Attachments In Messages
42. Capturing a Screen Recording
43. Enabling Do Not Disturb While Driving Mode

1. Maximizing Battery Life

There are several things you can do to increase the battery life of the phone.
- Lock the phone whenever you are not using it. To lock the phone, press the **Sleep/Wake** button at the top of the phone. Refer to *"Button Layout"* on page 17 for the location of the Sleep/Wake button.
- Keep the Auto-lock feature on and set it to a small amount of time. Refer to *"Changing Auto-Lock Settings"* on page 287 to learn how to change Auto-lock settings.
- Turn down the brightness and turn off Auto-Brightness. Refer to *"Adjusting the Brightness"* on page 290 to learn how.
- Turn on Airplane mode in areas where there is little or no signal, as the phone will continually try to search for service. Refer to *"Turning Airplane Mode On or Off"* on page 247 to learn how to turn on Airplane Mode.
- Turn off Wi-Fi when it is not in use. Refer to *"Using Wi-Fi"* on page 26 to learn how.
- Turn off Location Services when they are not in use. Refer to *"Turning Location Services On or Off"* on page 249 to learn how.
- Turn on the Grayscale accessibility feature. This will prevent you from seeing any colors, but is a great feature to use when your battery is running low. Refer to *"Managing Vision Accessibility Features"* on page 314 to learn how.

You can view a list of applications that are using up most of your battery. To view battery usage, touch the ![icon] icon, and then touch **Battery**. The Battery screen appears, showing all of the applications that are draining your battery, and the percentage of the battery that each has drained. Refer to *"Closing an Application Running in the Background"* on page 234 to learn how to cut down on the amount of battery used by applications. You can also turn on Low Power Mode from this screen. Low Power Mode reduces the performance, but increases the battery life of your phone.

2. Taking and Editing a Screenshot

To capture what is on the screen and save it as a photo, press the **Sleep/Wake** button and the **Volume Up** button at the same time. Release the buttons and the screen will momentarily flash white. The screenshot is saved to the 'Screenshots' album.

You can also touch the screenshot thumbnail in the lower left-hand corner of the screen to draw or write on it immediately. Touch and hold the same thumbnail to share it right away.

3. Scrolling to the Top of a Screen

Touch anywhere to the left or right of the ear piece at the top of the screen to quickly scroll to the top of a list, website, etc.

4. Saving an Image While Browsing the Internet

To save an image from Safari to the phone, touch and hold the picture until the Image menu appears. Touch **Save Image**. The image is saved to the 'Recently Added' album.

5. Inserting a Period

When typing a sentence, touch the space bar twice quickly to insert a period and a space.

6. Adding an Extension to a Contact's Number

When entering a number for a stored contact, you can add an extension that will be dialed following a short pause after the call is connected. While entering a number, touch the ＋✶♯ button in the lower left-hand corner of the screen, and then touch **Pause**. A comma appears, and you can now enter an extension. Each comma represents one second that the phone will wait after dialing the number.

7. Navigating the Home Screens

Typically, you navigate to another Home screen by touching the screen and sliding your finger to the left or right. Alternatively, touch one of the gray dots at the bottom of a Home screen to go to the previous or next screen.

8. Typing Alternate Characters

When typing a sentence, insert other characters, such as Á or Ñ, by touching and holding the base letter. A menu of characters appears above the letter. Slide your finger to a character to insert it.

9. Quickly Deleting Recently Typed Text

This feature is quite a secret. If you have just typed several lines of text and do not want any of it, just give the phone a good shake. A menu appears asking whether to undo the typing.
Touch **Undo**. The typed text is erased. Give the phone another shake to redo the typing. This works in any application, or while text messaging.

10. Resetting the Phone

If the phone or an application freezes up or is acting strangely, you may wish to reset the phone. This will NOT wipe any data, but simply restart the operating system. To reset the phone:
1. Press the **Volume Up** button and release.
2. Press the Volume Down button and release.
3. Press and hold the **Sleep/Wake** button until the phone completely shuts off. Continue to hold the button until the logo appears. The phone resets and starts up.

11. Calling a Phone Number on a Website

You can call a phone number on a website directly. The number will be blue and underlined, much like a link. Touch the number. The phone calls it. If the number is on a website, the phone will ask whether to call the number. Touch **Call**. This may not work with all websites.

12. Taking Notes

A convenient way to take notes is by using the built-in Notes application and emailing the notes to yourself. To take notes, touch the icon on the Home screen. Touch **New** at the top of the screen to add a note. Touch the icon and then touch **Mail** to email the note.

13. Recovering Signal After Being in an Area with No Service

Sometimes the phone has trouble finding signal after returning from an area where your network was not available. This issue can sometimes be fixed by turning Airplane Mode on and then back off. Refer to *"Turning Airplane Mode On or Off"* on page 247 to learn how.

14. Changing the Number of Rings Before the Phone Goes to Voicemail

There is a hidden way to change the number of times the phone rings before going to Voicemail. The maximum number of seconds the phone can ring is 30. Have a pen and paper ready, as you will need to enter a long number. To change the number of times the phone rings before going to Voicemail:
1. Turn off Call Forwarding. Refer to *"Turning Call Forwarding On or Off"* on page 324 to learn how.
2. Touch the icon and then touch the icon. The Keypad appears.
3. Dial ***#61#** exactly as it appears here and touch **CALL**. When the call is completed, the Voicemail Configuration screen appears.
4. Write down the number that follows "Forwards to." Skip the '+' since you will be typing it in later anyway.
5. Touch **Dismiss**. The call is ended.

6. Dial ***61*+XXXXXXXXXX*11*tt#** exactly as it appears here, where the X's represent the number you just wrote down and "tt" is the number of seconds you want for the phone to ring before going to Voicemail. For example, if the number you wrote down is 1234567890 and the number of seconds you prefer is 30, you would dial *61*+11234567890*11*30#. To make the plus sign appear when dialing a phone number, touch and hold **0**.
7. Touch **CALL**. The number of seconds the phone rings is changed and a confirmation appears.
8. Touch **Dismiss**. The call is ended.

Note: To change the ring time back, just repeat these steps. The number you wrote down in step three does not change, so you can proceed to step four if you know it. The default ring time for the phone is 20 seconds.

15. Deleting a Song in the Music Application

To delete a song from your phone, touch and hold a title of a song, and touch **Remove**. A confirmation appears. Touch **Remove Download** or **Delete from Library**. If you selected **Remove Download**, you can still stream the song from iCloud, but it does not take up space on your phone. If you selected **Delete from Library**, the song is hidden both in iCloud and on your phone. Deleting songs from the library is not recommended because restoring them involves a complicated process. Refer to the instructions below to learn how to unhide a deleted song.

To unhide a song in your library:
1. Open iTunes on your computer.
2. Click **Account** or click your name at the top of the window.
3. Click **Account Info** or **View My Account**. The Account Information screen appears.
4. Scroll down to the iTunes in the Cloud section, then click **Manage** next to Hidden Purchases. From this screen, you can unhide songs and albums.

16. Taking a Picture from the Lock Screen

To take a picture without unlocking the phone, slide your finger to the left. The camera turns on. Press the **Volume Up** button. The camera takes a picture.

17. Assigning a Custom Ringtone to a Contact

You can assign a custom ringtone to any contact in the Phonebook. To assign a ringtone to a contact:

1. Touch the [icon] icon. The Phonebook appears.
2. Find and touch the contact to whom you wish to assign a custom ringtone. The Contact Info screen appears. Refer to *"Finding a Contact"* on page 67 to learn more.
3. Touch **Edit** in the upper right-hand corner of the screen. The Contact Editing screen appears.
4. Touch **Ringtone**. A list of available ringtones appears.
5. Touch a ringtone. The ringtone plays.
6. Touch **Done**. The ringtone is assigned to the contact.

Note: Refer to *"Buying Music and Ringtones in iTunes"* on page 161 to learn how to purchase additional ringtones.

18. Opening the Photos Application without Closing the Camera

To open the Photos application while the camera is turned on, touch the photo thumbnail next to the [button] button. To return to the camera, touch **Camera** in the upper left-hand corner.

19. Inserting Emoticons

The Emoji keyboard contains over 460 emoticons that can be used when entering text. To learn how to add the Emoji keyboard, refer to *"Adding an International Keyboard"* on page 275, and touch **Emoji** in step 6. After adding the Emoji keyboard, touch the [smiley] key, if the Emoji keyboard is the only one that you have added, or touch the [globe] key if there are other keyboards in addition to English and Emoji. The Emoji keyboard appears. If you touched the [globe] key, you may need to touch it again to cycle through the keyboards until the Emoji keyboard turns on.

20. Hiding the Keyboard in the Messages Application

While reading a text message, you can hide the keyboard to view more of the conversation at once. Touch the last visible message in the conversation and slide your finger down to the keyboard. The keyboard is hidden.

21. Controlling Web Surfing Using Gestures

Instead of touching the ⟨ and ⟩ buttons to go back and forward, respectively, you can touch the right or left edge of the screen and slide your finger to the left or right, respectively.

22. Navigating the Menus Using Gestures

Instead of touching the text in the upper left-hand corner of the screen to return to the previous menu, just touch the left-hand side of the screen and slide your finger to the right. This works in most applications as well, such as the Music application.

23. Pausing or Cancelling an Application Download

If you are downloading more than one application at a time, you may wish to pause one of the downloads so that one of the other applications downloads first. To pause an application download, touch the application icon of the application that you wish to pause. Touch the icon again to resume the download. You may also cancel the download by deleting the application. Refer to *"Deleting an Application"* on page 235 to learn how.

Note: If you cancel a download by deleting the application, you will still be charged if the application was not free. You may still download the application later. Refer to "Buying an Application" *on page 229 to learn how.*

24. Making a Quick Note for a Contact

You may take a quick note for a contact without having to edit the entire contents of the contact. To make a quick note for a contact, touch **Notes** on the contact's information screen. Touch **All Contacts** at the top of the screen to save the note.

25. Using a Search Engine that Does Not Track Your Searches

Safari now allows you to use a new search engine, called DuckDuckGo. This search engine comes from a start-up company, and allows you to search the Web without tracking your searches like Google. Refer to *"Changing the Search Engine"* on page 129 to learn how to change your search engine to DuckDuckGo.

26. Preventing Applications from Refreshing in the Background

Certain applications, such as Podcasts and Weather will refresh their content even when the application is closed. This can drain your battery more quickly. To prevent applications from refreshing in the background:

1. Touch the ![icon] icon. The Settings screen appears.
2. Touch **General**. The General Settings screen appears.
3. Touch **Background App Refresh**. The Background App Refresh screen appears.
4. Touch the ![switch] switch next to 'Background App Refresh'. The ![switch] switch appears and the feature is turned off.

27. Leaving Your Home Screen Free of Icons

If you are a wallpaper connoisseur, you may wish to leave your main Home screen empty. You can move all of your icons to other screens and leave your main Home screen empty. Now you can look at your wallpaper all day long without the intrusion of those pesky icons.

28. Call Waiting in FaceTime

FaceTime allows you to accept another call while you are already on a call. To accept a call and end the current one, touch **End & Accept**. To reject an incoming call, touch **Decline**.

29. Viewing Battery Usage

If your battery is dying too quickly or if you are curious how your battery is being used, you can check the percentage of your battery that is used by each application. To view the battery usage, touch the icon. The Settings screen appears. Touch **Battery**. The Battery screen appears. Check the Battery Usage section to determine how your battery is being used.

30. Attaching Any File Type to an Email

In addition to attaching photos and videos to an email, you can attach other files, such as those that are in your iCloud or Google Drive. To attach a file to an email, touch and hold text in the email, then touch **Add Attachment** from the Text menu.

31. Viewing Favorite Contacts Using 3D Touch

To quickly view your Favorites, 3D Touch (firmly press) the icon. The list of your Favorites appears.

32. Moving the Text Cursor Like a Computer Mouse

Whenever you use the virtual keyboard, you can move the text cursor freely as if you are using a mouse. 3D Touch (firmly press) the screen and move your finger in any direction.

Help Me! Guide to the iPhone X

33. Saving Data by Sending Smaller Pictures

You can conserve your data by reducing the size and quality of photos when you send them via text message. To reduce photo size and quality in text messages:

1. Touch the ⚙ icon. The Settings screen appears.
2. Touch **Messages**. The Messages settings screen appears.
3. Touch the ⚪ switch next to 'Low Quality Image Mode'. The feature is turned on. To turn off the feature, touch the 🔘 switch.

34. Filtering Email to Customize Your Inbox

By default, the Mail application sorts your email by date, with the most recent emails at the top. Although you can search your email, sometimes you do not know precisely what you're trying to find. You can filter your email to easily find specific emails, such as those that are unread, flagged, or which contain attachments. To filter email, touch the ⊜ button in the bottom left-hand corner of the screen. Then, touch **Filtered by** and select as many filters as you need. Touch **Done** to filter your email.

35. Using 3D Touch in the Control Center

You can use 3D Touch in the Control Center to access additional features. 3D Touch (firmly press) one of the following icons to perform the corresponding action:

 - Change the brightness of the flashlight.

 - Set a quick timer for 1 minute to 120 minutes.

 - Copy the last result of a calculation.

 - Quickly capture a photo, selfie, video, or slo-mo.

Tips and Tricks

36. Deleting Unused Applications Automatically

Your phone can free up some space by automatically deleting unused applications. When an application is deleted, its data remains on the phone in case you want to reinstall it in the future. To turn on automatic application deletion:

1. Touch the ⚙ icon. The Settings screen appears.
2. Touch **iTunes & App Store**. The iTunes & App Stores screen appears.
3. Touch the ⚪ switch next to **Offload Unused Apps**. The phone will now delete unused applications automatically. To turn off the feature, touch the 🔘 switch next to **Offload Unused Apps**.

37. Disabling In-App Ratings and Reviews

Applications will often ask you for ratings and reviews. You can disable these notifications if you are not interested in receiving them. To turn off rating and review notifications:

1. Touch the ⚙ icon. The Settings screen appears.
2. Touch **iTunes & App Store**. The iTunes & App Stores screen appears.
3. Touch the 🔘 switch next to **In-App Ratings & Reviews**. Applications will no longer notify you to leave a rating or review. To turn on the feature, touch the ⚪ switch next to **In-App Ratings & Reviews**.

38. Scanning a Document in the Notes Application

You can scan a document in the Notes application and then mark it up. To scan a document in the Notes application:

1. Touch the ⊕ icon and then touch **Scan Documents**.
2. When the camera turns on, line up the document in the center of the frame and touch the ⬜ button. The document is scanned.
3. Touch **Keep Scan** to save the document in the Notes application. Or, touch **Retake** to rescan.

359

39. Sharing Your Wi-Fi Password Over the Air

You can send your Wi-Fi password directly to another phone as long as the phone that is trying to connect to your Wi-Fi network has iOS 11 installed. To share your Wi-Fi password:

On the phone that is trying to connect:
1. Touch the icon. The Settings screen.
2. Touch **Wi-Fi**. The Wi-Fi Networks screen appears.
3. Touch the switch next to 'Wi-Fi'. Wi-Fi turns on and a list of available networks appears.
4. Touch the network to which you would like to connect. The Wi-Fi Password prompt appears.

On the phone that is already connected:
1. After step 4 above is completed, a notification appears on your phone.
2. To share your Wi-Fi password, touch **Share Password**. The phone that is trying to connect is automatically connected to the Wi-Fi Network.

40. Shutting Down Your Phone without Using the Sleep/Wake Button

In case something happens to your Sleep/Wake button, you can always shut down your phone using the screen. To shut down your phone:
1. Touch the icon. The Settings screen appears.
2. Touch **General**. The General Settings screen appears.
3. Scroll to the bottom and touch **Shut Down**. A confirmation appears at the top of the screen.
4. Touch the slider and move your finger to the right. The phone turns off.

41. Viewing and Deleting All Attachments in Messages

You can view and delete all of the attachments received in the Messages application in one convenient location. To view and delete message attachments:
1. Touch the icon. The Settings screen appears.
2. Touch **General**. The General Settings screen appears.

Tips and Tricks

3. Touch **iPhone Storage**. The iPhone Storage screen appears.
4. Scroll down and touch **Messages**. The Messages screen appears.
5. Touch **Review Large Attachments**. The Attachments screen appears.
6. Touch and hold an attachment and slide your finger to the left to delete it. You can also touch **Edit**, select the attachments you wish to delete, and touch the  icon.

42. Capturing a Screen Recording

To capture a screen recording, including the audio in the recorded applications:
1. Touch the bottom of the screen and slide your finger up. The Control Center appears.
2. Touch the  icon. The phone begins a three-second countdown and then begins recording.
3. To stop recording, touch the bottom of the screen and slide your finger up to display the Control Center. Then touch the ■ icon.

To record audio from the microphone while recording, force touch the 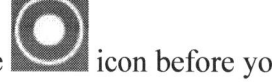 icon before you begin to record. Then, touch the 🎤 icon.

If you do not see the  icon, add the Screen Recording control in the Control Center. To add the screen recording control:
1. Touch the icon. The Settings screen appears.
2. Touch **Control Center**. The Control Center settings appear.
3. Touch **Customize Controls**. The Customize screen appears.
4. Touch ⊕ icon next to **Screen Recording**. The Screen Recording control is added to the Control Center.

43. Enabling Do Not Disturb While Driving Mode

When you turn on Do Not Disturb While Driving Mode, you will not receive any phone calls, text messages, or notifications while you are driving. To enable Do Not Disturb While Driving:
1. Touch the icon. The Settings screen appears.

2. Touch **Do Not Disturb**. The Do Not Disturb screen appears.
3. Touch **Activate** under **Do Not Disturb While Driving**. The Activate screen appears.
4. Touch **Automatically** to enable the phone to turn on the mode when it detects that you are driving. However, be aware that the phone has no way to tell whether you are a passenger in a car or in a train.
5. Touch **When Connected to Car Bluetooth** to activate the mode when you connect to your car's Bluetooth. This method is somewhat more reliable than the automatic method.
6. To activate the mode manually, add the Do Not Disturb While Driving icon to the Control Center and then touch the icon. To add the icon, touch **Control Center** on the Settings screen and then touch **Customize Controls**. Touch the icon next to **Do Not Disturb While Driving**.

When someone texts you while you have Do Not Disturb While Driving mode enabled, they receive an automated reply. This reply will inform them that they can text the word "urgent" with no other text in the message to push their message through. This way, people can still reach you in case of an emergency.

Troubleshooting

Table of Contents

1. Phone does not turn on
2. Phone is not responding
3. Can't make a call
4. Can't surf the web
5. Screen or keyboard does not rotate
6. iTunes does not detect phone when connected to a computer
7. Phone does not ring or play music, can't hear while talking, can't listen to voicemails
8. Low microphone volume, caller can't hear you
9. Camera does not work
10. Phone shows the White Screen of Death
11. "DEVICE needs to cool down" message appears
12. Display does not adjust brightness automatically

1. Phone does not turn on

If the phone does not power on, try one or more of the following tips:
- **Recharge the phone** - Use the included wall charger to charge the battery. If the battery power is extremely low, the screen will not turn on for several minutes. Do NOT use the USB port on your computer to charge the phone.
- **Replace the battery** - If you purchased the phone a long time ago, you may need to replace the battery. Contact Apple to learn how.
- **Reset the phone** - This method will not erase any data. Hold down the **Home** button and **Sleep/Wake** button at the same time for 10 seconds. Keep holding the two buttons until the logo appears and the phone restarts.

2. Phone is not responding

If the phone is frozen or is not responding, try one or more of the following. These steps solve most problems on the phone.

- **Exit the application** - If the phone freezes while running an application, hold the **Home** Button for six seconds. The application quits and the phone returns to the Home screen.
- **Turn the phone off and then back on** - If the phone is still frozen, try pressing the **Sleep/Wake** button to turn the phone off. Keep holding the **Sleep/Wake** Button until "Slide to Power Off" appears. Slide your finger from left to right over the text. The phone turns off. After the screen is completely black, press the **Sleep/Wake** button again to turn the phone back on.
- **Restart the phone** - Hold the **Home** button and **Sleep/Wake** button at the same time for 10 seconds or until the logo appears.
- **Remove Media** - Some downloaded applications or music may freeze up the phone. Try deleting some of the media that may be problematic after restarting the phone. Refer to *"Deleting an Application"* on page 235 to learn how to delete an application. You may also erase all data at once by doing the following:

Warning: Once erased, data cannot be recovered. Make sure you back up any files you wish to keep.

1. Touch the icon. The Settings screen appears.
2. Touch **General**. The General Settings screen appears.
3. Touch **Reset**. The Reset screen appears.
4. Touch **Erase All Content and Settings**. A confirmation dialog appears.
5. Touch **Erase**. The phone is restored to factory settings.

3. Can't make a call

If the phone cannot make outgoing calls, try one of the following:

- If "No Service" is shown at the top of the screen, the network does not cover you in your location. Try moving to a different location, or even to a different part of a building.
- Try walking around to find more signal.
- Turn off Airplane Mode if you have it turned on. If that does not work, try turning Airplane Mode on for 15 seconds and then turning it off. Refer to *"Turning Airplane Mode On or Off"* on page 247 to learn how.
- Make sure you dialled an area code with the phone number.
- Turn the phone off and back on.

4. Can't surf the web

If you have no internet access, there may be little or no service in your area. Try moving to a different location or turning on Wi-Fi, if available. Refer to *"Using Wi-Fi"* on page 26 to learn how to turn on Wi-Fi. If you still cannot access the Web, refer to *"Phone is not responding"* on page 364 for further assistance.

5. Screen or keyboard does not rotate

If the screen does not rotate, or the full, horizontal keyboard does not appear when you rotate the phone, it may be one of these issues:
- The application does not support the horizontal view.
- The phone is lying flat. Hold the phone upright to change the view in applications that support it.
- The rotation lock is on. The rotation is locked if the icon appears next to the battery life at the top of the screen. Touch the bottom of the screen and slide your finger up to access the Control Center. In the control center, touch the icon to unlock the rotation. On an iPad, if you do not see the icon in the Control Center, then the rotation can be controlled using the Side switch above the Volume Controls.

6. iTunes does not detect phone when connected to a computer

If iTunes does not detect the phone when connecting it to your computer, try using a different USB port. If that does not work, turn the phone off and on again while it is plugged in to the computer. If the phone indicates that it is connected, the problem might be with your computer. Try restarting your computer or reinstalling iTunes. Otherwise, refer to *"Phone is not responding"* on page 364 for assistance.

7. Phone does not ring or play music, can't hear while talking, can't listen to voicemails

Make sure the volume is turned up. Refer to *"Button Layout"* on page 17 to find the Volume Controls. Check whether you can still hear sound through headphones. The headphone jack is located on the top of the phone. If you can hear sound through headphones, try inserting the headphones and taking them out several times. Sometimes the sensor in the headphone jack malfunctions.

8. Low microphone volume, caller can't hear you

If you are talking to someone who can't hear you, try the following:
- Take off any cases or other accessories as these may cover up the microphone.
- When you first take the phone out of the box, it comes with a piece of plastic covering the microphone. Make sure to take this plastic off before using the phone.
- If the caller cannot hear you at all, you may have accidentally muted the conversation. Refer to *"Using the Mute Function During a Voice Call"* on page 56 to learn how turn Mute on or off.

9. Camera does not work

If the phone camera is not functioning correctly, try one of the following:
- Clean the camera lens with a polishing cloth.
- Take off any cases or accessories that may interfere with the camera lens on the back of the phone.
- Hold the phone steady when taking a picture. A shaky hand often results in a blurry picture. Try leaning against a stationary object to stabilize your hand.

Troubleshooting

- If you cannot find the 📷 icon on your Home screen, try the following:
1. Touch the ⚙ icon. The Settings screen appears.
2. Touch **General**. The General Settings screen appears.
3. Touch **Restrictions**. The Restrictions screen appears.
4. Touch **Disable Restrictions**. The Restrictions Passcode screen appears.
5. Enter the passcode that you set up when you enabled the restrictions. All restrictions are disabled.

10. Phone shows the White Screen of Death

If the phone screen has gone completely white, try restarting or restoring the phone. Refer to *"Phone is not responding"* on page 364 to learn how.

11. "DEVICE needs to cool down" message appears

If you leave the phone in your car on a hot day, or expose it to direct sunlight for too long, one of the following may happen:
- Phone stops charging
- Weak signal
- Screen dims
- Phone breaks completely
- "DEVICE needs to cool down" message appears, where DEVICE refers to the type of iOS 11 phone that you have.

Before using the phone, allow it to cool. The phone works best in temperatures between 32°F and 95°F (0°C to 35°C). While it is turned off, store the phone at temperatures between -4°F and 113°F (-20°C to 45°C).

12. Display does not adjust brightness automatically

If the phone does not brighten in bright conditions, or does not become dimmer in dark conditions, try taking any cases or accessories off. A case may block the light sensor, located at the top of the phone. Also, check to make sure that Auto-Brightness is turned on. Refer to *"Adjusting the Brightness"* on page 290 to learn how to turn on Auto-Brightness.

Index

"

"DEVICE needs to cool down" message appears, 375

A

Accessing Application Shortcuts Using 3D Touch, 35
Accessing Control Center Quick Actions Without 3D Touch, 15
Accessing Quick Settings through the Control Center, 12, 33
Adding a Bookmark to the Home Screen, 124
Adding a Drawing in an Email, 15, 220
Adding a Keyboard Shortcut, 284
Adding a New Contact, 67
Adding a Voice Message to a Conversation (iMessage Only), 106
Adding an Extension to a Contact's Number, 357
Adding an International Keyboard, 281
Adding and Viewing Bookmarks, 120
Adding Content to Your Wish List, 177
Adding Texted Phone Numbers to the Phonebook, 99
Adjusting Accessibility Settings, 320
Adjusting General Settings, 293
Adjusting Language and Keyboard Settings, 277
Adjusting Phone Settings, 330
Adjusting Siri Settings, 276
Adjusting Sound Settings, 266
Adjusting Text Message Settings, 343
Adjusting the Brightness, 296
Adjusting Wireless Settings, 252
Answering a Call Automatically, 16
Answering Phone Calls Automatically, 327
Application Store Redesign, 13
Archiving Emails, 213
Assigning a Custom Ringtone to a Contact, 360
Assigning a Passcode Lock, 298
Attaching a Picture or Video to an Email, 206
Attaching Any File Type to an Email, 364

B

Blocking Phone Numbers, 64
Blocking Pop-Up Windows, 128
Blocking Specific Numbers, 338
Blocking Unknown Senders, 352
Browsing Photos, 143
Browsing Photos by Date and Location, 153
Button Layout, 19
Buying an Application, 234
Buying Music and Ringtones in iTunes, 164
Buying or Renting Videos in iTunes, 167

C

Call Waiting in FaceTime, 364
Calling a Contact, 48
Calling a Favorite, 51
Calling a Phone Number on a Website, 358
Calling the Sender from within a Text, 97
Camera does not work, 375
Can't make a call, 372
Can't surf the web, 373
Capturing a Screen Recording, 12, 369
Capturing a Video, 142
Capturing and Viewing a Live Photo, 162
Changing Application Settings, 240
Changing Auto-Lock Settings, 293
Changing Email Options, 216
Changing the Contact Sort Order, 78
Changing the Default Signature, 213
Changing the Keyboard Layout, 290
Changing the Number of Rings Before the Phone Goes to Voicemail, 359
Changing the Operating System Language, 287
Changing the Region Format, 291
Changing the Search Engine, 131
Changing the Wallpaper, 312
Charging the Phone, 22
Clearing the History and Browsing Data, 131
Closing an Application Running in the Background, 239
Composing a New Text Message, 82
Connecting to a Wi-Fi Network Automatically, 16
Controlling Siri's Voice, 273
Controlling Web Surfing Using Gestures, 362
Copying, Cutting, and Pasting Text, 87
Creating a Photo Album, 149
Creating a Playlist, 183
Creating an Icon Folder, 26
Customizing Cellular Data Usage, 257
Customizing Notification and Alert Sounds, 272
Customizing Spelling and Grammar Settings, 277
Customizing the Smart Search Field, 136

D

Deleting a Contact, 72
Deleting a Photo, 149
Deleting a Photo Album, 153

Deleting a Song in the Music Application, 360
Deleting a Text Message, 99
Deleting an Application, 240
Deleting Unused Applications Automatically, 15, 366
Dialing a Number, 46
Disabling In-App Ratings and Reviews, 15, 367
Display does not adjust brightness automatically, 376
Downloading Media, 179

E

Editing a Photo, 145
Editing a Photo Album, 151
Editing Contact Information, 74
Editing iTunes Account Information, 228
Editing Live Photos, 13
Editing Preset Text Message Responses, 340
Enabling Do Not Disturb While Driving Mode, 13, 370
Entering an Alternative Character on the Keyboard, 14
Erasing and Restoring the Phone, 308

F

Filtering Email to Customize Your Inbox, 366
Finding a Contact, 69
Flagging an Important Email, 211
Focusing on a Part of the Screen, 143
Formatting Text, 201
Forwarding a Text Message, 94

G

Getting Started, 19

H

Handwriting a Message, 114
Hiding the Keyboard in the Messages Application, 361

I

Inserting a Period, 356
Inserting Emoticons, 361
Installing a SIM Card, 23
iTunes does not detect phone when connected to a computer, 374

L

Leaving a Group Conversation, 106
Leaving Your Home Screen Free of Icons, 364

Low microphone volume, caller can't hear you, 374

M

Making a Call Over Wi-Fi, 60
Making a Quick Note for a Contact, 363
Making an Emergency SOS Call, 17, 63
Making Voice and Video Calls, 46
Managing and Using Widgets, 42
Managing Applications, 223
Managing Contacts, 67
Managing Hearing Accessibility Features, 324
Managing Memories in Photos, 162
Managing Notification Settings, 16, 309
Managing Open Browser Tabs, 126
Managing People in Photos, 158
Managing Photos and Videos, 139
Managing Physical & Motor Accessibility Features, 326
Managing Vision Accessibility Features, 320
Marking Up and Sharing Screenshots, 14
Maximizing Battery Life, 355
Moving an Email in the Inbox to Another Folder, 209
Moving Multiple Application Icons at Once, 17
Moving the Text Cursor Like a Computer Mouse, 365

N

Naming a Conversation, 106
Navigating the Home Screens, 357
Navigating the Menus Using Gestures, 362
Navigating the Screens, 25
Navigating to a Website, 118

O

Opening the Most Recent Note from the Lock Screen, 14
Opening the Photos Application without Closing the Camera, 361
Organizing Applications into Folders, 239
Organizing Icons, 26

P

Pausing or Cancelling an Application Download, 362
Phone does not ring or play music, can't hear while talking, can't listen to voicemails, 374
Phone does not turn on, 371
Phone is not responding, 372
Phone shows the White Screen of Death, 375
Playing Music, 179
Preventing Applications from Refreshing in the Background, 363

Putting a Caller on Hold (hidden button), 58

Q

Quickly Deleting Recently Typed Text, 357

R

Reading a Stored Text Message, 94
Reading Email, 195
Reading User Reviews, 239
Receiving a Text Message, 90
Receiving a Voice Call, 55
Recording a Time-Lapse Video, 157
Recovering Deleted Photos, 157
Recovering Signal After Being in an Area with No Service, 358
Redeeming a Gifted Application, 245
Referring to Another Email when Composing a New Message, 201
Registering with Apple, 164
Replying to an Incoming Call with a Text Message, 55
Replying to and Forwarding Email Messages, 204
Resetting All Settings, 308
Resetting the Home Screen Layout, 306
Resetting the Phone, 358
Restricting Access to Private Information, 316
Returning a Recent Phone Call, 53

S

Saving an Image While Browsing the Internet, 356
Saving Data by Sending Smaller Pictures, 365
Scanning a Credit Card Using the Phone's Camera, 138
Scanning a Document in the Notes Application, 16, 367
Screen or keyboard does not rotate, 373
Scrolling to the Top of a Screen, 356
Searching for a Photo, 155
Searching for an Application to Purchase, 228
Searching for Media in iTunes, 171
Searching the Phone or Web for Content, 42
Sending a Digital Touch, 115
Sending a Picture Message, 102
Sending an Animoji, 115
Sending an Application as a Gift, 241
Setting a Reminder to Return an Incoming Call, 56
Setting the Amount of Time to Keep Messages, 348
Setting the Default Ringtone, 270
Setting the Expiration Time for Audio Messages, 350
Setting Up a Face ID Lock, 302
Setting Up a Virtual Private Network (VPN), 259
Setting Up the AutoFill Feature, 134
Setting Up the Mail application, 190

Sharing a Contact's Information, 74
Sharing a Wi-Fi Password Over the Air, 17
Sharing Your iTunes Account with Family, 173
Sharing Your Location in a Conversation, 108
Sharing Your Wi-Fi Password Over the Air, 368
Shutting Down Your Phone without Using the Sleep/Wake Button, 17, 368
Signing In to a Different iTunes Account, 226
Signing In to an iTunes Account, 223
Starting a Conference Call (Adding a Call), 58
Starting a FaceTime Call, 65
Switching Accounts in the Mail application, 197
Switching Between Applications, 14, 237

T

Taking a Picture, 139
Taking a Picture from the Lock Screen, 360
Taking and Editing a Screenshot, 356
Taking Notes, 358
Text Messaging, 82
Tips and Tricks, 354
Translating a Phrase Using Siri, 13
Troubleshooting, 371
Turning 24-Hour Mode On or Off, 304
Turning Airplane Mode On or Off, 252
Turning Automatic Application Updates On or Off, 245
Turning Bluetooth On or Off, 263
Turning Call Forwarding On or Off, 330
Turning Call Waiting On or Off, 334
Turning Caller ID On or Off, 336
Turning Data Roaming On or Off, 259
Turning Group Messaging On or Off, 348
Turning Guided Access On or Off, 324
Turning iMessage On or Off, 343
Turning Keyboard Clicks On or Off, 272
Turning Location Services On or Off, 254
Turning Lock Sounds On or Off, 272
Turning MMS Messaging On or Off, 347
Turning Night Shift On or Off, 296
Turning Private Browsing On or Off, 134
Turning Raise to Listen On or Off, 352
Turning Raise to Wake On or Off, 318
Turning Read Receipts for a Single Conversation On or Off, 116
Turning Read Receipts On or Off in iMessage, 346
Turning 'Send as SMS' On or Off, 346
Turning the Character Count On or Off, 347
Turning the International Assist On or Off, 338
Turning the Phone On and Off, 23
Turning the Subject Field On or Off, 347
Turning Vibration On or Off, 266
Turning Volume Button Functionality On or Off, 270
Turning Wi-Fi Calling On or Off, 342
Typing a Search in Siri, 13

Typing Alternate Characters, 357

U

Unsubscribing from an Email List, 216
Using 3D Touch in the Control Center, 366
Using a Search Engine that Does Not Track Your Searches, 363
Using Additional Audio Controls, 183
Using iMessage Applications, 116
Using Interactive Notifications, 45
Using iTunes, 164
Using Music Controls on the Lock Screen, 12
Using Siri, 246
Using Tapback in a Message, 115
Using the Cover Sheet, 35
Using the Digital and Optical Zoom, 142
Using the Flash, 142
Using the iTunes Radio, 188
Using the Keypad During a Voice Call, 57
Using the Mail Application, 190
Using the Music Application, 179
Using the Mute Function During a Voice Call, 58
Using the New Notification Center - Cover Sheet, 12
Using the Safari Web Browser, 118

Using the Speakerphone During a Voice Call, 56
Using the Spell Check Feature, 90
Using Wi-Fi, 28
Using Wi-Fi to Download an Application, 237
Using Wi-Fi to Sync Your Phone with Your Computer, 265

V

View a List of All Attachments in Messages, 18
Viewing All Attachments in a Conversation, 110
Viewing an Article in Reader Mode, 131
Viewing and Deleting All Attachments in Messages, 369
Viewing Battery Usage, 364
Viewing Emails in Conversation View, 217
Viewing Favorite Contacts Using 3D Touch, 365
Viewing Recently Closed Tabs, 136
Viewing Sender Information from within a Text, 98

W

What's New in iOS 11?, 11
Writing an Email, 199

Other Books from the Author of the Help Me Series, Charles Hughes

Help Me! Guide to the iPhone 7
Help Me! Guide to the iPhone 6
Help Me! Guide to the iPhone 5S
Help Me! Guide to the iPhone 4
Help Me! Guide to the iPad Air 2
Help Me! Guide to the iPad Air
Help Me! Guide to the iPad 2
Help Me! Guide to the Apple Watch
Help Me! Guide to the iPod Touch
Help Me! Guide to the iPad Mini
Help Me! Guide to iOS 11
Help Me! Guide to iOS 10
Help Me! Guide to the Kindle Fire HDX
Help Me! Guide to the Google Pixel
Help Me! Guide to the Nexus 7
Help Me! Guide to the Galaxy S8
Help Me! Guide to the Galaxy S6
Help Me! Guide to the Galaxy S4
Help Me! Guide to the HTC One
Help Me! Guide to the Kindle Touch
Help Me! Guide to the Samsung Galaxy Note
Help Me! Guide to the Kindle Fire HD 6
Help Me! Guide to the Kindle Fire TV

Help Me! Guide to the iPhone X

Author: Charles Hughes

This book is also available in electronic format from Amazon.com

All Rights Reserved. Copyright © 2016 Charles Hughes.

Printed in Great Britain
by Amazon